Modern Introductions to Philosophy

General Editor: D. J. O'CONNOR

The titles of the volumes in this series are:

MODERN MORAL PHILOSOPHY
W. D. Hudson

THE PHILOSOPHY OF LANGUAGE
Bernard Harrison

POLITICAL PHILOSOPHY
Derek Crabtree

THE LOGIC OF EMPIRICAL ENQUIRY
P. H. Nidditch

AN INTRODUCTION TO THE PHILOSOPHY
OF RELIGION
Kai Nielsen

PHILOSOPHY OF HISTORY
R. F. Atkinson

THE THEORY OF KNOWLEDGE
D. W. Hamlyn

MODERN DEDUCTIVE LOGIC
R. J. Ackermann

AESTHETICS
Ruth Saw

ROBERT J. ACKERMANN is professor of philosophy at the University of Massachusetts. An author of several books, he received his Ph.D. from Michigan State University in 1960. He was a Fulbright Lecturer at the University of Exeter, England, 1964–65; Guggenheim Memorial Foundation Fellow, 1968–69; and has taught at the University of Pennsylvania and Washington University in St. Louis.

MODERN DEDUCTIVE LOGIC

*An Introduction to Its Techniques
and Significance*

Robert John Ackermann

MACMILLAN

First published in the United States 1970
First published in the United Kingdom 1970

Published by
MACMILLAN AND CO LTD
London and Basingstoke
Associated companies in New York Toronto
Dublin Melbourne Johannesburg and Madras

SBN (boards) 333 08080 7
(paper) 333 11138 9

Printed in Great Britain by
RICHARD CLAY (THE CHAUCER PRESS) LTD
Bungay, Suffolk

Preface

The general attitude toward the significance of modern deductive logic expressed somewhat implicitly in the text of this book can be stated here in a direct fashion. Modern deductive logic as embodied in standard logical systems is a subtle and ingenious tool for investigating various questions of the soundness of a wide range of mathematical argument, but it is a rather poor and insensitive tool (unless extremely carefully handled) in evaluating the soundness of non-technical argument. In this respect, modern deductive logic differs little from the theory of the syllogism, which preceded it historically. The soundness of syllogisms is very important with respect to a certain style of exposition, and to master material presented in that style, a study of the syllogism is required. But people do not ordinarily argue or think in syllogisms. Similarly, axiomatization of mathematical and some scientific material is the only known method of grounding intelligent discussion of certain foundational problems, and a study of modern deductive logic is required to master the relevant axiomatizations. The problems which the logical systems introduced in this book are ultimately designed to solve are thus simply beyond the grasp of many undergraduates. Predicate Logic, which is in one form or another the second logical system usually introduced to beginning students, is already powerful enough to test the soundness of most of the arguments of modern algebraic theory. There is little wonder that a student unfamiliar with the mathematical arguments should be baffled by an instrument ideally suited to testing their soundness.

Apart from its mathematical and scientific applications, one may well wonder whether modern deductive logic has enough philosophical value to assume a major place in the curriculum assigned to philosophy students. Like any fairly precise area of subject matter, logical systems provide a number of intrinsically fascinating technical problems. It is possible to become totally entranced with technical minutiae in the same way that one may become addicted to crossword puzzles. In defense of this preoccupation, one may cite the non-utilitarian tradition of philosophy, if not of pure research. Such a defense, while logically impregnable, often seems to outsiders plainly disingenuous. The importance of logic, and its justification in the philosophy curriculum, seems rather to appear in the realization that logic is often most relevant to philosophical interests precisely where it fails to provide an appropriate assessment of validity. This fact has been somewhat obscured by the arrogance of some practicing logicians in assuming that their current systems should provide the standard for determining whether arguments are sound or defective and inherently confused. Quite often the failure of validity in standard systems points to an interesting way in which the standard systems contain presuppositions which are not appropriately matched in the subject matter of the argument. The existence of precise systems can give such observations a definite form which is useful in trying to give the relevant presuppositions an explicit status. This point of view is well illustrated in the important philosophical perspectives provided by such investigations as [H2] and [P4], listed in Further Reading at the end of this volume. We will consequently take the importance of logic to be directly related to its limitations.

In this book I have attempted to present the standard logical systems of modern logic along with an explicit introduction to the presuppositions embodied in their symbolism. I have tried to make this discussion accessible to beginners without introducing too many falsehoods in the process of simplification. The emphasis in modern logic is on rigor, precision, and close attention to detail. Important as these properties are in using logical systems to assess arguments, a careful attempt to exhibit them from the beginning without sufficient informal discussion of why they are invoked can repel students who might be attracted by the purposes which demand these tiresome accompaniments. I have tried to balance discussion of detail against a desire to give the student a sufficiently wide perspective to enable him to decide whether further study of logical systems and their application would prove interesting. Some conventional topics have been entirely omitted. There is, for example, no discussion of "use" and "mention," or of the syllogism. My defense is that these are best avoided rather than hastily dealt with. The distinction between use and mention, for example, is sufficiently given in an English grammar for the kind of argument the student is likely to encounter, and its important connection with such topics as impredicative definitions requires rather advanced discussion of certain mathematical points. An instructor may choose to add particular treatment of truth-tables and of natural deduction rules for direct proof to the general discussion of closely related topics in the text.

An introductory book such as this is obviously dependent on the prior work of a great many people, and is entirely derivative of the material cited in Further Reading except for various pedagogical strategies. In order to avoid submerging the logic in the footnotes, I have avoided careful and explicit documentation of all of my intellectual debts, a practice which seems in conformity with the style of most introductory texts. Nevertheless, there is a certain residual problem with illustrations and exercises, which are often unavoidably similar in some respects to illustrations and exercises appearing elsewhere. I have consciously adapted one illustrative sentence each from Noam Chomsky, Peter Geach, P. F. Strawson, and Paul Ziff in Chapters 5 and 9. Except for these debts, and those noted in Further Reading, this treatment of modern deductive logic seems sufficiently different to warrant entry into an area nearly saturated with good books. My hope is that students and instructors will find the discussions of the nature and difficulties of abstracting from ordinary language to logical symbolism a stimulating introduction to an interesting philosophical problem that is too frequently ignored in logic textbooks.

The exercises considerably augment the material in the chapters, as well as providing necessary drill in manipulatory techniques associated with the symbolism. As a result, it is useful to do the exercises along with reading the text if later chapters are to be comprehensible. Answers are programmed in the following sense. Each exercise directs the reader to a numbered answer at the end of the book. Sometimes the numbered answer will not be a complete answer, but will provide a hint or method of attack to be employed should difficulty be found in working the exercise. Each such hint then directs the reader to another numbered answer, where the solution can be found. Since the numbered answers are correlated with the exercises in a helter-skelter fashion, this structure should considerably facilitate self-study on the part of the student.

Robert Ackermann
University of Massachusetts

Contents

PART ONE
MATHEMATICS AND MODERN LOGIC

1. Abstraction and Appropriateness

In order to understand the way in which the symbolic systems of modern logic can be used to solve various problems about the cogency of argument, it is instructive to consider the familiar use of mathematical systems to solve a wide range of practical problems. The close relationship to be described is no accident of history. Features of the use of mathematical systems that can be discerned by philosophical analysis have been the most important models for the twentieth-century construction of symbolic logical systems.

To take an everyday example, suppose that a housewife wishes to bake a one-pound sponge cake, but has a recipe book giving directions for a four-pound cake only. The resourceful housewife would solve this problem by an elementary application of school mathematics. Her difficulty can be analyzed into a series of quite specific problems such as the following: If six tablespoons of butter are required for a four-pound cake, how many are required for the one-pound cake? Our baker should have no difficulty in hitting on the fact that the answer is obtained by a simple division. Provided that she does not immediately see the answer to her problem, she may set up a simple mathematical equation and obtain a solution for it before she begins baking. The specific recipe problem can then be solved as a simple consequence of solving this mathematical problem: What is the value of "x" in the equation "$6/x = 4/1$"? Since a simple calculation shows that

"$x = 1\frac{1}{2}$," she knows that $1\frac{1}{2}$ tablespoons of butter are required for the one-pound cake. In finding a recipe for the one-pound cake, the housewife finds a mathematical problem related to her practical problem, solves the mathematical problem, and then finds the solution to her practical problem. In practice, the housewife might say that she divides six tablespoons of butter by four to obtain her new recipe. But as butter is divided by kitchen utensils and not by numbers, this account blends together the practical and mathematical problems that would be distinguished in any philosophical account of her success with the new recipe.

The housewife's use of a simple equation highlights two characteristics of the use of mathematical systems to solve practical problems: the *abstractness* of mathematical problems, and the *appropriateness* of the mathematical problems which are used to obtain the correct solution to practical problems.

Solving a mathematical equation depends only on a knowledge of elementary algebra. The equation used to solve the baker's recipe problem described a relationship between certain numbers, and had nothing to do, by itself, with tablespoons of butter. A building contractor whose practical problem was to mix a one-ton batch of concrete using directions for a four-ton batch requiring six 100-pound bags of cement might use the same equation to find the number of 100-pound bags of cement required for the smaller batch. When we use mathematical problems to solve practical problems, we *abstract* a mathematical problem by using various numbers to represent important quantities involved in the practical problem, while ignoring some of the detail of the practical problem as irrelevant to its solution. In the baking example, it is not relevant that tablespoons of butter are being considered, since we might just as well be considering bags of cement, but the number of tablespoons or bags of cement is relevant. The baking problem and the concrete problem have the same abstract mathematical form, and that is why they may be solved by the same mathematical equation.

Abstracting to a mathematical problem is often quite simple, but the solution to the mathematical problem will provide a solution to the practical problem only in the case where an *appropriate* mathematical problem has been abstracted. With luck, one might solve the practical problem by a guess, or by solving an inappropriate mathematical problem, but we will overlook the lucky in order to simplify our presentation. Suppose that a boy wished to build a Tinkertoy crane one fourth the size of a Tinkertoy crane illustrated on his Tinkertoy box. If six pulleys were required for the illustrated one, he might abstract to the same mathematical equation used in the baking problem in an effort to find the solution. But this time the solution to the equation suggests that 1½ pulleys should be used to make the smaller crane. Something has gone wrong. The right answer to the mathematical equation has been found, but an *inappropriate* mathematical problem has been abstracted from the practical problem. The appropriateness of a mathematical problem depends upon a suitable analogy between the mathematical operations involved in its solution and physical operations involved in solving the practical problem. For example, dividing numbers can be quite analogous to dividing physical objects. We can divide numbers by numbers so as to obtain numbers, and tablespoons of butter by a knife to obtain tablespoons of butter, but when we divide a pulley with a knife we may well end up with a useless piece of wood rather than a pulley. Unless each Tinkertoy pulley in the large crane can be matched by a pulley one fourth as large, it may not be possible to build the smaller crane. Clearly, if we cannot build the smaller crane, then there is no mathematical problem whose solution will tell us how to build it. A practical problem is amenable to mathematical solution if and only if an appropriate mathematical problem may be abstracted from the problem. Only past experience with successful solutions of practical problems similar to one that we are attacking may give us a reasonable conviction that the problem is open to mathematical analysis.

Logicians may be confronted with an argument given in some practical context. A significant problem may then be whether the argument is cogent, that is, whether the conclusion of the argument is properly justified by the premises offered in its support. In this book we will treat the problem of the cogency of a given argument as the practical problem which the logician is usually interested in solving. The modern logician attacks this problem by abstracting from the argument a logical problem whose solution provides an answer to the question of whether the argument is cogent. Abstracting a logical problem will be quite analogous to abstracting a mathematical problem. Aside from learning the technical manipulations required to abstract and solve logical problems, therefore, our main attention must be directed to whether the logical problem abstracted in a particular context can be regarded as appropriate, that is, one whose solution provides the correct answer to the original problem. It will turn out that the question of appropriateness is very subtle and difficult, just as it is for many applications of mathematical systems.

Given the analogy between the use of mathematical systems and logical systems that has been suggested, and which has been consciously exploited by modern logicians, we may well ask in advance whether logical systems can secure an advantage in determining the cogency of argument which is in any way comparable to the manifest powers associated with the intelligent use of mathematical systems. It does not require elaborate justification to claim that some explicit use of mathematical systems is required for normal adult life in industrialized societies. A great deal of early schooling in such societies is devoted to instruction in arithmetic and in geometrical systems, some mastery of which underlies even such simple skills as making correct change. On the other hand, it is quite possible to live a normal adult life in an industrialized society without explicit instruction in logical systems. It may therefore seem required that logicians make some case for the value of mastery of their notations and systems beyond the mere possibility of usefulness suggested by the analogy with the usefulness of mathematical systems.

The usefulness of a study of logical systems would be put beyond doubt if it could be established that students of logic learn to reason more cogently and more cleverly than their untutored counterparts. Many students have seemed to assume that this is the object of courses in logic, to teach one to reason logically, and have later expressed disappointment at failure to attain this goal.

We can usefully compare the purpose of instruction in logical systems with that of instruction in mathematical systems. What can be taught in the obvious sense about mathematical systems is their structure as well as those techniques related to the structure which make possible the solution of fixed mathematical problems. But it is also quite clear that instruction in mathematics will not create mathematicians who can find the required appropriate mathematical problems for novel practical problems, or who can make new discoveries within the study of mathematical systems. Creativity may appear under the stimulation of examples, or as a result of contact with other creative persons, but very little is known about general methods of developing creative ability.

In a logic course, we introduce various logical systems and the rather dull techniques involved in solving fixed logical problems. By itself, mastery of these techniques will not enable one to construct cogent arguments which are very interesting, and it will not enable one to abstract appropriate logical problems in order to test the cogency of the argumentation of others. These are skills that will hopefully follow the mastery of techniques, but which are in no sense guaranteed by their mastery. We will find out that being a skillful logician involves creative insight just as much as does being a creative mathematician.

Honesty now compels a brief return to the problem of the justification of the study of logical systems. It remains true that explicit knowledge of logical systems is not a requisite for normal, everyday adult life. The reason for this should become apparent when we survey the presuppositions involved in abstracting to appropriate logical problems in the context of given arguments. Much of everyday argument is embedded in such a thick mat of particular information that abstraction to logical form effects very little economy and power. For instance, if you argue that Henry (who is a close friend) is likely to be at The Black Horse Inn by imagining yourself in Henry's place and guessing at what he would be doing, you are probably relying on a great mass of integrated particular information about Henry that could not be abstracted to logical notation with any useful resulting economy. In everyday argument, just a few conclusions are usually drawn from a great deal of assimilated biographical and local information. Here modern logic is of limited application. We can reason well in these circumstances because successful patterns of argument are embedded in our speech without our explicit awareness; our speech may exhibit grammatical regularities that we do not recognize explicitly, and which we may not be able to state.

The advantage of using modern logical systems is shown primarily in the analysis of mathematical, scientific, and sometimes philosophical argumentation, where a great many consequences are to be drawn from a few clear and simple abstract ideas. In these areas, argumentation may involve entities so abstract or so peculiar that the intuition provided by habitual patterns of successful inference may fail to provide a satisfactory test of cogency. Here modern logic has been of considerable help in stating and testing the cogency of complex argument.

2. Arguments and Validity

The notion of an argument is used in such a variety of contexts that it cannot by itself provide a suitable basis for an abstraction to a logical test of cogency. People are sometimes said to be having an argument when they are simply shouting at one another. Again, a certain kind of movie may be said to be an argument against war. In order to have a firm basis for abstracting logical problems, logicians have found through experience that it is helpful to define an argument as a certain kind of sequence of sentences. The sentences of an argument must all be such that if certain facts obtain, they are true, and if these facts do not obtain, they are false. Since the relevant facts may not be known when an argument is advanced, it may not be known whether or not the sentences in an argument are true or false. Nevertheless, each sentence in an argument must be of the kind which would be true or false if we came to know certain related facts. A particular sentence used on some occasion to make a claim that would be true or false if certain facts were known will, for the time being, be called an *assertion*. An assertion is not just a sentence, but a sentence used in some context to make a factual claim. For example, if you find a sentence written on a piece of paper left lying around by someone, that sentence is just a sequence of English words (let us say) until it is discovered what the author was doing when he wrote the sentence down. An actual argument will clearly be a sequence of assertions, but

we let the sentences used to make these assertions constitute
the basis for abstraction to a logical form. In doing this, we
will switch back and forth between talk about sentences and
talk about the assertions which they would be used to make
in some context. This should not cause any confusion provided that we treat the sentences in unknown contexts as
though they were used to make assertions. When an argument
is presented in a book, for example, we treat the sentences as
though they were used to make the assertions that they could
be used to make in some ordinary context.

An argument is a claim that some assertion in a sequence of
assertions follows from the other assertions made previously
in the argument. The assertion which is claimed to follow
from the others is called the *conclusion* of the argument,
and the assertion or assertions it is said to follow from are
called the *premise* or *premises* of the argument. The word
therefore can be inserted before the conclusion of an argument (if it does not already appear there) in order to identify
it for the purposes of abstraction. It should be clear that many
informal arguments of science and everyday life can easily
be recast as sequences of sentences expressing assertions in
this technical sense in order to provide a basis for abstraction
to the notation of logical systems.

These remarks do not give us a definition of argument
which results in a definite determination in every case of
whether some sequence of sentences satisfies the definition.
We have to say that someone has presented an argument if
we can see such an idealized sequence in what he has actually
written or said. Logic does not operate independently of these
considerations. To abstract to logical forms, we will have to
suppose that we can recognize, in a given context, the assertions which have been presented. We want to determine
whether someone has argued well, even though we do not
know whether the conclusion of his argument is true or false,
or whether each premise is true, or even, in some cases, when
we are sure that the conclusion is false. There is nothing
strange or esoteric about this: We can often agree that an
opponent has argued well in support of his position, even

though we are not prepared to accept it because we think that he has the facts wrong, or has overlooked certain important facts.

A typical reason for advancing an argument is to convince someone who accepts the premises of the argument as true that he must also accept the conclusion as true. This motivation for advancing an argument will enable us to sharpen the notion of arguing well or of providing a cogent argument into the logician's definition of a *valid deductive argument*. *An argument is defined as a valid deductive argument if its premises could not all be true while its conclusion was false.* An argument, as given, may have premises which are true or false, and a conclusion which is true or false. If, as the argument is presented, we can establish that the premises are all true and the conclusion false, we have shown that the argument is invalid. Suppose that this is not the circumstance, but we can imagine a possible world, that is, a set of facts, such that in this hypothetical world the premises of the argument could all be true while the conclusion was false. Again, we would see that the truth of the conclusion does not intuitively follow from the joint truth of the premises. If either the actual world or a possible world is such that the premises of the argument could be jointly true while the conclusion was false, then the argument is invalid. Otherwise, the argument is valid. We can describe an argument as valid in a more positive manner by saying that we can assess an argument as valid if a systematic survey of possible worlds shows that there are no circumstances in which the premises of the argument could be jointly true while the conclusion was false. The reason we will abstract arguments to logical forms is precisely to obtain a systematic way of checking through the possible worlds related to the form in an effort to determine whether a set of facts making the premises true while the conclusion was false could be found. The validity of an argument is not determined by the truth or falsity of the particular assertions which occur in it, given the world as we think it is, but by all the patterns of truth and falsity of its constituent assertions when the total range of relevant possible worlds is examined. The definition of *valid deductive argument* given here must be carefully studied, since the logical systems we are about to introduce can make sense only as a way of implementing the search through possible worlds that has been intuitively described in connection with this definition.

The usefulness of the notion of a valid deductive argument is a consequence of its definition. Now, we would not normally bother to advance an argument to someone if we knew the truth or falsity of all of the premises and the conclusion. If the conclusion is known to be true, for example, an argument can hardly convince us that it is more true. In abstract studies, we might be interested to determine whether a certain assertion follows from other assertions where we know that all of the assertions involved are true, but we can remember this one exception to the general remark that we do not normally advance an argument whose conclusion we know is true. The power of logical techniques is that they can often show us that an argument is deductively valid by means of a symbolic test of all of the relevant worlds. Sometimes, then, we can know that an argument is valid even though we do not know whether each assertion in the argument is actually true or false.

Suppose that we determine that some argument is valid, and only later find out that the conclusion of the argument is actually false. From the validity of the argument and the fact of the falsity of its conclusion, we can conclude that at least one of the premises of the argument is also false. For if all of its premises were true, and its conclusion false, it would not be valid, contrary to what we have already established. This simple pattern has many practical applications, particularly in the test of scientific theories. An experiment can cause the abandonment of a scientific theory if it shows that some deductive consequence of that theory is false. This is a little overdrawn in view of scientific practice, since theories with false consequences may be retained provided that they yield true consequences in a wide range of cases and there are no alternative theories of greater power available. But the rough logic of experimental testing of theories or hypotheses is an immediate consequence of validity.

In other cases, we may know both that certain arguments are valid and that their premises are true. This is often the case in the construction of mathematical systems where certain axioms are simply set down by stipulation and declared true of certain mathematical objects. By finding valid consequences of these axioms, one can find other assertions of an interesting kind which reveal further truths about the mathematical objects. The consequences of the axioms of plane geometry are established in this fashion in modern treatises. (See, for example, [F2].) We can thus see that the knowledge that certain arguments are valid, coupled with either a knowledge that their premises are true, or that their conclusions are false, can be of immense practical application in mathematics and in science.

We will now turn to some general remarks about abstraction in logical systems. One abstractive step is already taken when we construe an argument as an explicit sequence of sentences. This abstractive step may appear in the use of mathematics when one clarifies the practical problem to be solved by asking certain questions. The crucial step of abstraction occurs when the clarified practical problem is abstracted to an explicit logical or mathematical problem to be solved solely by logical or mathematical techniques. In testing the validity of an argument, we abstract to a pattern of logical symbols known as a *logical form*. The logical form provides the logician with the recipe for the possible worlds which he must check through to determine whether the abstracted argument is valid.

There is an important constraint on the abstraction to logical forms which can provide an insight into the symbols to be used in logical abstraction. Somehow, an appropriate logical form must exhibit the pattern of facts which determine the truth or falsity of the assertions in the argument. In the form, this pattern is generalized so that from it we may determine all the patterns of fact in the different possible worlds which may make the assertions in the argument true or false. As a minimum requirement for a good logical symbolism, we might expect that if two assertions in an argument are the same, that is, true or false together no matter what possible world is considered, then they should be abstracted to the same symbol or to equivalent patterns of symbols in the logical form. Otherwise, differences in patterns of symbols abstracting assertions should somehow be correlated to the differences we see with respect to the facts that make them true or false.

The whole matter of abstraction would be easy if assertions were transparently simple. For example, if any two different sentences were always used to make independent assertions, that is, assertions which might each be either true or false depending on the facts, then logic would be trivial. We could construct one simple calculus that would determine validity in every case. Let an argument be a sequence of *n* sentences. Then the conclusion is a sentence either identical with one of the premise sentences or it is not. In the former case, the argument would be valid, since any facts making the premises jointly true would make the conclusion, as identical with one of them, true also. In the latter case, the argument would be invalid, since by assumption some possible world is such that the conclusion could be false while all of the premises (each different from the conclusion) could be true. Validity of argument would then turn out to be trivial repetition of a sentence in every case. We are saved from the triviality of validity by the complexity of language.

The existence of complex assertions has resulted in the development of a number of distinct kinds of logical form which logicians have found it profitable to employ in assessing validity. There are different kinds of logical form tailored to fit different levels of complexity of assertion, just as there are different mathematical problems tailored to fit various kinds of practical problems.

To show the invalidity of an argument it is not always necessary to abstract to a logical form. If someone offers an argument, and we can consistently suppose that the facts are such that the premises are jointly true while the conclusion is false, we have shown the argument invalid by counterexample. Much ordinary criticism of argument proceeds in this fashion, and it is a perfectly sound way of showing an argument invalid.

But since the skill involved in thinking of counterexamples is not very systematic, and is often hampered by the (false) assumption that certain possible worlds could not occur, failure to find a counterexample on the intuitive level may either mean that the argument is valid, or that we simply haven't been clever enough yet to invent an appropriate counterexample. In order to achieve a systematic approach, we need to abstract logical forms.

When we have abstracted to a logical form, it is not possible to tell in general whether the complexity of the form matches the complexity of the argument in a manner which makes the logical form an appropriate test of the validity of the original argument. Logicians have solved this problem by adopting a conservative philosophy which will insure that all dubious cases are assessed as invalid arguments. In working with a particular logical form for an argument, we can conclude from an assessment of validity that the argument is valid, and can be freely used in further argument without fear of counterexample. On the other hand, an assessment of an argument as invalid in terms of a particular logical form may merely mean that the form is inappropriate to the argument, and not that the argument is actually invalid.

The logician has the attitude of a bridge builder. To be safe, a good bridge builder will draw up plans satisfying so many safety factors that he can be certain that his bridge will stand. In this context, we will pass over the philosophical puzzles which purport to show that we can never be certain of anything. If the builder learns more and more about the materials he is using, he may reduce the early safety factors and build some bridges that he is equally certain will stand that would have been ruled out by the earlier safety factors. The bridge builder uses safety standards that are contrary to fact, in that he assumes that the materials he is using are less safe than in fact he thinks they are. After abstracting to a logical form, a logician will deliberately assume that the factual patterns which determine the truth or falsity of the assertions abstracted can be more varied than he may in fact think they can be. If he makes rather wilder assumptions about the inde-

pendence of the assertions than may seem appropriate, he
then allows for the maximum possibility that the conclusion
could be false while the premises were jointly true. If an
argument is assessed as valid under these circumstances, he
can reasonably conclude that it is valid. On the other hand,
if it is assessed as invalid, it may well turn out that if reasonable restraints on the assumed independence of the assertions
can be added, the argument will in fact be valid. For example,
the logician could adopt the test for validity mentioned earlier
as the assumption that any two different sentences could be
regarded as used to make independent assertions in every
context. He would then find that only quite trivial arguments
would be valid, and he would miss most of the valid arguments that he might come across. Nonetheless, his attack
would be conservative in the sense that relaxation of his
standards could only be expected to expose new valid arguments, and not to show that arguments previously assessed as
valid were actually invalid. It is important to understand this
conservative attitude if the logical forms we abstract later are
not to seem inappropriate to a silly degree on many occasions.

In this book we will develop two conceptions of logical
form and the tests for validity related to them. Sentential Logic
forms are abstracted under assumptions so stringent that any
argument assessed as valid on their basis may reasonably be
regarded as valid in any more advanced test of validity. When
we abstract Predicate Logic forms, we will take a much closer
look at the structure of individual assertions, and many arguments will be assessed as valid in this more complicated logical
system that would not pass the test of Sentential Logic. Predicate Logic will extend Sentential Logic in the sense that it will
widen the class of valid arguments without finding any argument assessed as valid by Sentential Logic to be invalid in
the extended test. These two logical systems are considered by
most contemporary logicians to be adequate to the discovery of
validity in all important scientific and mathematical contexts.
In this sense, the material to be mastered in Part Two and
Part Three is the indispensable foundation for an understanding of the techniques and significance of modern logic.

PART TWO
SENTENTIAL LOGIC

3. Abstracting SL Forms

The first logical forms to be explicitly introduced are known as Sentential Logic forms, or SL forms. We will hereafter use SL to abbreviate *Sentential Logic*. In defining an argument in the logician's sense, it was assumed that we could recognize assertions in order to construct sequences of sentences corresponding to arguments in the technical form. It is clear that we can use this insight to assign simply the same symbol to both of any pair of sentences sufficiently simple that we can see that they are true or false together in any conceivable circumstances. For example, the sentences "John loves Mary" and "Mary is loved by John" are not identical, but in the context of most arguments they would be used to make assertions true or false together, so that they could be abstracted to the same symbol. The difficulties which arise in abstracting to SL forms are concerned with pairs of sentences which are used to make assertions neither obviously equivalent nor obviously independent in their truth-values. The truth-value of an assertion is always *truth* or *falsity*, depending on the relevant facts. Since experience will enable us to see equivalences that might otherwise be obscure, we need some fairly objective criterion of equivalence and independence in order to have a common symbolism for SL forms.

The symbols which we will use to abstract SL forms are capital letters (of the alphabet), parentheses, and a few special logical symbols. Capital letters, sometimes with primes or sub-

scripts, will be used to abstract the simplest equivalent assertions in a given argument in a sense of *simple* to be developed
shortly. Parentheses and logical symbols will be used to abstract the structure of complex assertions which may be
thought of as having the simplest assertions as constituents.
We will now examine the way in which SL analysis of sentences
to obtain SL forms can find a complex assertion to be suitably
represented as a structure having simpler components.

Suppose that the assertion "It is raining" is abstracted to
the capital letter "A." Another assertion, for example, "It is
not raining," could be an assertion claiming that the assertion
abstracted to "A" was false. Any facts making the one
assertion true would make the other assertion false. If some
assertion has been abstracted to a capital letter, and another
assertion is true in exactly the circumstances which make the
first assertion false, and vice versa, then this second assertion
is known as the *negation* of the first. The negation of an
assertion is abstracted by enclosing the SL symbol abstracting
the assertion to be negated within parentheses, and prefixing
the left-hand parenthesis with a tilde. In terms of the example,
"It is not raining" would be abstracted to "$\sim (A)$," a complex
SL symbol which can be read "not A." The purpose of the
parentheses is merely to indicate the exact abstracted assertion
which a tilde negates. This does not matter when only a single
capital letter is within the parentheses, but later we will see
that quite complex SL forms may need to be enclosed in the
parentheses in order to abstract complex arguments.

The context of an argument must provide the essential clues
to negation. By virtue of our description of negation, a sentence and its negation must each take a different truth-value
on any possible circumstances. What about a pair of sentences
like the "It is raining" and "It is not raining" of our example?
We can imagine circumstances of weather in which the one
would not seem clearly false while the other was clearly true.
But this is why we take abstraction relative to the context of
an argument. For tennis players and soccer players, meteor-
ological conditions might differentiate more or less sharply
rain from lack of rain; the same conditions could cause sus-

pension of tennis because of rain while a soccer match might take place on an adjoining field. The appropriateness of abstraction must be closely related to the circumstances in which an argument is offered.

The SL symbolism for an abstracted assertion and its negation has an obvious symmetry. If we see "A" and "$\sim (A)$" among the symbols of an abstracted argument, we know that one of these abstracts an assertion and the other the negation of that assertion. But it is not important from the standpoint of logic which is considered the assertion and which its negation. The symbols only remind us that when we search through possible worlds in an effort to determine validity, these pairs of symbols must never be given the same truth-value in the same possible world. That is all that they tell us, since each will be true and the other false in any possible world. If both an assertion and its negation appear in an argument, the usual convention is to abstract the assertion not containing an explicit grammatical negation into the SL form which does not contain an initial tilde. This is how we abstracted in the example. If an assertion appears without a corresponding negation in some argument, we may abstract it to an SL form with or without a tilde, as we please. It does not matter if it contains grammatical negation, since such negation only takes on significance in a possible world if there is a sentence which must have the other truth-value to be contrasted with it.

Let two assertions be abstracted to "A" and "B," respectively, since they are not obviously equivalent. There are two common ways of making a complex assertion which would have these two abstracted assertions as constituents. One may make an assertion claiming that both of the assertions are true, or one may make an assertion claiming that at least one (and possibly both) of the assertions is true. "$(A \wedge B)$" will be used to abstract an assertion that both of the assertions abstracted to "A" and "B" are true. This complex symbol will be called the *conjunction* of "A" and "B," and it can be read "A and B." "$(A \vee B)$" will be used to abstract an assertion that at least one of the assertions abstracted to "A" and "B" is true. This complex symbol will be called the *disjunction* of *"A"* and *"B,"* and is to be read *"A or B."*

Each of the complex symbols we have introduced so far has an important property: If we know whether or not the assertions abstracted to capital letters are true or false, we also know whether the assertion abstracted to the complex symbol is true or false. Any complex assertion whose truth or falsity can be determined from the truth or falsity of certain other assertions is called a truth-functional assertion of the other assertions. The negation of an assertion, the conjunction of two assertions, and the disjunction of two assertions are all truth-functional assertions of simpler assertions. If a negated assertion is true, the negation of that assertion is false, and vice versa. If both assertions in a conjunction are true, then the conjunction is true. Otherwise the conjunction is false. If at least one of the assertions in a disjunction is true, then the disjunction is true. Otherwise it is false. These three truth-functional assertions are sufficient to abstract all of the truth-functional assertions in any argument. Every truth-functional assertion of simpler assertions can be abstracted using some combination of negation, disjunction, and conjunction. In this sense, our symbolism for abstraction is complete.

After this, we will call any symbolism which abstracts an assertion, no matter how simple or complex, an *SL form.* An argument, since it is a sequence of assertions, could be abstracted to a sequence of SL forms which we could call an *SL argument form.* An SL argument form would correspond to the general notion of a logical form discussed in Chapter 2.

Before we begin to abstract SL argument forms, we will return to our definition of valid deductive argument. We defined an argument as deductively valid if circumstances could not be such that all of its premises were jointly true while its conclusion was false. This is equivalent to saying that an argument is *not* deductively valid if circumstances can be such that all of the premises are jointly true while *the negation of the conclusion* is true also. *The importance of this equivalent formulation cannot be overemphasized in terms of the test for validity we are about to introduce.* Instead of abstracting an argument to an SL argument form as described in the last paragraph, we will abstract an argument to an *SL argument consistency form*. An SL argument consistency form will be a sequence of SL forms abstracting the premises and the negation of the conclusion of the original argument. The point of abstracting an SL argument consistency form rather than an SL argument form is that when we attempt to show an argument invalid by examining possible worlds, we will be trying to make all of the SL forms in the SL argument consistency form abstract true assertions. The slight complication brought about by remembering to abstract the negation of the conclusion is made up for by the uniformity of our attack in trying to find circumstances in which all of the SL forms in an argument consistency form would be true.

To find an SL argument consistency form, we set down the premises and the negation of the conclusion of the original argument as *n* numbered lines. Further, we omit the word "therefore" before the conclusion, which is now negated, and write "∼ (CON)" at the right-hand side of the last line to remind ourselves that we are abstracting the negation of the conclusion of the original argument. After we have set down these *n* numbered lines, we attempt to abstract SL forms from them which will exhibit as much truth-functional structure as seems appropriate. If any of the assertions in the argument are seen to be negations, or conjunctions, or disjunctions of simpler assertions, we use capital letters to abstract the simpler assertions, and abstract the complex assertion in the manner we have previously indicated. The complex SL form then replaces the English sentence which originally appeared as a line of the SL argument consistency form. A complex SL form may contain a capital letter which in turn abstracts an assertion which is a truth-functional assertion of simpler assertions. If so, it may be abstracted to a complex SL form which then replaces the capital letter in the original complex SL form. Analysis of truth-functional structure is continued in this manner until no remaining truth-functional assertions seem unanalyzed. At any time during this process of analysis when it is seen that two assertions are sufficiently simple to have no truth-functional structure, and yet make equivalent assertions in the context of the argument, they should be abstracted to the same capital letter if they are not already so abstracted. Otherwise, new capital letters should always be used at each abstraction to a more complex SL form in order to express the conservative strategy that assertions not shown equivalent will be treated as independent. If some premise or the negation of the conclusion of the original argument escapes this analysis unabstracted to an SL form because it has no truth-functional structure and is not equivalent to any assertion which turns up in the course of the analysis of other assertions in the argument, it is abstracted to a capital letter. The form resulting from the completion of this line of SL analysis is called a *most sophisticated SL argument consistency form* for the original argument. "Most sophisticated" suggests that the greatest amount of truth-functional structure has been exhibited, and as a result we will also call the capital letters appearing in a most sophisticated SL argument consistency form the *simplest constituent assertions* of the original argument. The assertions which they abstract will also be called the *simplest constituent assertions* of the original argument. When we have abstracted a most sophisticated SL argument consistency form for a given argument, we are ready to begin the logical test for SL validity.

The procedure described in the last paragraph for finding a most sophisticated SL argument consistency form for a given argument may seem rather complex, but it is fairly easy to work through in actual examples. To illustrate the procedure and provide some comment on using it in practice, we will now work a few examples.

The first example is provided by an argument which has been partially abstracted to this sequence of sentences:

> If the Yankees do not win, the manager is to be fired. But the manager is not to be fired and the stadium is not to be sold.
> Therefore, the Yankees will win.

A first step is to negate the conclusion of the argument, dropping the word "therefore" and marking this step by "~ (CON)." The new sequence is then written down as three numbered lines:

(1) If the Yankees do not win, the manager is to be fired.
(2) But the manager is not to be fired and the stadium is not to be sold.
(3) The Yankees will not win.   ~ (CON)

Clearly, line (2) is an assertion which asserts both "The manager is not to be fired" and "The stadium is not to be sold." Both of these conjuncts contain grammatical negations, so we may abstract them respectively to "~ (D)" and "~ (E)." The conjunction may then be abstracted to the complex SL form "(~ (D) ∧ ~ (E))." In general, it is a good strategy to look for assertions in an argument which can be treated as conjunctions, since they are often quite easy to recognize. By contrast to line (2), for example, line (1) may appear to have no recognizable truth-functional structure to the untrained eye. When this happens, it is useful to try paraphrases of the original sentence to see if truth-functional structure can be exposed. For example, the sentence in line (1) is no doubt used to make an assertion which would be considered false in the event that it turns out that "The Yankees will not win" is true while "The manager will be fired" is false. We can abstract the latter assertion to "*D*," since we have used "~ (D)" to abstract the apparent negation of this assertion within the context of the argument. Let "*D*" abstract "The manager will be fired" and "~ (C)" abstract "The Yankees will not win." Making use of our previous observation that line (1) makes a false assertion if both "~ (C)" and "~ (D)" abstract true assertions, we might abstract line (1) as the negation of the conjunction of the assertions abstracted to "~ (C)" and "~ (D)." The resulting complex SL form "~ (~ (C) ∧ ~ (D))" is an acceptable abstraction of line (1). It is important to notice that this complex SL form is *not* a conjunction, but the negation of an SL form which is in turn a conjunction. In fact, the negation of a conjunction is always equivalent to a disjunction, as will be proved somewhat later. For the moment, we can see that another look at line (1) may indicate that this sentence is no doubt used to make an assertion which is equivalent to the assertion that at least one statement, "The Yankees will win" and "The manager will not be fired," is true. Using abstractions we have already introduced, this could be abstracted to the complex SL form "$(C \lor D)$." We will use this SL form to abstract line (1). Line (1) may be abstracted by paraphrasing it either as "It is not the case that the Yankees will not win and the manager will not be fired" or as "Either the Yankees will win or the manager will be fired." The former paraphrase requires two steps of abstraction: first, the abstraction of the negation of "The Yankees will not win and the manager will not be fired," and then the abstraction of the conjunction. The latter paraphrase requires only a single abstraction to a disjunctive SL form. We use the latter because it seems simpler. As a general strategy, if some line is not fairly clearly a conjunction, or the negation of some other sentence, we look for a paraphrase in terms of disjunction. Disjunction appears in the subtlest grammatical disguises, but once recognized, it is quite easy to abstract. Our example is now abstracted except for line (3), the negation of the conclusion of the original argument. But line (3) is plainly equivalent to the negation of one disjunct of the SL form abstracting line (1), and we can abstract line (3) to "$\sim (C)$." None of the assertions abstracted to "C," "D," or "E" shows any further truth-functional structure. Therefore, collecting SL forms and replacing the original lines by the appropriate forms, we obtain the following most sophisticated SL argument consistency form for this first sample argument:

(1)　$(C \lor D)$
(2)　$(\sim (D) \land \sim (E))$
(3)　$\sim (C)$　　　　　　　　　$\sim$ (CON)

The discussion of this first example may seem rather over-elaborate, but the techniques involved in abstracting a most sophisticated SL argument consistency form for any argument are quite well illustrated here. It is just a question of para-phrasing again and again until we find truth-functional structure that we can abstract, or conclude that there is no truth-functional structure to be abstracted. The only com-plication introduced by more complex arguments is one of keeping track of the levels of analysis that may be reached in the course of abstraction. A good way to do this is to ab-stract to an SL argument consistency form, and then trans-form this to more and more sophisticated SL argument con-sistency forms until no capital letter abstracts a sentence with further truth-functional structure, and all equivalent simplest constituent assertions have been abstracted to the same capital letter. We will illustrate this by abstracting a most sophisticated SL argument form for an argument containing a premise whose truth-functional structure is more complex than that of any sentence we have so far abstracted. The argu-ment to be abstracted is this:

> Either he left the switch off, and there is no danger of fire, or he left the switch on, and again there is no danger of fire.
> For in the latter case, the relay would have shut off. There-fore, there is no danger of fire.

We can immediately set this down in argument consistency form:

(1)   Either he left the switch off, and there is no danger of fire, or he left the switch on, and again there is no danger of fire.

(2)   If he left the switch on, the relay would have shut off.

(3)   There is danger of fire.   ~ (CON)

Lines (2) and (3) are quite amenable to the methods we employed in the last example. Using "*O*" to abstract "He left the switch on," "*R*" to abstract "The relay would have shut off," and "*D*" to abstract "There is danger of fire," we can abstract line (2) to the SL form "($\sim (O) \lor R$)" and line (3) to "*D*." We now turn our attention to line (1). Line (1) is clearly a disjunction, so we may abstract it to "($M \lor N$)," where "*M*" abstracts "He left the switch off and there is no danger of fire" and "*N*" abstracts "He left the switch on and there is no danger of fire." We can now set down the following SL argument consistency form for the argument:

(1)　$(M \lor N)$
(2)　$(\sim (O) \lor R)$
(3)　D　　　　　　　　　　$\sim$ (CON)

This is clearly not sophisticated enough, since "*M*" and "*N*" obviously abstract assertions with further truth-functional structure. Now, "*M*" abstracts the conjunction of "He left the switch off" and "There is no danger of fire." But these conjuncts should be abstracted to "$\sim (O)$" and "$\sim (D)$," respectively, in view of previous abstractions in the SL argument consistency form. So the assertion abstracted to "*M*" can be abstracted to "($\sim (O) \land \sim (D)$)," showing further truth-functional structure. Similarly, the assertion abstracted to "*N*" can be abstracted to "($O \land \sim (D)$)." These new SL forms showing greater truth-functional structure can then replace "*M*" and "*N*" in the previous SL argument consistency form to obtain this more sophisticated SL argument consistency form:

(1)　$((\sim (O) \land \sim (D)) \lor (O \land \sim (D)))$
(2)　$(\sim (O) \lor R)$
(3)　D　　　　　　　　　　　　$\sim$ (CON)

This is a most sophisticated SL argument consistency form for the original argument since none of the simplest constituent assertions of the argument consistency form have any additional truth-functional structure. When replacing SL forms by more complex SL forms, care must be taken to replace the simpler form with the more complex form exactly where it occurs in the less sophisticated SL argument consistency form. The way we use parentheses will then insure that the sentence is correctly analyzed. Line (1) of the most sophisticated SL argument consistency form just given is in fact basically a disjunction, each of whose disjuncts is a conjunction, exactly the structure that it should have on our analysis.

The techniques of abstraction using paraphrase where necessary and of replacement of SL argument consistency forms with more sophisticated SL argument consistency forms as greater truth-functional structure is located prove sufficient to abstract a most sophisticated SL argument consistency form for any argument. Except for some skill involved in discovering useful paraphrases, these techniques are quite mechanical and trivial, requiring nothing but greater attention to detail as arguments become more complex.

We pause for a moment to consider the significance of a most sophisticated SL argument consistency form. The most sophisticated SL argument consistency form that we find for a given argument does not, by itself, tell us whether the original argument is valid. A most sophisticated SL argument consistency form merely abstracts a precise logical problem which remains to be solved. It corresponds to the mathematical problem whose solution will solve some practical problem. Validity remains to be determined by appropriate manipulation of the symbolic patterns exhibited in the most sophisticated SL argument consistency form.

Exercises

1. The expressions "$\sim (A)$," "$(A \lor B)$," and "$(A \land B)$"
are read "not A," "A or B," and "A and B," with capital
letters pronounced as letters of the alphabet. It is helpful
in discussing SL forms to be able to read them in this code.
In reading complex SL forms, emphasis and pauses must
be used to indicate the structure. "$(\sim (\sim (A)) \land B)$" and
"$\sim (\sim (A) \land B)$" would be read "(not(not A)) and B"
and "not (not A and B)," the parentheses and spacing
indicating what parts must be read quickly and with less
emphasis. To read a complex SL form, one must first
grasp the structure in order to find a correct rhythm and
emphasis for its pronunciation. With this in mind, read
the following SL forms:
   a. $(\sim (S) \land E)$
   b. $\sim (S \land E)$
   c. $(C \lor \sim (S \land E))$
   d. $\sim (\sim (\sim (P) \lor C))$
   e. $(\sim (S) \land E) \lor \sim (S \land E)$

   (See Answer No. 62.)

2. Parentheses are merely a convenience, used in order to
keep track of the exact disjuncts of a disjunction, and so
forth. Many parentheses are actually redundant, and may
be omitted. We can considerably reduce the visual complexity of our symbolism with no loss in its exactness if
we use parentheses more flexibly. If one pair of parentheses encloses another pair, it is clear that the outer pair
is redundant, and may be dropped. If an entire SL form
is enclosed in a pair of parentheses, these outermost

parentheses may be omitted. If any tilde negates a single capital letter rather than a more complex SL form, the parentheses surrounding the capital letter may be dropped. After this, we will use these simplifications, but we will always imagine that all of the parentheses are actually in the SL form for the purposes of manipulating it according to the rules we will introduce later for developing proofs. Some of the following expressions are SL forms which have been simplified by the conventions just suggested, and some of these expressions could not be obtained from SL forms by omitting parentheses according to these conventions. Decide which expressions could be simplifications of SL forms, and restore the missing parentheses in these cases:

a. $\sim P \vee Q$
b. $\sim P \vee Q \wedge R$
c. $(\sim P \vee \sim Q) \wedge R$
d. $\sim P \wedge Q \wedge R$
e. $\sim (\sim P) \vee P$ (See Answer No. 18.)

3. Using the simplifications in parenthesis notation introduced in the last exercise, abstract the following arguments (assuming some normal context) to most sophisticated SL argument consistency forms:

   a. Either Australia or England will win the Test Match. Therefore, South Africa will not win the Test Match.
   b. The triangles are similar. But if the triangles are isosceles, then they are similar. Therefore, the triangles are isosceles.
   c. Either the police or the fire departments were called, or he was not protected by insurance and had to pay all court costs. But the records show that the police and fire departments were not called. Therefore, he had to pay court costs.
   d. Either Jack did not steal the goods, or he was in the building and did not leave before midnight. But if he left before midnight, the watchman would have seen him leave. The watchman did see him in the building at 9 P.M. Therefore, he stole the goods.

   (See Answer No. 9.)

4. Testing for SL Validity

•

How are we to determine the validity of an argument from a most sophisticated SL argument consistency form that we have abstracted from it? The definition of validity suggests that the argument will be valid if and only if it is not the case that circumstances could be such that all of the SL forms in the most sophisticated SL argument consistency form abstract true assertions. For if all of the SL forms could abstract true assertions, it would be possible for all of the premises of the original argument to be jointly true while its conclusion was false. Our method of attack in testing for validity will be to determine whether all of the SL forms in a most sophisticated SL argument consistency form for an argument can be regarded as abstracting jointly true assertions.

To begin with, if we know whether the simplest constituent assertions abstracted to capital letters in a most sophisticated SL argument consistency form are each true or false, we could determine whether more complex SL forms abstract true or false assertions because of the significance of truth-functional structure. For example, if "*P*" and "*Q*" abstract simplest constituent assertions in these circumstances, and "$(P \wedge Q)$" is a more complex SL form occurring in the most sophisticated SL argument consistency form, we know that "$(P \wedge Q)$" abstracts a true assertion if and only if both "*P*" and "*Q*" abstract true assertions. If we knew, therefore, whether each simplest constituent assertion in a most sophisticated SL argument consistency form abstracted a true assertion or a false assertion, we could determine the truth value of every more complex SL form also occurring in the most sophisticated SL argument consistency form. From our discussion of validity, we know that an argument will be invalid just in the case that the SL forms abstracting its premises and the negation of its conclusion in a most sophisticated SL argument consistency form could all be true in some possible world. For purposes of SL analysis, possible worlds are described by deciding for each simplest constituent assertion in a most sophisticated SL argument consistency form whether it abstracts a true or a false assertion. The test for SL validity can now be rather simply stated: An argument is SL valid (or simply valid, given our conservative viewpoint) if there is no way of describing a possible world in which all of the SL forms constituting a most sophisticated SL argument consistency form for that argument would abstract true assertions.

In giving a test based upon possible worlds, we are explicitly assuming that each simplest constituent assertion in an argument may be true or false independently of the other simplest constituent assertions. This assumption of independence is very strong, and does not correspond to our actual use of language. Suppose, for example, that "P" abstracts "The ball is red" and "Q" abstracts "The ball is colored," the ball referred to in each assertion being the same one in the context of some argument. We cannot imagine facts which would make "The ball is red" true, and "The ball is colored" false. But in testing for validity, we will speak of the possible world in which "P" abstracts a true assertion and "Q" abstracts a false assertion. Now, where the sentences are related in the manner just sketched, the logician could safely suppose that the two sentences were not independent. But there are many borderline cases of independence. Two sentences may be such that some scientists regard them as related by a law of nature, while other scientists are skeptical that any such law of nature exists, and treat the sentences as independent. If each logician were to decide borderline cases as he saw fit, there would be no objective standard for SL validity. In order to have a simple, uniform, objective test for SL validity, the logician decides to treat each pair of distinct simplest constituent assertions as though they were independent.

The assumption of independence may be regarded as a "safety factor" insuring that an SL valid argument will remain valid no matter what new factual discoveries might be made in science. Treating all pairs of simplest constituent assertions as independent can be defended by the principle of conservatism. The class of all possible worlds includes every possible way of describing the truth values of the simplest constituent assertions of an argument while ignoring any constraints which might be imposed by the meaning of words or by the discoveries of science. Suppose an argument is declared SL valid because there is no possible world in which the SL forms constituting a most sophisticated SL argument consistency form abstracted from it are jointly regarded as abstracting true assertions. Then suppose that two or more pairs of distinct simplest constituent assertions of this argument are discovered not to be, in actual fact, independent. This amounts to saying that there cannot be as many possible worlds relevant to determining the truth or falsity of the simplest constituent assertions as are considered in the SL test. But if the argument is valid in all possible worlds as defined by the SL test, it would remain so if some of the possible worlds were struck out as a result of other considerations. The test for SL validity may thus be regarded as a test in every conceivable, and perhaps even some inconceivable, circumstances. It follows from this that when an argument has been shown SL valid, it is simply valid. When we develop the PL test for validity later, we will have a means of expressing dependence between pairs of nonequivalent sentences. When these dependencies are expressed as premises of an argument, it will turn out that some arguments judged to be SL invalid will prove to be valid on the basis of this subtler test. But no argument assessed as SL valid will turn out to be invalid when examined by PL methods of analysis.

A direct approach to SL validity is to evaluate the assertions abstracted by the SL forms of a most sophisticated SL argument consistency form in every possible world. If n is the number of different capital letters in a most sophisticated SL argument consistency form for some argument, then we can quite easily calculate that there are 2^n possible worlds to be considered in testing for validity. Each capital letter abstracts a simplest constituent assertion, which may be true or false independently of the others. Consider the simplest constituent assertions in any order. There are two choices of truth-value for the first assertion. For each of these choices, there are two choices for the second assertion, and 2^2 or 4 possible worlds to be described for the first two assertions. If there is a third simplest constituent assertion, it may be considered as extending each of the 4 possible worlds to either of two possible worlds, depending on whether the third assertion is considered to be true or false. There are then $2^2 \times 2$, or 2^3, or 8 possible worlds involving three simplest constituent assertions. This method of extension can obviously be continued to yield the formula 2^n for giving the number of possible worlds involving n distinct simplest constituent assertions. As n increases, the number of possible worlds becomes very large, and the direct method of examining a most sophisticated SL argument consistency form in each possible world would obviously be tedious, with considerable possibility of error in mere bookkeeping. It is thus obviously desirable to circumvent the direct method in favor of some method of testing for validity which will show a useful economy of effort as the number of distinct simplest constituent assertions in an argument becomes rather large.

The shorter method we will employ is known as the method of proof. We will begin by assuming that each most sophisticated SL argument consistency form abstracts an invalid argument, that is, that there is a possible world in which all of the SL forms in the most sophisticated SL argument consistency form abstract true assertions on some possible assignment of truth-values to the simplest constituent assertions in the argument. Then we will conduct a *systematic* search for the possible world satisfying our assumption. This search will always terminate after a finite number of steps either with a description of the possible world satisfying our assumption, or with a contradictory outcome that will show the original assumption to have been wrong. The method of proof will consequently always enable us to determine whether an argument is SL valid or SL invalid.

We start a proof for a particular argument by writing down the n lines of the most sophisticated SL argument consistency form that we have abstracted from it. This time, of course, we will assume that each of these lines abstracts a true assertion. If these lines abstract true assertions, we can add other SL forms as further lines which must also abstract true assertions. Each line which is added will be justified by a rule of proof showing that the newly added line must abstract a true assertion if the earlier lines abstract true assertions. The rules of proof will operate by simplifying complex SL forms into their truth-functional constituents, so that as lines are added to a proof, the SL forms added become simpler and simpler until we reach SL forms abstracting simplest constituent assertions which must abstract true assertions if the original SL forms of the proof abstracted true assertions. These simplest constituent assertions, which must be true if the original SL forms of the proof abstract true assertions, then either describe the possible world that we were looking for, or they are contradictory, and describe no possible world. In the latter case, we will be able to show that the original assumption was unjustified, and the SL forms in the most sophisticated SL argument consistency form cannot all abstract true assertions. It is an immediate consequence that the original argument to be tested is SL valid, or simply valid.

We will now introduce rules of proof which will justify the addition of new lines to an SL proof on the understanding that a new line must abstract a true assertion if the previous lines abstracted true assertions. Any SL form occurring as one of the first n lines of a proof will be one of the following kind:

(A) an SL capital letter,
(B) a conjunctive SL form,
(C) the negation of an SL form, or
(D) a disjunctive SL form.

SL forms of kind (A) are quite easy to deal with. If a line of a proof is an SL capital letter, then on the assumption that there is a possible world in which this line is true, that possible world must be such that the simplest constituent assertion abstracted to the capital letter is a true assertion. But we cannot and need not simplify further, since this information is part of the description of the possible world that we are looking for.

Now consider any line of a proof which is a conjunctive SL form. On the assumption that such a form abstracts a true assertion, we are also committed to the view that each SL form abstracting one of the conjuncts is true, since a conjunction is true if and only if both of its conjuncts are true. We can simplify a conjunctive SL form by writing down either or both of its conjuncts as further lines of the proof. We will express this fact by introducing a pair of rules of proof which we represent in the following fashion:

$p \land q \vdash p$ CS_1 (conjunctive simplification$_1$)
$p \land q \vdash q$ CS_2 (conjunctive simplification$_2$)

We read these rules as follows:

CS_1: "p" may be deduced from "$p \land q$."
CS_2: "q" may be deduced from "$p \land q$."

The way in which these rules are used can be illustrated by an example. We first write down one of the most sophisticated SL argument consistency forms abstracted in Chapter 3 as the first n lines of a proof:

(1) $C \lor D$
(2) $\sim D \land \sim E$
(3) $\sim C$ $\sim$ (CON)

Line (2) is a conjunctive SL form. If we wish to use CS_1 to simplify it, we must first show that an SL form can be substituted for "p" and an SL form substituted for "q" in the expression "$p \land q$" of the rule so that line (2) of the proof is obtained. (Small letters "p," "q," and "r" will be used to

state rules of proof. The small letters are not SL forms, and
neither are any of the expressions in the rules. Instead, the
small letters stand for SL forms, and are simply a convenient
way of talking about the total range of SL forms. Any conjunctive form can be obtained, like line (2), from the expression
"$p \wedge q$" when one SL form is substituted for "p" and another
is substituted for "q." Thus we can use the expression
"$p \wedge q$" to talk about all conjunctive SL forms.) Having
shown that line (2) is an SL form which may be obtained
by substitution in the left-hand side of rule CS_1, we can now
write down the SL form which is described by the same substitution into the right-hand side of the rule as a new line of
the proof. To keep track of the justification of a new line in
a proof, we cite on the far right of the line the number of the
earlier line from which it is obtained, followed by the symbol
for the rule whose application provides the justification for
adding the new line. It is not necessary to keep track of the
substitution employed, since this can be determined from the
lines involved along with the rule cited. Using CS_1 to simplify
line (2), we could add a line (4) to our sample proof which
would look like this:

(4) $\sim D$ (2) CS_1

If both CS_1 and CS_2 have been used to simplify a conjunctive SL form, then we may cross out the twice simplified conjunction to indicate that it can be simplified no further, and to
remind ourselves that the assumption that it is true is entirely
justified if we can find a possible world in which the lines
obtained from it abstract true assertions. Crossing out previous
lines will not be part of the rules of proof, but simply a procedure designed to facilitate proofs by concentrating our
attention on lines that may still require simplification. Using both CS_1 and CS_2, we now extend our sample proof by
another line and cross out line (2) as follows:

(1) $C \vee D$
(2)   ~~$\sim D \wedge \sim E$~~
(3) $\sim C$ $\sim$ (CON)
(4) $\sim D$ (2) CS_1
(5) $\sim E$ (2) CS_2

Since none of the remaining lines is a conjunctive SL form, we cannot add any further lines to this proof with our present rules.

We now turn our attention to lines of proofs which are of kind (C), that is, negations of SL forms. Clearly, a negation could be the negation of an SL form of any of kinds (A)–(D), so that rules of proof for negation will prove rather numerous, although they will be quite simple individually. First, we consider a line of a proof which is the negation of an SL capital letter. Such a line can abstract a true assertion if and only if the SL capital letter which it negates abstracts a false assertion. But this gives us direct information about the possible world which we are looking for, and we do not simplify further. Looking back at our sample proof, lines (3)–(5) inform us that a possible world satisfying the assumption that lines (1)–(3) jointly abstract true assertions is given by the possible world in which the simplest constituent assertions abstracted to "*C*," "*D*," and "*E*" are all false.

We next consider lines of proof which are negations of SL forms which are in turn negations. Clearly, the negation of the negation of an SL form can abstract a true assertion if and only if the negation of the SL form abstracts a false assertion, and the negation of the SL form abstracts a false assertion if and only if the SL form abstracts a true assertion. Consequently, the negation of the negation of an SL form abstracts a true assertion if and only if the SL form abstracts a true assertion. Negations of negations of SL forms can be simplified by adding this rule:

$$\sim (\sim p) \vdash p \qquad \text{DN (double negation)}$$

As above, if we add a new line by applying DN, we cite the number of the previous line on the right followed by "DN." We may also cross out the old line on the same philosophy that permitted crossing out in the case of a simplified conjunction.

The remaining cases of kind (C) to discuss are lines of proof in which an SL form is the negation of either a conjunctive or a disjunctive SL form. Underlying the simplification of such SL forms is the following important fact: The negation of a conjunctive SL form is equivalent to a disjunctive SL form, and the negation of a disjunctive SL form is equivalent to a conjunctive SL form. The rules which give the exact equivalences are somewhat complicated when they are first encountered, because of subtleties of form introduced by the presence of negations of SL forms. We will give a justification in detail for only one of these simplifying rules, since when it is understood, the rest of the rules can be seen as just trivial variations of the underlying idea. The simplifying rule to be discussed in detail is this:

$$\sim (p \wedge q) \vdash \qquad \sim p \vee \sim q \qquad \text{DM}_1 \quad (\text{DeMorgan}_1)$$

A line of a proof which can be obtained by substitution of an SL form for "p" and an SL form for "q" in the left-hand side of DM_1 can abstract a true assertion if and only if the SL form obtained by the same substitution into "$p \wedge q$" is false. But then the line of proof abstracts a true assertion if and only if at least one of the SL forms substituted for "p" or for "q" abstracts a false assertion. This is equivalent to saying that the line of proof abstracts a true assertion if and only if at least one of the SL forms which may be obtained by the same substitution into "$\sim p$" or "$\sim q$" abstracts a true assertion. Again, this is equivalent to saying that the line of proof abstracts a true assertion if and only if this same substitution into "$\sim p \vee \sim q$" results in an SL form abstracting a true assertion. We can repeat this line of argument with "$\sim p$" or "$\sim q$" instead of "p" or "q" throughout, using DN to eliminate any double negations. The slightly different variations yield three additional rules for simplifying the negation of a conjunction:

$$\sim (\sim p \wedge q) \vdash p \vee \sim q \qquad \text{DM}_2$$
$$\sim (p \wedge \sim q) \vdash \sim p \vee q \qquad \text{DM}_3$$
$$\sim (\sim p \wedge \sim q) \vdash p \vee q \qquad \text{DM}_4$$

Corresponding rules for the simplification of the negation of a disjunction are easily made available by a closely related line of argument. We will discuss this rule in some detail:

$$\sim (p \lor q) \vdash \sim p \land \sim q \qquad \text{DM}_5$$

A line of proof which can be obtained by substitution of an SL form for "p" and an SL form for "q" in the left-hand side of DM_5 can abstract a true assertion if and only if the SL form obtained by the same substitution into "$p \lor q$" abstracts a false assertion. But the line of proof then abstracts a true assertion if and only if both of the SL forms substituted for "p" and "q" abstract false assertions. This is equivalent to saying that the line of proof abstracts a true assertion if and only if both SL forms obtained by the same substitution into "$\sim p$" and "$\sim q$" abstract true assertions. Again, this is equivalent to saying that the line of proof abstracts a true assertion if and only if this same substitution into "$\sim p \land \sim q$" results in an SL form abstracting a true assertion. By repeating this line of argument with "$\sim p$" or "$\sim q$" for "p" or "q" throughout, and using DN to eliminate double negations, we can add these three further rules for simplifying the negation of a disjunction:

$$\sim (\sim p \lor q) \vdash p \land \sim q \qquad \text{DM}_6$$
$$\sim (p \lor \sim q) \vdash \sim p \land q \qquad \text{DM}_7$$
$$\sim (\sim p \lor \sim q) \vdash p \land q \qquad \text{DM}_8$$

By using rules DM_1–DM_8, we can simplify any negation of a conjunctive or disjunctive SL form, and we may also cross out the simplified line.

We now turn to lines of proof which are of kind (D), that is, disjunctive SL forms. A disjunctive SL form can abstract a true assertion if and only if at least one of its disjuncts abstracts a true assertion. The difficulty with handling disjunctive forms is that this information by itself does not entitle us to say that either of the disjuncts is true. Now, suppose that during a proof we obtain a line which is the negation of one disjunct of a disjunctive SL form which appears as another line of the proof. The negation of the disjunct can abstract a true assertion if and only if the disjunct abstracts a false assertion. We can conclude under these circumstances that the other disjunct abstracts a true assertion, so that we can add the disjunct as a further line of the proof. Either disjunct, of course, may be shown false by some other line of the proof. Using DN to simplify the negation of the negation of some SL form, we have four new rules of proof provided by this line of reasoning:

$$p \lor q, \sim p \vdash q \qquad \text{DS}_1 \quad \text{(disjunctive syllogism}_1\text{)}$$
$$p \lor q, \sim q \vdash p \qquad \text{DS}_2 \quad \text{(disjunctive syllogism}_2\text{)}$$
$$\sim p \lor q, p \vdash q \qquad \text{DS}_3 \quad \text{(disjunctive syllogism}_3\text{)}$$
$$p \lor \sim q, q \vdash p \qquad \text{DS}_4 \quad \text{(disjunctive syllogism}_4\text{)}$$

These rules are different from previous rules of proof in that a sequence of two expressions appears on the left-hand side. If two lines of a proof can be obtained by substitution into the two expressions on the left-hand side of the proof, then we may add the SL form obtained by the same substitution into the right-hand side of the rule as an additional line of the proof. On the far right we cite the numbers of the pair of lines from which the new rule is derived, along with the symbol for the appropriate rule. It should be noted that it does not matter in which order the relevant pair of lines happens to occur earlier in the proof, since the argument underlying the rules is not dependent on the order of the lines of a proof. After DS_1 or DS_2 has been used to simplify a disjunctive SL form, we may cross out the disjunctive form for convenience, since we know that only one of its disjuncts can abstract a true assertion, and that disjunct appears as a later line of the proof.

If a disjunctive SL form occurs as a line of a proof but no other line of the proof is the negation of one of its disjuncts, we will not be able to simplify the line by DS_1–DS_4. We may simplify such a disjunction with an *auxiliary rule of proof* now to be introduced. The idea behind the auxiliary rule is this. If a disjunctive SL form abstracts a true assertion, then at least one of its disjuncts must abstract a true assertion. Therefore, we can temporarily guess that one disjunction abstracts a true assertion and then see whether we can describe a possible world in which all of the earlier lines of proof can jointly abstract true assertions along with this disjunct. If we can describe such a possible world, then the disjunction can abstract a true assertion along with all of the earlier lines in the same possible world, since the truth of the disjunct guarantees the truth of the disjunction. The auxiliary rule is as follows:

If a disjunctive SL form occurs as a line of a proof, we may write down either disjunct of the line as a new line of the proof, citing on the right-hand side of the new line the number of the line which is the relevant disjunctive SL form followed by "D," and prefixing the number of the new line with an asterisk.

The purpose of the asterisk is to remind us that a prefixed line is a guess at the description of a possible world in which the first *n* lines of the proof jointly abstract true assertions. But this line is not deducible from earlier lines, since it may be the other disjunct only which can abstract a true assertion jointly with the earlier lines of the proof. We cannot therefore justify the claim that a prefixed line can abstract a true assertion jointly with preceding lines of the proof at the time when it is added.

In order to keep proofs as short as possible, we will assume that the same rule is not applied twice to the same line in the course of developing a proof. Then, using auxiliary rule D along with the previously given rules of proof, we can *completely simplify* the most sophisticated SL argument consistency form which initiates a proof by adding lines to the proof until we reach a point at which no line of the proof can be simplified by a rule so as to add a further line to the proof.

When a most sophisticated SL argument consistency form has been completely simplified in a proof using this process of development, exactly one of the following two descriptions will apply to the completely simplified proof: Either (i) no two lines of the proof consist of some SL form and its negation, or (ii) two lines of the proof consist of some SL form and its negation.

First, suppose condition (i) holds. Then the assumption that the first n lines of the proof jointly abstract true assertions can be consistently held. We can describe a possible world demonstrating that this assumption is correct. Let every line of the proof which is either an SL capital letter or the negation of an SL capital letter be regarded as abstracting true assertions. The more complex SL forms of the proof can then be seen to abstract true assertions if these simplest constituents do. The last conjunction (if any) appearing as a line of the proof abstracts a true assertion because both of its conjuncts do, and the last disjunction (if any) abstracts a true assertion because at least one of its disjuncts abstracts a true assertion. Further, the last complex negated SL form abstracts a true assertion if and only if the lines following from it abstract a true assertion. We can work out the truth-values of earlier and earlier lines of the proof by using these facts about the truth-values of the lines of the proof until we establish directly that the first n lines abstract true assertions. But in this case, the premises of the original argument can be jointly true while its conclusion is false. Therefore, *if condition (i) holds, the original argument is invalid.*

Now suppose that condition (ii) holds, and some SL form and the negation of that SL form are two lines of the proof. It follows that some SL capital letter and its negation must both abstract true assertions, which is absurd. Therefore, not all of the lines of the proof can abstract true assertions. We cannot conclude from this fact alone that the original argument is valid unless auxiliary rule D has not been used. If D has not been used, then the only assumption we have made is that the first n lines of the proof abstract true assertions. This is shown impossible if condition (ii) holds, so that in any possible world, at least one premise of the original argument must abstract a false assertion or the conclusion must abstract a true assertion, so that the argument is valid. But if D has been used, not only have we assumed that the first n lines of the proof abstract true assertions, but we have also guessed at the truth of certain disjuncts in adding each line prefixed by an asterisk. One or more of these guesses might be wrong in the sense that other guesses (that is, assuming the other disjuncts instead) would have led to a proof which was a complete simplification of the most sophisticated SL argument consistency form constituting the first n lines and in which condition (i) would hold. Therefore, if D is used one or more times in a proof, and condition (ii) holds when complete simplification has been obtained, the original argument is valid if and only if there is no alternative proof in which complete simplification can be obtained along with condition (i). In this case, we know that the premises and the negation of the conclusion cannot be jointly true in any possible world, and the original argument being tested is valid.

Actually, a proof does not have to result in complete simplification of the most sophisticated SL argument consistency form constituting its first n lines in order to show validity. If some SL form occurs as a line of a proof and the negation of that SL form occurs as another line of the same proof, then no possible world can be such that both of these SL forms abstract true assertions. We call a proof *blocked* if this occurs. A proof in which some most sophisticated SL argument consistency form is completely simplified and condition (ii) holds is a special case of a blocked proof. Now, if rule D is used in each of its applications in a proof so that complete simplification results, and condition (i) holds in this event, rule D is then said to be used *optimally*. Clearly, if we obtain a simplified proof in which D is used optimally, we can conclude that the original argument being tested is invalid. It should be carefully noted that if we obtain a blocked proof in which D has not been used, we can say (trivially) that rule D is used optimally, since no other way of using D could lead to alternative proofs in which complete simplification would occur and condition (i) would hold.

How can we determine whether rule D has been used optimally in a blocked proof? The obvious answer is to construct all of the alternative proofs which could result from making different choices whenever rule D was invoked. This is not easy to spell out in detail. We could imagine that we start one proof, and then double the number of proofs that we are working on whenever rule D must be used by extending the existing proofs first with one disjunct, and then with the other. If we continued to double the number of proofs that we were working on in this way, we would eventually produce a proof that the argument is invalid if there is one. If there is none, any way of using rule D is as good as any other whenever it must be used, and each blocked proof is one in which D is used optimally.

In order to have a systematic way to try alternative possibilities in a single column of proof lines, we now introduce a second auxiliary rule DS. If we find that we have reached a blocked proof and that the proof contains one or more uses of rule D, we search back through the lines of the proof for the last line (the one with the highest number) which was added to the proof by rule D. We then erase this line and every subsequent line in the proof. The line previously justified by rule D is replaced by the other SL form which rule D might have justified, and the line is justified by citing DS rather than D. DS is a rule of proof since we know that the disjunct which is added as a line when DS is used must abstract a true assertion jointly with the SL forms in preceding lines of the proof if the assumption that the first n lines abstract true assertions is not to be absurd. The line from which a line justified by DS is obtained should *not* be crossed out, however, since DS may have to be applied to it more than twice for reasons which will be made clear below.

Now suppose our first proof from a most sophisticated SL argument form is blocked, and at least one line in this proof is justified by an application of D. An application of DS now changes the last line of the original proof justified by D to a line justified by DS which is not prefixed by an asterisk. If we develop a proof from this line and it blocks, DS can be used to eliminate the asterisk prefixed to the next-to-last line of the original proof justified by D. A new proof now developed may contain a use of D. But if this proof blocks, and the next proof blocks, then DS will change the second-from-last line of the original proof justified by D to a line not prefixed by an asterisk. As long as proofs continue to block, DS will eliminate earlier and earlier lines of the original proof prefixed by an asterisk until either a blocked proof is obtained in which no line is justified by D (so that D is used optimally), or a complete simplification is obtained in which condition (i) holds. We then know whether the original argument was valid or invalid. The rule DS completes the SL test of validity. Having abstracted a most sophisticated SL argument consistency form, we can find a proof with this form as the first *n* lines which either shows the original argument to be valid, or to be SL invalid.

We will now finish the proof begun earlier as an illustration:

$$
\begin{array}{lll}
(1) & C \lor D & \\
(2) & \sout{\sim D \land \sim E} & \\
(3) & \sim C & \sim (\text{CON}) \\
(4) & \sim D & (2)\ \text{CS}_1 \\
(5) & \sim E & (2)\ \text{CS}_2 \\
(6) & D & (1)\ , (3)\ \text{DS}_1 \\
\end{array}
$$

This proof is blocked by lines (4) and (6), and D is used optimally. Therefore the original argument is valid since no possible world is such that lines (1)–(3) can jointly abstract true assertions.

We now provide an illustration of a blocked proof in which lines justified by rule D occur. Instead of erasing, we will cross out lines and their justification to indicate earlier work that would be erased. The first three lines of this proof are the

most sophisticated SL argument form for the second argument
that was abstracted in Chapter 3:

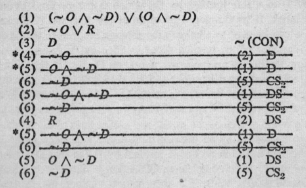

(1)	$(\sim O \wedge \sim D) \vee (O \wedge \sim D)$		
(2)	$\sim O \vee R$		
(3)	D	$\sim$ (CON)	
*(4)	~~$\sim O$~~	~~(2)~~	~~D~~
*(5)	~~$O \wedge \sim D$~~	~~(1)~~	~~D~~
(6)	~~$\sim D$~~	~~(5)~~	~~CS$_2$~~
(5)	~~$O \wedge \sim D$~~	~~(1)~~	~~DS~~
(6)	~~$\sim D$~~	~~(5)~~	~~CS$_2$~~
(4)	R	(2)	DS
*(5)	~~$O \wedge \sim D$~~	~~(1)~~	~~D~~
(6)	~~$\sim D$~~	~~(5)~~	~~CS$_2$~~
(5)	$O \wedge \sim D$	(1)	DS
(6)	$\sim D$	(5)	CS$_2$

The final proof consists of those lines numbered (1)–(6)
which are not erased. *Erased lines should be carefully studied
by the reader to see how they were first obtained, and why
their erasure is justified by an application of* DS. Since the
final proof is blocked and D is used optimally, the original
argument is valid.

We mentioned earlier that in adding a line justified by an
application of DS we do not cross out the line containing the
disjunctive SL form from which the new line is derived, even
though DS is a rule of proof. The reason is that a line added
by DS is provisional in that the proof developed from this
line may block, leading to erasure of this line along with
others in another application of DS. This happens in the
proof given. Notice that an erased line (5) is obtained from
line (1) by DS, just as is line (5) of the final proof. Line
(1) must be left intact for as many applications of DS as
may be required before a final proof is obtained. In general,
these remarks can be extended to all rules of proof. No lines
should be crossed out for convenience when any line of proof
is added which comes after some line prefixed by an asterisk.
In the given proof, we could have crossed out line (1) and

line (2) in the final proof compatibly with this restriction, but they have been left intact to facilitate the study of erased lines. The technical details of the SL test for validity are now complete.

Exercises

1. Suppose that some arguments have already been abstracted to the following most sophisticated SL argument consistency forms. Develop proofs from these most sophisticated SL argument consistency forms, and determine whether the original arguments were valid or invalid:

   a. (1) $\sim (A \lor B)$
      (2) $\sim A \lor \sim B$
      (3) A $\sim$ (CON)
   b. (1) B
      (2) $(\sim (A \land B) \lor M)$
      (3) M $\sim$ (CON)
   c. (1) $\sim A \lor (F \land \sim G)$
      (2) $\sim (\sim G \lor R) \lor \sim P$
      (3) $P \land \sim Q$
      (4) A $\sim$ (CON)
   d. (1) $(P \land Q) \lor (R \land S)$
      (2) $\sim P \lor \sim P$
      (3) $\sim S$ $\sim$ (CON)
   e. (1) $((\sim P \land Q) \lor R)$
      (2) $\sim (P \lor (\sim (Q) \lor R))$ $\sim$ (CON)
   f. (1) $\sim M \lor (A \land \sim L)$
      (2) $L \lor D$
      (3) $\sim (D \land K)$
      (4) $\sim (\sim A \lor \sim K)$
      (5) $M \lor P$
      (6) $\sim P$ $\sim$ (CON)
   g. (1) $H \lor \sim E$

$(2) \quad \sim S \wedge E$

$(3) \quad \sim E \vee \sim (D \wedge S)$

$(4) \quad D \vee \sim H \qquad\qquad\qquad \sim (CON)$

(See Answer No. 44.)

2. Develop proofs for the most sophisticated SL argument consistency forms which you abstracted in Exercise 3 of Chapter 3. Which of these arguments is valid?

(See Answer No. 1.)

3. Compare your answer to Exercise 2 with the original arguments as given in Exercise 3 of Chapter 3. Do your intuitions about validity agree with the results of your proofs in every case? Explain any disagreement.

(See Answer No. 67.)

4. Several times in the proofs required in Exercise 1, a sequence of lines was encountered in which one line was a disjunctive SL form, while another line was the negation of a conjunct occurring in one of the disjuncts of the disjunctive SL form. Clearly, if D is used to add the conjunctive disjunct, the proof will block, and the other disjunct can then always be added by DS. For example, in developing Exercise 1, part f., we can reach a point where the following two SL forms are lines (1) and (m) of the proof:

$(1) \quad \sim M \vee (A \wedge \sim L)$

$(m) \quad L$

If we add "$(A \wedge \sim L)$" as a line by D, the proof will block after one use of CS_2, and "$\sim M$" could then be added as a line by DS. Wherever such a pattern of lines appeared, we could see that "$\sim M$" could be added by rules of proof, so we might use a *derived* rule of proof to avoid repeating this pattern every time as follows:

$p \vee (q \wedge \sim r) , r \vdash p \qquad DS'$

This is a *derived* rule of proof, because we can establish that any line added to a proof by its use could be added by using D, CS_2, and DS', in that order, instead. Derived rules are merely conveniences allowing us to shorten proofs, but at the expense of having more rules to remember while developing a proof. Although we will not explicitly add any derived rules of proof, which of the following could be added as derived rules of proof, and what rules of proof would need to be cited to establish that they merely shortened patterns of lines permitted by the rules of proof given in Chapter 4:

   a. $p \lor (\sim q \land r), q \vdash p$
   b. $p \lor (q \land r), \sim r \vdash p$
   c. $p \lor \sim q, p \vdash \sim (\sim q)$
   d. $p \lor (\sim p \land q) \vdash q$
   e. $(p \lor q) \land (p \lor \sim q) \vdash p$ (See Answer No. 14.)

5. The purpose of a proof is merely to determine validity. If we need to use D, and we can *see* that one disjunct of the line to which it will be applied will block the proof, we might write down the other disjunct immediately, and go on. In making this shortcut, we cite the added line by writing "DS*" on the far right to remind ourselves that we think this line could be obtained in a regular proof by using D and then DS after the proof would block. We can use the insight leading to derived rules of proof in adding lines by DS*. A development of a most sophisticated SL argument consistency form containing lines justified by DS* will be called a *proof sketch*. A proof sketch may be sufficient to convince us that an argument which has been abstracted is either SL invalid or valid, but it is not a proof proper, since DS* amounts to making a conjecture as to what would happen when a proof was developed according to the usual rules. Develop proof sketches for the most sophisticated SL argument consistency forms d. and f. in Exercise 1 above, using DS* (and giving an informal explanation for its use) wherever you feel that it is justified.   (See Answer No. 4.)

6. Since a most sophisticated SL argument consistency form contains an SL form abstracting at least one premise, and an SL form abstracting the negation of the conclusion of the argument, a most sophisticated SL argument consistency form always has at least two SL forms as constituents. Many of the rules of proof, however, can be used to add lines to a proof which are justified by citing only one previous line of the proof and the rule involved. We could, therefore, develop a proof from a single SL form as the first line by using one of these rules to start the development, and then using the rules of proof in the usual way. Suppose that such a proof blocked with optimal use of D. Then this proof would disprove the assumption

that the sentence abstracted as the first line could be true in a possible world, and we could conclude that the sentence abstracted as the first line of the proof was false in every possible world. Such a sentence is known as a *contradiction,* and the SL form abstracting it, as a *contradictory* SL form. On the other hand, such a proof would establish that the negation of the contradiction abstracted as its first line was true in every possible world. The negation of a contradiction is known as a *tautology,* and the SL form abstracting it, as a *tautologous* SL form. We can thus use proofs to determine whether SL forms are tautologous or contradictory, and hence to determine whether sentences are tautologies or contradictions. To determine whether an SL form is contradictory, we develop a proof from it, and conclude that the SL form is contradictory if and only if the proof blocks. To determine whether an SL form is tautologous, we develop a proof from its negation, and conclude that it is tautologous if and only if the proof blocks. Tautologies and contradictions come in pairs. If we have an SL form and develop proofs from it and from its negation which do not block, then the SL form may be true or false in various possible worlds. We call such an SL form a *contingent* SL form. Which of the following SL forms are contradictory:

a. $P \wedge \sim P$
b. $(P \vee \sim Q) \wedge (\sim P \vee Q)$
c. $\sim (P \wedge \sim Q) \vee \sim P$
d. $P \vee (\sim P \vee Q)$
e. $\sim (\sim P \vee \sim P) \vee \sim P$
f. $\sim P \wedge (P \vee Q)$
g. $\sim ((\sim P \vee Q) \wedge (\sim Q \vee P)) \vee (P \wedge Q)$

(See Answer No. 61.)

7. Which of the SL forms given in Exercise 6 are tautologous? (See Answer No. 80.)

8. Suppose that an argument has a single premise and a conclusion. Assuming that the premise is not a contradiction, and that the conclusion is not a tautology, can the most sophisticated SL argument consistency form abstracted from the argument fail to have at least one SL capital letter occurring both in the SL form abstracting

the premise and the SL form abstracting the negation of the conclusion if the argument is valid?

(See Answer No. 33.)

9. We agree to call an assertion an *observation assertion* if its truth or falsity can be completely determined by a single observation of some kind. Some philosophers have suggested that all scientifically meaningful assertions (to be known as the *verifiable* assertions) are related to observation assertions as follows (see [A4], p. 13):

   (1) An assertion is *directly verifiable* if it is either an observation assertion or if an observation assertion follows from it by a valid argument in which any additional premises are also observation assertions, and which are such that the conclusion does not follow from them alone by valid argument.

   (2) An assertion is *indirectly verifiable* if a directly verifiable assertion follows validly from it by some argument in which any additional premises are either directly verifiable or independently known to be indirectly verifiable.

   (3) An assertion is *verifiable* if it is either directly verifiable or indirectly verifiable.

An objection to this proposal (see [C8], pp. 52–53) is that every assertion is verifiable if it is adopted, so that it fails to distinguish scientifically meaningful assertions from other assertions, which is its intention. For let "*O*," "*P*," and "*Q*" abstract three observation assertions which are independent of one another. None of these then follows from any of the others by valid deductive argument. Now let "*S*" abstract an arbitrary assertion not equivalent to any assertion abstracted to "*O*," "*P*," or "*Q*." Then we can construct an assertion which would be abstracted to the following SL form:

$(\sim O \wedge P) \vee (Q \wedge \sim S)$

We call this SL form, for convenience, "*R*." The assertion abstracted to *R* is directly verifiable, since one can argue validly from it and the assertion abstracted to "*O*" as premises to the directly observable assertion abstracted to "*Q*."

(a. Establish this by developing a proof.)

But the assertion abstracted to "*P*" follows from the assertions abstracted to *R* and "*S*."

(b. Establish this by developing a proof.)

Either the assertion abstracted to *"P"* follows from the assertion abstracted to *R*, or it does not. If it does not, *"S"* is indirectly verifiable.

(c. Satisfy yourself that *"S"* meets the definition above.)

If the assertion abstracted to *"P"* does follow from that abstracted to *R*, then since the assertion abstracted to *R* follows from the assertion abstracted to *"(Q $\wedge \sim S$),"* the assertion abstracted to *"P"* is a consequence of *"(Q $\wedge \sim S$)."*

(d. Justify this argument in detail.)

Since, by independence of the assertions abstracted to *"P"* and *"Q,"* this means that *"P"* is a consequence of *"$\sim S$."* The assertion abstracted to *"$\sim S$"* is indirectly verifiable. Therefore, either *"S"* or *"$\sim S$"* abstracts a scientifically meaningful assertion, so the assertion abstracted to *"S"* must be scientifically meaningful.

(e. Justify this argument in detail.)

It has been suggested that the definitions of verifiable assertions can be revised to meet this objection by requiring that all of the SL capital letters occurring in any SL forms abstracting premises used in an argument whose indirect verifiability is being tested abstract known verifiable assertions. This blocks the objection given (see [N1], pp. 88–89), since although the assertion abstracted to *R* is proved directly verifiable, it has *"S"* as a constituent which is not known to abstract a verifiable assertion. Indeed, the last part of the objection begs the question under this construal. But the suggested repair points up a difficulty in the definition of direct verifiability. It is possible to find an SL form which is a truth-function of *"O," "P,"* and *"S"* such that the assertion abstracted to *"O"* follows from this truth-function, but not from the assertion abstracted to *"P."* (As before, the assertions abstracted to *"O"* and *"P"* are independent, and *"S"* is arbitrary.) This truth-function, which contains the scientifically meaningless *"S,"* is thus directly verifiable, contrary to the intention of framing the definitions in the first place.

(f. Can you construct such a truth-function?)

(See Answer No. 85.)

5. Appropriateness in SL Abstraction

We have been construing arguments as sequences of assertions, and we have been supposing that assertions could be taken as sentences uttered or written on certain occasions in a fixed context with a fairly clear intention. Consequently, we have used talk about assertions and about sentences interchangeably in abstracting most sophisticated SL argument consistency forms from given arguments. But this is only a beginning of an explanation of the significance of SL abstraction, and we need to bring some philosophical analysis to bear on this simple characterization. In this chapter, we first examine the distinction between an assertion and a sentence, replacing it with a more subtle account of what is abstracted using SL techniques. After doing this, we will look at some of the problems raised in attempting an SL abstraction when the context of an argument is carefully considered.

Suppose Tom and Jim (one right after the other) both say, "It is raining." Can they be said to say the same thing? There is no definitive answer apart from context. Normally, we would say that they said the same thing. On the other hand, an acting coach who was trying to get Tom and Jim to affect a special accent for some dramatic production might feel that they had said different things, Tom getting the accent right, let us say, and Jim not. The acting coach is not interested in the import of their remarks as comment on the weather, but in their physical quality. Our usual attitude toward what is said is that of paying attention to what is meant by what is said, and not to *how* it is said, so that a wide variance in physical production would still be taken to make the same assertion. Indeed, this attitude is so common that we usually talk about what is meant by what is said even when we are discussing specific utterances. Let Herman speak German and Jim speak English, and suppose that Herman and Jim need bilingual Jane to interpret for them if they are to communicate. Herman says, *"Es regnet."* If Jim says to Jane, "What did he say?," Jane's answer is something like "He said that it is raining," but not "He said *'es regnet,'*" unless Jane is a weak humorist, or is trying to call attention to herself. Normally, again, if we're interested in what people say, we are interested in what they're saying, not in exactly how they say it.

What is said and how it is said are not, of course, completely independent. We might, for example, be interested in what some statesman has said at his news conference. A friend may say, "He said that there were no preconditions for talks, but it is not so much what he said as how he said it." Does this conflict with the claims just made? No—it merely points out that nuance, gesture, timing, and so on, may subvert the normal use of a sentence in order to use it to say something completely different. There are at least three preliminary distinctions to be drawn: the notion of a sentence as a physical utterance on a particular occasion (what we have been calling a *sentence*), the notion of what a sentence *typically* means or is used to say (after this, the *proposition* that it expresses), and the notion of what a sentence is used to say on a particular occasion (after this, the *statement* that it makes). This use of terms is stipulative, and it does not always mesh with ordinary language. For example, we don't always use "statement" to mean what was said as opposed to the sentence used. In institutionalized contexts, we may say, "He issued the following statement," and use this locution to introduce *exactly* the words that he uttered. Then why do we bother to draw these distinctions? To indicate that our abstraction from what we say on given occasions to SL argument forms must be an abstraction to SL forms which represent (strictly) the pattern of *statements,* and not the pattern of sentences or propositions. This is why the intuitive element in selecting an appropriate abstraction is so important. If we abstract mechanically from sentences or from propositions, we are obviously bound to assess inappropriate SL forms on at least some occasions, although the mechanical test of validity contains no errors.

The notion of a proposition is required to make sense of the notion of a statement, since it is only by subversion of the *ordinary* meaning of a sentence that it can be used to make an unusual claim. This is analogous to saying that counterfeit money can have significance only by contrast to real money. Without stability somewhere, flexibility is useless. But the notion of a proposition does more work than this. In one case, a pair of sentence tokens expressing different propositions can be used to make the same statement. And in another, a pair of sentence tokens expressing the same proposition may be used to make two different statements. To illustrate the former case, if Jim says on February 10 that it snowed five days before, and James says the next day that it snowed six days before, they obviously make the same statement, yet the propositions expressed by the sentences they are likely to utter are surely different. Snowing five days ago and snowing six days ago are two different things. In fact, much of the usefulness of the distinction between propositions and statements is caused by reference to times and places of utterance, as well as by the identity of the speaker of a particular sentence. In abstracting to SL forms, it is clear that it is different sentences *which make the same statement in the context of the argument that should be represented by the same SL form,* or at least by equivalent SL forms. It is useful to look at the pitfalls involved in abstracting arguments to SL forms without paying attention to the relevant subtleties of language and context.

First, we may consider the difference between two sentences abstracted to the SL forms *"S"* and *"∼S,"* or to any SL capital letter and its negation. It is clear from the symbolism that such pairs of sentences (strictly, as usual, the statements which they are used to make) must be such that if one is true, the other is false, and vice versa. The chief difference between SL forms and English appears in the fact that a pair of such sentences can exist in English which are appropriately true or false in the context of a given argument, but which are not necessarily different in truth-value in every context. For example, in an argumentative context in which the game being discussed cannot end in a tie, "The Hawks are losing" is roughly the negation of "The Hawks are winning." The Hawks and their opponents may be momentarily tied, but we can overlook this case by taking the details of the game's apparent momentum into account, or by letting "The Hawks are losing" include every case where they are not winning, covering by definition the case of a tie. In an argument during the course of the game, "S" and "$\sim S$" might suitably abstract these sentences given just this context. This obviously supposes as part of the context the fact that the Hawks are a sports team, that a game is under way, and so on. These suppositions, obviously, would not always hold. Before the start of a Hawk game, "The Hawks are winning" seems unintelligible. In these circumstances, the statement that would normally be advanced by this sentence is out of place, or possibly false, depending on our outlook. Restriction to a definite context may thus considerably aid SL abstraction by defining negations of various statements within the suppositions embodied in the context.

The contextual aspects of negation are much subtler than the resources of SL symbolism. A negation of a sentence in a context can be any sentence which says something incompatible with, or simply dissenting from, what some other sentence says. The negation of a sentence may not be clearly defined if too many such dissensions appear within the same argument. Consider the following sentence and the statement it may be supposed to make in some context: (See [K4], pp. 249–50.)

(1) The students believed that it had happened.

Now we can look at some ways in which a speaker might dissent from the statement made by this sentence:

(1a)   The students doubted that it had happened.
(1b)   The students did not believe that it had happened.
(1c)   None of the students believed that it had happened.
(1d)   Few of the students believed that it had happened.
(1e)   The students never believed that it had happened.
(1f)   The students rarely believed that it had happened.
(1g)   The students believed only momentarily that it had happened.
(1h)   The students were unable to believe that it had happened.

Each of (1a)–(1h) may be used to deny that (1) makes a true statement on some particular occasion, even though they seem to advance different statements dissenting from (1). For example, (1a) and (1b) may make different claims. Negation (1a) says that the student attitude was different from that suggested by (1), but (1b) may be used to claim that the students neither believed nor failed to believe that it had happened because they simply had no opinion on the matter. One could say, in this sense, "The students did *not* believe that it had happened, in fact they hadn't heard anything at all about it." Negations (1c) and (1d) express dissent from the number of students to which the belief is apparently attributed in (1), and (1e), (1f), and (1g) could be used to question various temporal suggestions of (1). Negation (1f) could be used to suggest that although (1) is literally true of a given class of students, the (possible) implication that all students so believe is wrong since few such classes form such a belief. Negation (1h) is peculiar. It could be the start of a long argument designed to show that certain (perhaps overlooked) evidence is available to show that (1) must be false. Does the existence of these eight negations of (1) indicate that (1) could be used to make at least eight different statements on various occasions? It is clear that (1) could be used to emphasize different aspects of some one situation, but all of these slightly different emphases may be construed as ways of looking at a single statement, one which is true if and only if the students referred to actually had the mentioned belief. Negations (1a)–(1h) merely suggest different ways in which (1) could be false in a context where various suppositions are implicit. Any of these statements might be regarded as *the* negation of (1) and appropriately symbolized if the context were such that only one kind of dissent were made from (1) in the course of an argument. Otherwise, none of these statements may strictly be regarded as *the* negation of (1), and different SL capital letters would be required for abstraction. The falsity of any of (1a)–(1h) does not establish the truth of (1). Looking back at our Hawks example, it is possible to regard all of (1) and (1a)–(1h) as unintelligible, or false, if there are no such students as those referred to in these sentences. The significance of negation thus seems quite closely tied to the contextual background of an argument.

In order to use the SL symbolism effectively, logicians have often introduced the locution "It is not the case that . . ." When the blank in this phrase is filled with a sentence, the result is a sentence which is the negation of the original. For example, the negation of "It is snowing" can be produced as "It is not the case that it is snowing." This may seem to be a barbarism, for it is certainly not a commonly used locution. If you say, "Jones is trying for the presidency," and I say, "No, that's not the case," my denial is usually context dependent, in the sense that I agree that there is a Jones, but do not agree that he has the relevant political ambitions. But in spite of context dependency, it is often useful to have an artificial negation at hand in order to formalize an argument in a reasonable way. For example, I may at one time suppose that either one or the other of two statements abstracted to "C" and "D" is true, and then later find that the facts are such that "C" cannot be true. I might then add "$\sim C$" to the premises of an argument containing the disjunction of "C" and "D" as a premise, even though it would be difficult to give a completely articulated statement which it might abstract. To be more definite, suppose that in some mathematical context I wish to assert the disjunction of "$x \sim +2$" and "$x \sim -4$." These possibilities might appear as the solutions of a quadratic equation. A negative value might be without physical significance for the practical problem with which some argument is concerned, and "$\sim C$" might thus be added as an additional premise, even though it would not be clear even in the context what statement this SL form abstracted. That is, we may not know from context, or we may not care, whether this statement claims that "x" is some irrational number other than "-4," or some rational number other than "-4." It doesn't matter, as we have the right value, therefore we need not work out the contextual implications. The artificial "$\sim C$" does quite nicely for our purpose. Sentences which we call the negations of other sentences do not always go into pairs of SL forms like "C" and "$\sim C$," although it may be quite legitimate so to abstract them for the purposes of assessing a particular argument. On the other hand, we may invent artificial negations in order to abstract conveniently from a given argument. In both cases, we must use the contextual clues to determine what pairs of sentences are such that they must differ in truth-value in the circumstances.

Our approach takes SL assessment as a practical tool for determining the validity of a given argument whose success is heavily dependent on the use of intuition to guide the relevant abstractions. This dependence on intuition is greatest in the context of ordinary argumentation, where a great deal of context is given by unexpressed supposition, and it becomes progressively less as argument becomes more scientific or mathematical and the suppositions are meant to receive explicit formulation. Some logicians have not been happy with so rough-and-ready an attitude. Their approach to formalization, which we will call the formalist approach, requires that all the relevant details of context be explicitly added to the statements that are used to present an argument before abstraction is undertaken. The formalist argues that this must be done if an exact significance is to be given to the SL forms abstracting an argument. On this understanding, a sentence like "The Hawks are winning" is really shorthand for some gargantuan sentence incorporating relevant context, something like "At 9 P.M. on March 5, 1968, at Kiel Auditorium in St. Louis, Missouri, U.S.A., Earth, the Hawks are playing the Lakers on the basketball court and have more points scored than the Lakers." There is something odd about taking this latter sentence as giving a more adequate or accurate reading of what the former sentence intends in the context of an argument about the game. It seems at once both too precise and too loose. It is too loose because one can imagine bizarre circumstances defeating any attempt to spell out the context in every detail. For example, the statement might have been about a charity volleyball game being played between the two teams, while the reformulation fails. This is not a proof that the formalist approach won't work, but it seems very difficult to suppose that context in an ordinary situation can be successfully described in detail to the point of circumventing every possible ambiguity that might be worried about on some philosophical grounds. On the other hand, the apparent precision of the reformulation, even if it were accurate, has some odd consequences. If the speaker's watch were wrong by a few minutes, and the history of the game suitable, the elaborate paraphrase might be false because it had incorrectly tied the statement to a temporal sequence. If one tries to mention time without explicit reference to an instant by use of a phrase like "Whatever time it is now, . . ." no increase in precision is actually effected. The approach of formalism, while it would preserve the technical significance of SL symbolism in every context, seems to force us to adopt elaborate paraphrases which cannot be known to correspond accurately to the statements that we are actually making.

We turn now to the abstraction of conjunction in a context. The SL form "$P \wedge Q$" is supposed to abstract a true statement if and only if both "P" and "Q" abstract true statements. Further, statements abstracted to "$P \wedge Q$" and to "$Q \wedge P$" should be equivalent in the sense that they are true or false together no matter how a relevant possible world is described. Conjunction is often marked in a sentence by the word "and." If "and" is flanked by two sentences in some complex sentence, we can usually abstract the complex statement being made by a conjunctive SL form unless the occurrence of "and" has temporal significance, and means roughly "and then." A simple test for temporal significance is to reverse the sentences which flank "and" to determine whether an equivalent statement would be advanced by the new sentence. If an equivalent sentence does not result, we have seen that the properties of a conjunctive SL form would not make abstraction appropriate. For example, the complex sentence "She got married and she had a baby" is *not* usually equivalent (in context) to "She had a baby and she got married," the latter having overtones not associated with the former in polite conversation. Only a conjunction without temporal significance may be abstracted to a conjunctive SL form if the abstraction is to be appropriate.

Many conjunctive statements are of a form known as conjunctive contractions, in which "and" appears but is not flanked by two *sentences*. Some examples are "She got married and had a baby," "The man is tall and thin," "The flag is black and white," "Apples and oranges are plentiful," and "Carrots and peas are a good mixed vegetable." Such contractions are appropriately abstracted to conjunctive SL forms only if they are equivalent to more cumbersome conjunctions which they may be said to contract. The reason for caution can be illustrated by our examples. Consider this argument:

The flag is black and white.
Therefore, the flag is black.

An appropriate flag would provide a counterexample, since we assert "The flag is black" only where the flag is plain black or nearly so, whereas a black and white flag may contain quite a small amount of black. If "The flag is black and white" is abstracted to "$P \land Q$," we would get the erroneous result that the argument was valid. The suggested test eliminates this case, since the non-equivalence of "The flag is black and white" with "The flag is black and the flag is white" is obvious.

These remarks should be sufficient to indicate that the pressures toward economy of expression in English do not generally result in constructions which exhibit neatly the relationship between a sentence and the facts which are relevant to its truth. This is partly because sentences are frequently asserted for some purpose other than communicating a fact in the relevant sense. We need therefore to avoid mechanical abstraction and ask ourselves in each case what statement is being made before abstracting.

In practice, the matter can be subtler than any simple tests we can devise. Consider the sentence "Joe and Bill had the opportunity." (See [G1], pp. 174–76.) Is this equivalent to "Joe had the opportunity and Bill had the opportunity"? Suppose the circumstances to be such that Joe and Bill as a team, or as a pair of persons, had the opportunity, say, to accomplish something requiring the abilities of both men. Then the former sentence would be true while the latter was false on a natural reading. If Joe and Bill have the opportunity but Bill refuses to seize it, and Joe does not have the opportunity with another partner, we may say that although both had the opportunity, Joe did not have it by himself. We can see from this example that our tests for conjunction can be far from decisive if the context is suitably subtle. The tests are useful, not as a mechanical procedure, but as a means of forcing some consideration of the *exact* significance of the context for the statements made in the course of advancing an argument.

Disjunction raises problems even more complicated than those broached by conjunction. This is related to an important fact. Whereas a conjunctive assertion is also the assertion of its conjuncts, a disjunctive assertion does not assert either of its disjuncts. A disjunction claims rather that one or the other of the disjuncts could be asserted if further facts were known. Difficulties in abstracting from disjunctive contexts seem to arise from this fact, although logicians have not agreed whether the difficulty is to be traced to differing kinds of disjunction, or to differing relationships between disjuncts which may nonetheless be disjoined by a common notion of disjunction.

Let us look at some sample disjunctive sentences:

(A)   Tom is either a member of the Kiwanis Club or the Elks Lodge, or maybe both.
(B)   Tom is either a member of the Kiwanis Club or the Elks Lodge, but not both.
(C)   Tom was born in either England or France.

Clearly, (A) is true if Tom is a member of one or both clubs, and (A) could be appropriately abstracted to the SL form "$M \vee N$" as a constituent of an argument. Now, (B) is true if Tom is a member of just one of the clubs, but false if Tom is a member of neither club, or of both. Consequently, (B) could be appropriately abstracted by this SL form:

$$(\sim M \wedge N) \vee (M \wedge \sim N)$$

This form abstracts a true statement if either the statement abstracted to "M" is true or the statement abstracted to "N" is true, but it abstracts a false statement if both "M" and "N" abstract true statements, or if they abstract false statements. We will let SL forms like "$M \vee N$" and "$(\sim M \wedge N) \vee (M \wedge \sim N)$" abstract what we will call *inclusive* and *exclusive* disjunction, respectively. Now let us turn to (C). Is (C) true or false when Tom is born both in England and in France? Since we can't imagine how this case could arise, the question doesn't seem to make sense, and we have a resulting difficulty with accepting either answer. There is consequently a temptation to propose a third kind of disjunction, let us call it *exclusion*, such that the joint truth of excluded disjuncts is simply not conceivable. An exclusion of two statements is *not* a truth-function of two statements, since it fails to have a truth-value when its component statements are both true.

A path to appropriate abstraction of disjunction may now seem fairly clear. If a disjunction is inclusive or exclusive, we can abstract to an appropriate SL form. If a disjunction is

.an exclusion, we do not abstract. But it was earlier claimed that a disjunction merely claims that one of its disjuncts could be asserted if enough further information were at hand. This claim is true of inclusive disjunction, exclusive disjunction, and exclusion. It was then said that the logician did not speculate on the independence of different simple statements, but assumed that they were always independent, in order to have a conservative and mechanical test for SL validity. Exclusion jars with this assumption because exclusion is patently a case where the assumption is wrong. But to recognize exclusion, and fail to abstract, the logician must explicitly recognize non-independence, something that he refuses to speculate about. It is literally the case, therefore, that one *cannot* recognize exclusion during the abstractive process, but must treat it as inclusive disjunction. Suppose we abstract using the truth-functional inclusive disjunction to abstract the non-truth-functional exclusion. In working out a proof, we may find a proof completely simplifying to a description of a possible world in which both disjuncts of an exclusion abstract true statements. Now, the rules of proof involving disjunction are all correct for either exclusion or inclusive disjunction. Therefore, if such a possible world is obtained, we could simply regard it as blocked, rather than as a description of a possible world showing the original argument invalid. If we did this, we might discover that some arguments judged SL invalid were actually valid, but not the reverse, so that this course cannot cause us to make a mistaken assessment that an argument is valid when it is invalid, although the reverse error is possible, a situation which is conservative in the appropriate sense. There are further subtleties in this matter, but the whole problem is meliorated considerably in practice by the fact that exclusions cannot arise in many areas of mathematical and scientific abstraction. We will see an example of this in the next chapter.

In abstracting from disjunctive sentences, we find immediately that the presence of "or" may be an even more unreliable guide to disjunction than the presence of "and" is to conjunction. Let us begin with two simple cases:

Apples or oranges are available for dessert.
Jack weighs more than Jim or Bob.

Typically, the former statement would be used to claim that both apples and oranges are available for dessert, and this would be appropriately abstracted to an SL form like "$P \wedge Q$" on the intuition that it was equivalent to "Apples are available for dessert and so are oranges." On the other hand, the statement might be made by a poor host about to serve dessert who remembers that the last of the oranges has been eaten, or the last of the apples, but can't remember which. Under such conditions, the statement would have to be abstracted to an SL form appropriate to an exclusive disjunction. The second of our examples is usually a conjunctive statement, but one can construct rather bizarre contexts in which it would not be so.

In addition to the presence of "either" and "or," disjunction can be indicated by such phrases as "only if," "unless," "if," and others. Consider these statements:

If switch A is pressed, the light glows.
If switch A is pressed, then the light glows.
The light glows only if switch A is pressed.
The light does not glow unless switch A is pressed.

These may all be equivalent to the following:

Either switch A is not pressed or the light glows.

The point is that we can imagine on a single occasion that any of these statements is false just in the case that switch A is pressed and the light does not glow. These equivalences put intuition to a severe test, in that we have to see that any of the locutions amounts to a disjunctive statement either disjunct of which could be true if enough further information were made available. These equivalences are easily abused in similar examples.

We now introduce a new symbol, "⊃." This symbol may be regarded technically as superfluous, since we will introduce it by definition into the SL symbolism in such a fashion that any SL form containing one or more of these symbols can be transformed into an equivalent SL form which has no occurrences of this symbol. The method for effecting this transformation is the following: Wherever some substitution into "∼ p ∨ q" appears as an SL form, possibly as a constituent of another SL form, it may be replaced by the expression which results from the same substitution into "p ⊃ q," and vice versa. Strictly, we should regard an expression like "P ⊃ Q" (read "P only if Q") not as an SL form but as an *abbreviation* of the SL form "∼ P ∨ Q." In practice, however, we can treat the symbol "⊃" as though it were a regular symbol of SL, but the transformation means that we must regard our understanding of its use and of its significance as derived entirely from our prior understanding of negation and disjunction, and the symbols used to abstract negated and disjunctive sentences. The use of the symbol "⊃" therefore adds nothing to the abstractive powers of SL or to the range of its proof techniques. Why do we introduce this obvious complication? There are at least two reasons. The first is that it can cause a considerable simplification of the typographical structure of SL forms. Suppose that some sentence is abstracted to the following SL form:

$$\sim (\sim P \vee Q) \vee R$$

Using the symbol "⊃," hereafter called "the conditional," this can be changed by definition into the following SL form:

$$(P \supset Q) \supset R$$

This SL form proves (after some practice) to be easier to read and understand than the SL form using only the symbols "∼" and "∨." The other reason is a consequence of the first, and it is that many of the formal systems of interest to logicians in the foundations of mathematics are much simpler to develop when the sign "⊃" is used to develop proofs.

Abstraction from English statements to SL forms containing "⊃" has given rise to the greatest controversies in the literature discussing the use of SL techniques for assessing the validity of everyday argument. There are two underlying facts which account for these controversies. Let "*A*" and "*B*" abstract simplest constituent statements in some argument, and consider the SL form "*A* ⊃ *B*" which may appear in the abstraction of the argument. For simplicity of discussion, suppose that the statement abstracted to "*A* ⊃ *B*" is of the following rough style:

If . . . , then _____.

In this case, we suppose the sentences abstracted to "*A*" and "*B*," or equivalent sentences, fill the blanks of this framework in order to construct the complex statement abstracted to "*A* ⊃ *B*." The symbol "⊃" is then taken to abstract the indicated conditional framework from this statement. Now, whereas conjunctive or disjunctive sentences seem either true or false depending on the truth or falsity of their conjuncts or disjuncts, it seems that conditional sentences may on certain occasions be neither true nor false, but inappropriate. We had a similar situation with negation earlier, but the difficulties there could be resolved by finding a suitable context. The difficulties with the conditional are harder to resolve. The sense of the context "If . . . , then _____" is not so much a matter of the truth or falsity of the antecedent (the sentence filling the blank ". . .") and the truth or falsity of the consequent (the sentence filling the blank "_____") as it is a matter of whether there is a reasonable connection between the antecedent and the consequent such that should the antecedent be true, it could be expected that the consequent would be true too. This connection can exist only where the truth of the antecedent seems at least relevant to the truth of the consequent. But we already know that the SL symbolism will reflect only equivalence or independence between simple enough statements, and is simply not sophisticated enough to reflect the notion of relevance. Thus we can construct intuitively silly arguments which no reasonable person would put forward, but which are valid under the SL test. To exhibit this problem, let "*A*" abstract the statement "Five is a larger number than three" and let "*B*" abstract the statement "Spiders eat cheese" or any other statement that might amuse the reader. Now consider this argument:

If five is a larger number than three, then spiders eat cheese.
Five is a larger number than three.
Therefore, spiders eat cheese.

Abstracting, we obtain this most sophisticated SL argument consistency form:

(1) $A \supset B$
(2) A
(3) $\sim B$ $\sim$ (CON)

It can be easily verified that this is SL valid. The principle of conservatism can defend this conclusion by pointing out that no inference from true statements to a false statement could occur in an argument of this form. But a distinction between the technical concept of validity and the intuitive concept of cogency which it was introduced to clarify is now apparent. We can very well feel that the argument is such that we cannot imagine circumstances in which it would be cogent, even though it is seen to be valid. This does not mean the rejection of SL, since we can continue to apply the SL test for validity only to arguments which pass certain intuitive tests or standards for cogency.

It might be noted that the problem of relevance can appear even for the conjunctive and disjunctive forms that we have already discussed, although the problem was not explicitly broached when these forms were introduced. Consider the following argument: (See [A3].)

John will arrive on the 10 P.M. plane.
Therefore, either John will arrive on the 10 P.M. plane or
he will arrive on the 11:30 P.M. plane.

After abstraction to an appropriate most sophisticated SL
argument consistency form, this argument can be seen to be
valid. This is also true of its corresponding conditional form:

John will arrive on the 10 P.M. plane.
Therefore, if John will not arrive on the 10 P.M. plane, then
he will arrive on the 11:30 P.M. plane.

Now, if the premise of either argument is true, then the disjunctive conclusion must be true, and both arguments are
valid. Nevertheless, these arguments seem odd, and an examination of this fact may be useful. In a particular context, with
John definitely expected at 10 P.M. on a given evening, both
conclusions would surely be regarded as false if there were no
11:30 P.M. plane for John to arrive on if he happened to miss
the 10 P.M. plane. When we spoke of a disjunction as asserting that one of its disjuncts would be assertible if more information were available, we didn't stress the fact that another supposition in ordinary language seems to be that either
could be assertible if more information became available. On
this basis, if "A" abstracts a premise of an argument, and
"$A \lor B$," the conclusion of the same argument, then the
conclusion would be cogent only if it is considered possible
that "B" could be asserted on the basis of additional information. But if "$\sim B$" is a consequence of known facts (which
may be part of the context of the argument) and this is seen
to be so, then "$A \lor B$" will not seem a cogent conclusion.
The import of this observation for the sample argument is
obvious. If there is no 11:30 P.M. plane, the conclusion
contains a disjunct which is not potentially assertible. By examining the intuitive equivalence of disjunctions and conditionals, and examining the context to make sure that the constituent statements of a disjunctive or conditional conclusion
are potentially assertible, we can get a rough check on the

cogency of arguments in ordinary language which pass the SL test of validity. Once again, cogency and validity will tend to coincide in mathematical and scientific contexts where background assumptions must be spelled out, even in practice. Here validity is a sufficient test of cogency.

Given the complexities of actual argument, and the pitfalls in abstraction discussed in this chapter, it should by now be plain that there are no shortcuts to the abstraction of an appropriate most sophisticated SL argument consistency form for a given argument. When confronted with textbook examples, it is good practice to imagine a concrete situation in order to provide sufficient context to give the abstraction some semblance of grounded appropriateness. For as we have seen, negation, conjunction, disjunction, and the conditional may be quite suitably abstracted in restricted contexts in order to provide an accurate assessment of SL validity.

Exercises

1. Discuss the abstraction of negations of the following sentences for various possible contexts. These sentences and their negations prove important in various problems of philosophical analysis:
   a. I believe that he has the gold.
   b. I don't want to go.
   c. I don't believe that he is right.
   d. I ought to see it through.
   e. He found an interesting fossil there not long ago.
   f. This is good wine.
   g. A person is just a living body.
   h. I broke the vase yesterday.   (See Answer No. 41.)

2. We have already seen that the legibility of the parenthesis notation can be improved by omitting parentheses which would not result in ambiguous SL forms. We now find some additional freedom by dropping parentheses from repeated conjunctions and repeated disjunctions. A repeated conjunction is a conjunction at least one of whose conjuncts is in turn a conjunction, and so on. For example, the following SL form abstracts a repeated conjunction:

   $A \wedge (B \wedge C)$

   If this were a line of a proof, we would finally add "A," "B," and "C" as lines of the proof by using CS_1 and CS_2 several times. But this would also be true if the SL form were this:

   $(A \wedge B) \wedge C$

We can therefore write this repeated conjunction as follows:

$A \wedge B \wedge C$

When we wish to add a line of proof from it, we can group its conjuncts as we please, since the same lines would finally be added to the proof. This is also the case if any of "*A*," "*B*," and "*C*" is replaced by a conjunctive SL form.

A similar, but slightly more complicated argument allows us to write a repeated disjunction as follows:

$A \vee B \vee C$

We may then group this either as "$(A \vee B) \vee C$" or as "$A \vee (B \vee C)$" in using D, DS, or DS* to add a line of proof. To take one case, suppose the proof should block after two uses of D to add "$(A \vee B)$" and then "*A*." "$A \vee (B \vee C)$" would then block when D is used to add "*A*" in one line. Other cases work out to be equivalent in a similar way. Repeated conjunctions and disjunctions are not infrequent in English, but some care must be taken to find genuine cases, just as in abstracting simple conjunction and disjunction.

Abstract this argument (example due to Paul Ziff):

> He ate and he ate and he ate.
>
> Therefore, he ate.

Is it valid?   (See Answer No. 2.)

3. Discuss difficulties in abstracting the following sentences to SL forms:

   a. He is the Father, Son, and Holy Ghost.
   b. He is the top scorer and passer on the team.
   c. He equates electrocution and death.
   d. John believes that Mary and Joe are guilty.
   e. Cassius has a lean and hungry look.
   f. Ice cream and candy are an inadequate diet.

                    (See Answer No. 23.)

4. Examine the following pair of arguments:

   a. Either I don't get a letter today and go to New York, or I do get a letter today and don't go to New York.
      Therefore, I'll either go to New York or not go.
   b. Either I don't get a letter today and sing the blues, or I do get a letter and sing for joy.
      Therefore, I'll either sing the blues or sing for joy.

Are these arguments (intuitively) both valid or both invalid? Abstract most sophisticated SL argument consistency forms for these arguments and develop proofs so as to obtain results fitting your intuition about their validity. What statements must these sentences be making in order to complete an analysis to your liking?

(See Answer No. 55.)

5. Abstract an SL form for the following sentence:
Either he wants to sell his house to Negroes or it's not the case that he wants to sell his house to Negroes.

Now suppose that in some suburb of a large city, the law requires houses listed with a realtor or house agent to be sold to anyone who meets the asking price. One could further suppose that realtors or house agents might not be interested in listing or showing houses in that suburb as a result. Then a man who definitely does not want to sell his house to Negroes, as well as a man who would like to, would likely try to sell his house by private advertisement. (Their fears are somewhat different.) The sentence quoted might be used to comment on someone who advertised privately, to the effect that he almost certainly holds one of two opposed attitudes. Is there any way of abstracting this statement differently from the nearly trivial statement that might be made about anyone selling his house elsewhere.   (See Answer No. 30.)

6. To develop proofs involving SL forms containing the conditional symbol, we need some additional rules of proof. First, we can add the following rules of proof and justify them by remarks given in Chapter 5:

$p \supset q \vdash \sim p \vee q$ MC   (material conditional)
$\sim (p \supset q) \vdash p \wedge \sim q$ DMC   (conditional negation)

Actually, these are the only two rules of proof that we need to add, since they enable us to eliminate the negation of a conditional SL form, and to convert any conditional SL form to an SL form containing the disjunctive symbol, for which we already have complete rules of proof. But to facilitate the development of proofs, we can add the following derived rules:

$p \supset q, p \vdash q$ MP   (modus ponens)
$p \supset q, \sim q \vdash \sim p$ MT   (modus tollens)

These rules are justified in application by citation on the

far right of a line, just as for the earlier rules of proof introduced in Chapter 4. Using MC, DMC, MP, and MT, develop proofs for the following most sophisticated SL argument consistency forms:

a.   (1) $P \supset Q$
      (2) $\sim P \supset R$
      (3) $\sim (\sim Q \supset R)$ $\sim$ (CON)

b.   (1) $P \supset \sim Q$
      (2) $\sim R \wedge Q$
      (3) $Q \supset (T \vee R)$
      (4) $\sim (T \vee P)$ $\sim$ (CON)

c.   (1) $B \vee T$
      (2) $(B \vee C) \supset (P \wedge Q)$
      (3) $\sim P$
      (4) $\sim T$ $\sim$ (CON)

d.   (1) $(E \wedge P) \supset Q$
      (2) $(E \wedge \sim P) \supset \sim Q$
      (3) $\sim (E \supset ((P \wedge Q) \vee \sim (P \vee \sim Q)))$
              $\sim$ (CON)   (See Answer No. 6.)

7. Abstract appropriate most sophisticated SL argument consistency forms for the following arguments in an assumed context. You may use "$\supset$" if you wish in abstracting. Assess the validity or SL invalidity of each argument by developing a proof:

a. If either Jones or Smith wins the nomination, then the campaign will be well financed and victory will be certain. Therefore, either Jones will not win the nomination or the campaign will be well financed.

b. Jack will believe that Tom is a Communist only if Tom wears a red shirt in the parade.
But Tom has no red shirt.
So Jack will not believe that Tom is a Communist.

c. There's some cheese in the pantry if you want some. Therefore, there's some cheese in the pantry.

d. If Harvey takes logic, he will not be a sophomore next year, and if he doesn't take logic, then he will fall in love with Jane.
If he will not be a sophomore, then he will not have fallen in love with Jane.
Therefore, Harvey will take logic.

e. If God cannot prevent evil, He is not omnipotent, and

      if He can but does not, He is not completely good.
      Therefore, there is no evil.

f. It is false that if I had diabetes, I should be glad to
     have it.
     Therefore, I have diabetes.

g. If he enters the tournament, then if he does his best,
     he will not only win the first round but go on to win
     the cup and set a tournament record.
     If he plays his usual game, he will win the cup but
     not set a tournament record.
     Therefore, if he plays in the tournament and does his
     best, he will not play his usual game.

h. If this match were scratched, it would surely light.
     However, this match will not light.
     Therefore, it isn't scratched.   (See Answer No. 74.)

8. A professor says that to pass his course, one must either
write a passing paper or a passing exam. (See [P1].) This
could apparently be abstracted as follows:

$$C \supset (P \vee E)$$

Suppose that he then says that it is not necessary to write
a passing paper or a passing exam. We might try to abstract this as follows:

$$\sim (C \supset P) \wedge \sim (C \supset E)$$

But from these two SL forms, strictly the statements that
they abstract, we can argue validly to the statement that
would be abstracted to this SL form:

$$C \wedge \sim P \wedge \sim E$$

But this SL form cannot jointly abstract a true statement
along with the first SL form. What has gone wrong?
                           (See Answer No. 54.)

9. Suppose that as a result of a riot, it is established that
twenty people are killed. Let "*A*" abstract the statement
"Twenty people are killed" in this context. Now, if this
statement is true, so is the statement "Twenty people are
killed or forty people are killed," which may be abstracted
to "*A* $\vee$ *B*." Now, by extending this line of argument, we
can show that an SL form abstracting the statement "Between twenty and forty people were killed" can be obtained as a long repeated disjunction. Now suppose that a
journalist not in sympathy with the rioters prints this last
statement and not the first established statement in his

newspaper, and defends this against criticism by saying that he has printed a true statement if the facts are as his critics say. What is he probably being accused of, and is his defense supported by logic?   (See Answer No. 17.)

10. It has often been pointed out that "$(P \supset Q)$" and "$(P \supset \sim Q)$" are consistent, that is, that they can jointly abstract true statements in circumstances where "P" abstracts a false statement. But in ordinary language, sentences which can be abstracted to these two SL forms are regarded as inconsistent in many contexts. An example due to Strawson (see [S5], p. 85) is this:

If it rains, the cricket match will be called off, and If it rains, the cricket match will not be called off.

Given what was said earlier, we might suppose that the felt conflict is due to the fact that a conditional is asserted only when it traces out a path that events will take if certain other events are realized. In this case, distinct paths are traced out from the event of rain. Can you, with this hint, describe a condition that would distinguish which of these two sentences is true and which is false even if it doesn't rain?   (See Answer No. 35.)

11. It is often said that SL can illuminate the structure of philosophical arguments. An interesting example is presented in [S1]. Find a copy of Plato's dialogue *Protagoras* and assess the following statements. According to Sayre in [S1], the following statements are introduced into the dialogue, the number in parentheses indicating the line of the dialogue which establishes the existence of a statement making the appropriate claim:

   (1)   Courage and knowledge are distinct parts of virtue. (349c)

   (2)   Pleasure is identical with good, and pain with evil. (351e)

   (3)   Knowledge of good and evil can be overcome in practical decisions by momentary pleasure and pain. (352c)

The purpose of the discussion is to investigate Protagoras' assertion of the claim embodied in (1). In the lines following, it is claimed by Sayre that Socrates forces Protagoras to assert (2), and to see that if (2) is asserted, (3) must be false. Socrates also makes Protagoras admit that the negation of (3) entails the negation of (1). We abstract (1) to "P," (2) to "Q," and (3) to "R." Then the falsity of the statement abstracted to "R" can be expressed by the SL form "$R \supset \sim R$," which abstracts a true statement if and only if "R" abstracts a false statement. Using this trick, we abstract Protagoras' admissions as follows:

Q
$Q \supset ((R \supset \sim R) \wedge (\sim R \supset \sim P))$

The statement abstracted to "$\sim P$" follows by valid argument from the statements abstracted to these SL forms as premises.

a.   Show that this argument is valid.

Does this abstraction help you to grasp Socrates' line of argument in the dialogue?   (See Answer No. 45.)

12. Which of the following are tautologous SL forms:

   a. $((P \supset \sim P) \supset \sim P)$
   b. $(\sim P \supset Q) \supset (\sim Q \supset \sim P)$
   c. $((P \wedge Q) \supset R) \supset ((P \wedge \sim R) \supset \sim Q)$
   d. $(P \supset (Q \supset R)) \supset (Q \supset (P \supset R))$
   e. $\sim (P \supset Q) \supset \sim P$
   f. $((P \vee Q) \supset R) \supset ((P \supset R) \wedge (Q \supset R))$

                              (See Answer No. 25.)

6. Switching Networks

We have been using SL techniques to assess the validity of given arguments. It is clear from the examples in the last chapter that arguments in ordinary contexts are likely not to fit the suppositions behind SL abstraction closely, so that our assessment of validity is no better than the appropriateness of the abstracted most sophisticated SL argument consistency form, and the appropriateness of such a form depends upon the exercise of intuition in grasping the statements being made by the use of various sentences in a fixed context. In this chapter, we will show how the SL symbolism can be used to solve some problems of (simple) scientific interest, where features of the abstracted SL forms will correspond quite closely to features of the subject matter being abstracted.

Suppose we have a supply of simple on-off switches, which we represent as follows:

If we write "ON" above the switch box, as in Fig. 1, we will suppose that this represents a *closed* switch, that is, a switch which allows electricity to flow through it. On the other hand, if we write "OFF" below the switch, as in Fig. 2, this will represent an *open* switch, that is, one which will not allow electricity to flow through it. Assuming that the battery is working properly, and so forth, Fig. 1 and Fig. 2 illustrate these conventions in terms of a very simple electrical circuit:

Figure 1

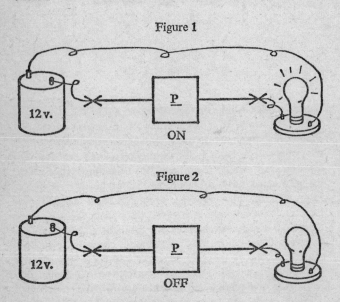

ON

Figure 2

OFF

We will assume that each simple switch is such that at any time it is either closed or open, so that formally the switches have exactly one of these characterizations at any given moment. This feature parallels the assumption that simple statements are either true or false. We will label simple switches with SL capital letters or the negations of SL capital letters.

Simple switches can be wired together to form more complex switches of two terminals, which can be inserted into an electric circuit in the place of simple switches. Two simple switches, "*P*" and "*Q*," can be wired together in two basic ways:

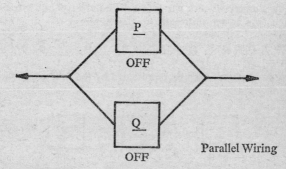

Series Wiring

Parallel Wiring

For convenience, we will label switches "OFF" if we are merely discussing how they are wired together. A series switch consisting of two simpler switches wired in series will be closed if and only if both of its constituent switches are closed. This can be seen from the illustration. Formally, this is just like a conjunction, true if and only if both of its conjuncts are true. If "P" and "Q" are simple switches wired in series to make a complex switch, we could abstract this switch to the notation "$P \wedge Q$." Similarly, a parallel switch of two switches will obviously be such that it will be closed if either one of its constituent switches is closed. Formally, this is like a disjunction, which is true if and only if either (or both) of its disjuncts is true. If "P" and "Q" are simple switches wired in parallel to make a complex switch, we could represent the complex switch as "$P \vee Q$." Negation is somewhat harder to visualize. A switch labeled "$\sim P$" has to be open when a switch labeled "P" is closed, and vice versa. Further, we need to account for various switches all labeled "P" or all labeled "$\sim P$." In practice, it is not difficult to construct a switching mecha-

nism which will close or open a number of switches simultane-
ously, or which will operate two sets of simple switches simul-
taneously, opening all the switches in one set when closing all
those in the other, and vice versa. We will imagine such
mechanisms in use if our complex switches were to receive a
physical embodiment in practice.

Suppose we have a rather complex switch made up of
many simple switches wired in series and in parallel, for example, the switch abstracted to this SL form:

$$(P \land Q \land R) \lor (P \land \sim Q \land R) \lor (P \land Q \land \sim R \land S).$$

This switch could also be represented by the following switching diagram:

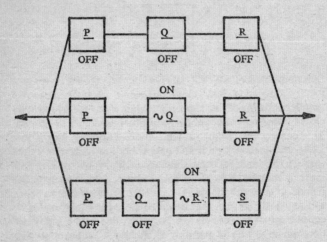

The point of mentioning the way in which SL forms can be
used to abstract simple switching networks is to indicate that
simple switching networks are abstracted quite precisely by SL
forms. This is because the properties of the SL forms are
more nearly analogous to the properties of switching networks than they are to the properties of ordinary sentences.
A simple switch is either closed or open. There are de-

fective switches in practice, but we can plausibly suppose that
a manufacturing process can surmount practical problems for
switching networks of a fixed simple kind. On the other hand,
as we have seen, it is not always easy to determine whether a
sentence used in some context actually makes a statement, and
this difficulty is partly intrinsic in the way we use ordinary
language. We can also see that problems of temporality, which
raise problems for abstraction from statement to SL forms, are
not existent for switching networks. A series wired switch,
for example, is closed only when both of its constituent
switches are closed, and the order in which the constituents
happen to be closed does not matter. Further, as any two
differently labeled switches can be closed or open independently of one another, the assumption of independence for SL
capital letters in SL forms abstracting switches is met exactly.

An obvious question is whether abstraction of simple
switching networks to SL forms is useful in the solution of
any problems about switches. We call a diagram or an SL
form abstracting a complex switch a *switching network*. A
problem which may be attacked by means of such representa-
tion is the simplification problem. The *simplification problem* is this. Suppose that we have a suitable switching network
for some purpose which has been constructed by lucky guess or
trial and error. Let the simple switches in such a network cost
fifty pennies each while the cost of wiring them can be considered negligible. Then we may want to find out whether
our switching network is simplest in this sense: We may
want to know whether the switching network we have is
such that there is no switching network which behaves just like
it but contains a smaller number of simple switches. Here we
regard two occurrences of a switch labeled "*P*" as being two
switches, since each costs fifty pennies. This interest in
simplicity in switching networks has obvious economic consequences if we are intending to manufacture these switching networks as computer components.

We will call two complex switches *functionally equivalent*
if and only if, when all simple switches of the same label in
both switches are either all open or closed (allowing for

negations of single switches), the two switches themselves are either both open or both closed. Obviously, the switch (if it exists) with *fewest* constituent simple switches of a functionally equivalent pair of switches is the simpler switch for our purpose, and the one we would prefer to manufacture. Let us suppose that we start with a switching network containing twenty constituent simple switches. We could manufacture all possible switching networks of one to nineteen constituent simple switches, trying various labelings of the constituent switches and testing them for functional equivalence. In order to complete this survey, or even to take advantage of a lucky insight, we need a method for determining whether two switches are functionally equivalent. Of course, we could try all the permutations of opening and closing the constituent simple switches of the two complex switches in otherwise similar circuits. But functional equivalence can be determined by the use of SL proofs.

Consider the following pair of switches:

$P \wedge P, P$

It is clear just from examination that these switches are functionally equivalent, since either is open only when the simple switch "P" is open. Regarding these as SL forms, we could construct the following pair of most sophisticated SL argument consistency forms from them:

(1) $P \wedge P$
(2) $\sim P$ $\sim$ (CON)
    and
(1) P
(2) $\sim (P \wedge P)$ $\sim$ (CON)

Suppose both of these most sophisticated SL argument consistency forms have proofs which block, so that they are forms abstracting valid arguments. Then the pair of SL forms with which we started must abstract statements which are true or false together in every possible world. Suppose, to the contrary, that they could differ in truth-value. Let "*P*," for example, abstract a true statement and "*P* $\wedge$ *P*," a false statement in some possible world. In this case the proof for the second most sophisticated SL argument consistency form given above would not block, contrary to our assumption. Now, utilizing the analogy between the truth-values of simplest constituent statements of an argument and the open or closed condition of simple switches, we can see that truth-functionally equivalent pairs of SL forms will abstract functionally equivalent pairs of switches, and that truth-functional equivalence can be found by developing a pair of proofs using SL techniques.

Now suppose, in the above argument, that we replaced "*P*" with some complex switch. The pair of proofs for the more complex switches would also block in the same number of steps using the same rules of proof. Therefore, we will write down the equivalence we have found as follows:

$$p \wedge p \dashv\vdash p$$

This means that any substitution of an SL form for "*p*" in both sides of this equivalence will result in a truth-functionally equivalent pair of SL forms which would abstract functionally equivalent switches. We can work out other equivalences in the same way, by finding pairs of blocked proofs derived from a pair of SL forms, and then noting that any pair of proofs with more complex switches replacing any of the simple switches will also block in the same fashion. Utilizing this approach, we can establish the following useful equivalences:

$p \wedge p \dashv\vdash p$	FE$_1$
$p \vee p \dashv\vdash p$	FE$_2$
$p \wedge q \dashv\vdash q \wedge p$	FE$_3$
$p \vee q \dashv\vdash q \vee p$	FE$_4$
$p \wedge (q \wedge r) \dashv\vdash (p \wedge q) \wedge r$	FE$_5$
$p \vee (q \vee r) \dashv\vdash (p \vee q) \vee r$	FE$_6$
$p \wedge (q \vee r) \dashv\vdash (p \wedge q) \vee (p \wedge r)$	FE$_7$

$$p \lor (q \land r) \dashv\vdash (p \lor q) \land (p \lor r) \qquad \text{FE}_8$$
$$(p \land q) \lor (p \land \sim q) \dashv\vdash p \qquad \text{FE}_9$$
$$p \lor (p \land q) \dashv\vdash p \qquad \text{FE}_{10}$$
$$p \lor (\sim p \land q) \dashv\vdash p \lor q \qquad \text{FE}_{11}$$
$$\sim p \lor (p \land q) \dashv\vdash \sim p \lor q \qquad \text{FE}_{12}$$
$$p \lor (q \land \sim q) \dashv\vdash p \qquad \text{FE}_{13}$$
$$p \lor (q \lor \sim q) \dashv\vdash q \lor \sim q \qquad \text{FE}_{14}$$

Now suppose that two switches are shown to be functionally equivalent by substitution into one of FE_1–FE_{14}. As switches they are interchangeable, and we cannot tell them apart (except by the number of component simple switches). Consequently, if the more complex of such a pair appears in a switching network, we can replace it with its functional equivalent, thus effecting an economy in the manufacture of the switch.

We will now show how a complex switch can be simplified using these equivalences. Consider a switch abstracted to this SL form:

$$(P \land Q \land R) \lor (P \land \sim Q \land R) \lor (P \land Q \land \sim R \land S)$$

This switch was diagramed earlier in this chapter. To simplify this switch, we can first consider the following SL form as giving the left-hand disjunct of the SL form under one grouping of parentheses:

$$(P \land Q \land R) \lor (P \land \sim Q \land R)$$

We can work out a simpler equivalent for each disjunct of this switch. By substitution into FE_3 we obtain the following as a switch equivalent to the first disjunct:

$$(P \land (R \land Q))$$

By FE_5, this is in turn equivalent to the following:

$$((P \land R) \land Q)$$

In the same manner, FE_3 and FE_5 give this switch as equivalent to the second disjunct:

$$((P \wedge R) \wedge \sim Q)$$

Replacing disjuncts with their equivalents, we then obtain the following SL form as an equivalent of the left-hand disjunct of the original switch:

$$((P \wedge R) \wedge Q) \vee ((P \wedge R) \wedge \sim Q)$$

A substitution into FE_9 shows this to be functionally equivalent to the following far simpler switch:

$$(P \wedge R)$$

Most simplifications will follow this pattern. We use FE_1–FE_8 to group conjunctions or disjunctions in the proper order for a use of one of FE_9–FE_{14}, for it is clear to inspection that these four equivalences are the ones which may markedly simplify a complex switch. Now let us go back to the original switch with our simplification replacing the first disjunctive component:

$$(P \wedge R) \vee (P \wedge Q \wedge \sim R \wedge S)$$

We can simplify this slightly using FE_7:

$$P \wedge (R \vee (Q \wedge \sim R \wedge S))$$

Looking ahead, we can see that FE_{11} will simplify this by simplifying the second conjunct after grouping and ordering. FE_3 and FE_5 show the following switch to be functionally equivalent to the second conjunct:

$$(R \vee (\sim R \wedge (Q \wedge S)))$$

Use of FE_{11} on this and replacement of the result for the second conjunct above gives us the following SL form abstracting a switch functionally equivalent to the one with which we started:

$$P \wedge (R \vee (Q \wedge S))$$

In terms of economy, we have saved \$3.00 in the cost of manufacturing the original switch by finding this functional equivalent.

We have seen how SL proofs may be used to find equivalences between switching networks, and how these equivalences may be used to simplify such networks. Now we will show how SL can be used to solve another kind of problem. Suppose we have a supply of switches labeled "P," "Q," "R," "$\sim P$," "$\sim Q$," and "$\sim R$," and we want to construct a switching network which will be a closed complex switch if and only if various specified combinations of these simple switches being closed actually hold in the network. For example, suppose that we want the complex switch to be closed if and only if *exactly one* of the switches labeled "P," "Q," or "R" is closed. Switches with these labels may occur as often as required in the network, provided that they are all closed or open together. It is easy to see how to do this. We can wire a series switch of the switches "P," "$\sim Q$," and "$\sim R$." This switch will be closed if and only if "P" is closed, and "Q" and "R" are open. Similarly, the switches "$\sim P \wedge Q \wedge \sim R$" and "$\sim P \wedge \sim Q \wedge R$" handle the other two cases. A switching network which is the parallel wiring of these three series switches will be closed if and only if one of them is closed, and it can be represented by the following diagram: (note that the switch is represented in just one of the eight configurations made possible when "P," "Q," and "R" are on or off) It is easy to see how to get other switching networks realizing fixed conditions. There are two trivial cases. A switch which is closed under all conditions can be realized either as a plain wire (no switch) or by the parallel wiring of a simple switch and its negation. A switch which is always off can be obtained by the series wiring of a simple switch and its negation. Once a

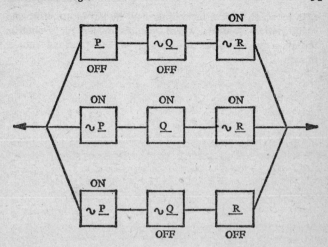

switch has been constructed to realize fixed conditions, it may be simplified by the techniques given earlier in the chapter. The combination of the two techniques may be used to design and then simplify quite complicated switching networks.

Finally, we should note that the use of SL techniques to attack switching problems involves a considerable departure from our earlier use of SL techniques to assess the validity of given arguments. For we have been using SL forms to abstract not statements but switches. Of course, we can convert many problems about switches directly into arguments. A man claiming the functional equivalence of two switches may be arguing that if either switch is on, so will be the other, and this argument can be directly abstracted by letting the SL form abstracting each switch abstract instead the claim that the switch is closed when certain of its constituent simple switches are closed. Most of the problems about switches we have been solving could be converted into slightly artificial arguments about whether certain switches are closed or open under certain conditions, but the details are tedious, and would result in no interesting insight. Instead, we let the novel use of SL symbolism in this chapter indicate the variety of

uses to which logical techniques may be put in scientific and
mathematical contexts where features of logical symbolism
are directly analogous to features of the practical subject
matter.

Exercises

1. Simplify the following switches:
   a. $(P \wedge Q) \vee (\sim P \wedge R) \vee \sim R$
   b. $(P \wedge \sim Q) \vee Q \vee (P \wedge R)$
   c. $((P \wedge Q) \vee R) \wedge ((\sim Q \wedge \sim R) \vee (Q \wedge \sim R))$
   d. $(\sim P \wedge Q \wedge R) \vee (Q \wedge S \wedge R) \vee (P \wedge \sim S \wedge R)$
      $\vee (P \wedge \sim Q \wedge R \wedge S)$
   e. $(\sim P \wedge Q \wedge \sim R) \vee (P \wedge \sim Q \wedge \sim R) \vee (P \wedge Q$
      $\wedge \sim R)$ (See Answer No. 82.)

2. Diagram the following switch:
   $(P \wedge Q) \vee (\sim Q \wedge \sim R) \vee (P \wedge \sim R)$
   Verify from the diagram or by inspection that simply
   omitting the disjunct "$(P \wedge \sim R)$" results in a functionally
   equivalent switch. Try to simplify the switch using the
   methods discussed in Chapter 6.   (See Answer No. 88.)

3. Design a switch using simple switches "P," "$\sim P$," "Q,"
   "$\sim Q$," "R," and "$\sim R$" as components such that the
   switch is closed if and only if at least two out of the three
   switches "P," "Q," and "R" are closed. Simplify the
   switch after you have designed it.
   (See Answer No. 29.)

4. Design a switch using simple switches "P," "$\sim P$," "Q,"
   "$\sim Q$," "R," and "$\sim R$" as components such that the
   switch is closed if and only if exactly two out of the three
   switches "P," "Q," and "R" are closed. Simplify the
   switch.   (See Answer No. 59.)

5. Consider the following network:

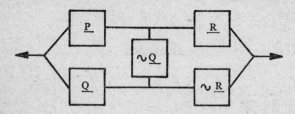

Can this be expressed as a switch which consists solely of a number of switches which are wired in parallel?

(See Answer No. 12.)

6. We have used equivalences FE_1–FE_{14} to show that switches are functionally equivalent. Switches which are functionally equivalent may replace each other in a switching network without any change in the characteristics of the complex network. But as the switches which are functionally equivalent are given as SL forms, we can make use of our analogy between closed and open switches and true and false statements to claim this: SL forms which are equivalent by substitution into FE_1–FE_{14} are also truth-functionally equivalent. Any truth-functionally equivalent SL forms are true together or false together in any possible world. A pair of SL forms can be shown to be truth-functionally equivalent (hereafter just *equivalent*) if they can be obtained by substitution into FE_1–FE_{14} or if the pair of most sophisticated SL argument consistency forms obtained by taking one as the first line and the negation of the other as the second line in each are both those of valid arguments. Just as functionally equivalent switches can replace each other anywhere in switching networks, so equivalent SL forms can replace each other in complex SL forms without changing the truth-values of the pair of complex SL forms in any possible world. Which of the following pairs of SL forms are equivalent:

a. $\sim (P \wedge Q) \vee R, \sim P \vee (\sim Q \vee R)$
b. $\sim (P \wedge Q) \vee R; \sim (P \wedge \sim R) \vee \sim Q$
c. $\sim P \vee (Q \wedge R), (\sim P \vee Q) \wedge (\sim P \vee R)$
d. $\sim A, (\sim A \vee B) \wedge (\sim A \vee \sim B)$

(See Answer No. 48.)

7. Look back at the rules of proof DN and DM_1–DM_8. Which of these can be regarded as giving equivalent SL forms after substitution so that the symbol "⊢" can be replaced by the symbol "⊣ ⊢"?

(See Answer No. 34.)

8. Observe the significance of the symbol "⊣ ⊢" as used to express an equivalence. Since pairs of SL forms obtained by substitution into both sides of an equivalence are equivalent SL forms, *either* may be deduced from the other, and an equivalence may be regarded as a two-way rule of proof. Using equivalences, we could develop proofs which did not add only simplified SL forms as new lines, but also added equivalent SL forms (sometimes more complex) as new lines. We could, on this basis, have two new general rules of proof:

SLE_1: If some line of a proof is an SL form Θ, and Θ is equivalent to another SL form Δ, then Δ may be added as a new line of the proof. The equivalence used and "SLE_1" are cited on the far right after the number of the line from which the new line is obtained.

SLE_2: If some line of a proof is an SL form containing an occurrence of an SL form Θ as a (truth-functional) constituent, and Θ is equivalent to another SL form Δ, then the SL form obtained by replacing Θ with Δ may be added as a new line of the proof with the usual citation on the far right. The new SL form is equivalent to the SL form from which it is obtained.

These qualify as rules of proof since they could not take us from an SL form abstracting a true statement to an SL form abstracting a false statement. Using these new rules of proof, and the equivalences FE_1–FE_{14} along with equivalences DNE and DM_1E–DM_8E (the equivalences obtained from rules of proof DN and DM_1–DM_8 by replacing "⊢" with "⊣ ⊢"), we could construct a kind of proof which we will call an *equivalence derivation*. An equivalence derivation starts with a single SL form as its first line and adds lines of proof using only rules SLE_1 and SLE_2 in conjunction with the equivalences just cited. Each new line added to such a proof is an SL form equivalent to all of the preceding lines. We have not proved this, but it is quite obviously true that equivalence between SL forms is *transitive:* If an SL form Θ is equivalent to an SL form Δ, and Δ is equivalent to an SL form Γ, then Θ is equivalent to Γ. Which of the following are true claims about SL forms:

a.   All tautologous SL forms are equivalent.

b.   All contradictory SL forms are equivalent.

c.   All contingent SL forms are equivalent.

d.   Some contingent SL forms are equivalent.

e.   If an SL form Θ is equivalent to an SL form Δ, then Δ is equivalent to Θ.

f.   If an SL form is equivalent to an SL form Θ, then it is identical with Θ.

g.   If an SL form Θ is equivalent to an SL form Δ, then $\sim \Theta$ (the negation of Θ) is equivalent to $\sim \Delta$.
     (See Answer No. 3.)

9. Any SL form can be shown to be equivalent to an SL form in which negations are negations of capital letters only. The SL form in which negations are negations of capital letters only can always be found by developing an equivalence derivation. By inspection of DM_1E–DM_8E, it is easy to see that negations of conjunctive and disjunctive SL forms can be replaced by equivalent disjunctive or conjunctive SL forms in which the negation signs negate simpler SL forms. This is the basis of the strategy. Suppose we start with the SL form "$R \wedge \sim (P \wedge \sim Q)$." We get an equivalence derivation to an SL form of the appropriate kind in one step as follows:

(1) $R \wedge \sim (P \wedge \sim Q)$

(2) $R \wedge (\sim P \vee Q)$ (1) SLE_2, DM_3E

Find equivalence derivations from the following SL forms to SL forms in which negations are of capital letters only:

a. $\sim (P \vee Q)$

b. $\sim (\sim (\sim P) \vee (\sim Q \wedge R))$

c. $(\sim P \vee Q) \wedge \sim (P \wedge \sim Q)$

d. $\sim (\sim P \vee \sim Q) \vee \sim (\sim P \vee Q)$
     (See Answer No. 51.)

10. Suppose we have a tautologous SL form Δ which does not contain any occurrences of "$\supset$," for example, "$P \vee \sim P$." Let "$\vee$" and "$\wedge$" be exchanged throughout Δ

so as to obtain another SL form Θ. Θ is known as a *dual* (often called *the* dual) of Δ. How are Θ and Δ related?
(See Answer No. 19.)

11. How could you *systematically* find a complex switch Θ which would be closed when and only when some arbitrary complex switch Δ was open? (See Answer No. 40.)

PART THREE
PREDICATE LOGIC

7. Abstracting PL Forms

The undesired consequences of the SL assumption that the simplest constituent assertions in an argument are independent can be illustrated by this example:

All men are mammals.
All mammals are warm-blooded.
Therefore, all men are warm-blooded.

This argument is valid, since its conclusion could not be false while its premises were true, but it is SL invalid. The failure of the SL test is related quite directly to the SL assumption of independence. It should be suspected that independence might fail here because of the fact that various terms, such as "men," occur in more than one simplest constituent statement of the argument. Informally, we can perhaps grasp the validity of this argument as follows. Let *"a"* be a name for any particular man. Then we could let *"Ha,"* *"Ma,"* and *"Wa"* stand as shorthand for the following sentences:

"Ha" for *"a* is a man."
"Ma" for *"a* is a mammal."
"Wa" for *"a* is warm-blooded."

"Ha," *"Ma,"* and *"Wa"* are symbolic expressions like SL capital letters in that they abstract statements which have no

discernible truth-functional structure. Now, if the first premise of the argument above is true, then the sentence which could be abstracted by a slight extension of SL methods to "~ *Ha* ∨ *Ma*" must also be true. For if all men are mammals, then "*a*," if a man, is also a mammal. We chose the name "*a*" so that it is the name of a man, and we might suppose that we could write down the abstraction "*Ha* ∧ *Ma*" and suppose that it abstracts a true statement. Given our assumptions, it *is* true, but the truth of this statement does not follow from the first premise alone, but from the first premise along with the additional claim that there is at least one man and "*a*" is his name, a claim which we have smuggled into our use of "*a*," but which does not follow from the first premise. Similarly, if the second premise is true, then "~ *Ma* ∨ *Wa*" must abstract a true statement. From now on, we will call any test for validity using SL techniques but in which more complex symbols than SL capital letters are used to abstract simplest constituent assertions or statements an *extended SL test* for validity. Clearly, such extensions can be completely justified by enlarging the definition of an SL form to accommodate the more complex symbols. By using an extended SL test for validity, we can show that the statement abstracted to "~ *Ha* ∨ *Wa*" follows from the statements abstracted to "~ *Ha* ∨ *Ma*" and "~ *Ma* ∨ *Wa*." Now, the conclusion, "All men are warm-blooded," can be false if and only if there is some man who is *not* warm-blooded. If this man were the one named "*a*," then "*Ma* ∧ ~ *Wa*" would abstract a true statement, but this cannot be jointly true with the statement abstracted to "~ *Ma* ∨ *Wa*," whose truth follows from the joint truth of the premises of the argument. Given the premises, "*a*" must be warm-blooded if "*a*" is a man. Suppose then that some man other than "*a*" is not warm-blooded. Using "*b*" as a name for that man, we can carry through a similar analysis to show that at least one of the premises must be false. Since the premises of the argument cannot be jointly true while the conclusion is false, the argument is surely valid.

In indicating the validity of this argument, we have used

lower-case letters as names of individuals, and we have used upper-case letters to stand for properties which could be attributed to these individuals. Analysis of sentences into two similar components should be familiar from grammatical analysis, where it is often useful to analyze a sentence into its subject and predicate. PL analysis ("PL" will abbreviate "Predicate Logic") will proceed by refining and extending traditional grammatical analysis to look for common names and common predicates in the sentences of an argument that indicate their dependence. To develop PL analysis, we first turn our attention to simple declarative sentences in which the distinction between subject and predicate is obvious to grammatical intuition. We will assume that these simple sentences have no truth-functional structure, so that they could represent the simplest constituent statements in a most sophisticated SL argument consistency form for some argument. We will abstract these simple sentences to what we will call PL *expressions*. PL *forms* will be introduced later as abstractions from the PL expressions about to be introduced.

In a sufficiently simple declarative sentence, the subject of the sentence is a word or phrase occurring in the sentence which refers to some identifiable individual or object, and the whole sentence will be said to make a claim (represented by the predicate) about that subject. For example, consider these three simple sentences:

Jim has red hair.
Jack has red hair.
Jim is six feet tall.

The first and third (in a suitably imagined context) have the same subject, Jim, while the first and second may be said to make the same claim about two different subjects. But these crude observations need considerable elaboration.

Consider the sentence "Jim has red hair." Here it is sufficiently obvious that Jim is the subject of the sentence, and that the predicate is the claim that he has red hair. Now we need to make a few remarks about the way in which subjects and predicates are to be abstracted in PL analysis. The subject of a sentence in a PL analysis is not the *word* which occurs in the sentence, but it is (in simple cases, anyway) the object of some referring expression or name which occurs in the sentence. We will call any word or phrase in a sentence which refers to an identified specific single object a *naming expression*. "Jim" is a naming expression in a suitable context, and so is "2 + 2," since it refers to the number four. When PL is elaborated for special purposes, descriptions or functions or both may be introduced to abstract relationships between various names or naming expressions referring to the same individual. But for the time being, we will let the lower-case letters "*a*," "*b*," "*c*," "*d*," and "*e*" (possibly with dashes or subscripts) abstract naming expressions each of which refers to a distinct, identifiable individual. These symbols will be known as the PL constants. We use the same PL constant to abstract two different naming expressions which we recognize as referring to the same individual or object. We use this freedom to abstract different naming expressions to the same PL constant in quite another way: We will say that we can abstract a naming expression in a sentence to a PL constant if and only if, when any other naming expression referring to the same object is substituted for the first naming expression, the resulting sentence is one which has the same truth-value as the first no matter what the underlying facts are. Thus, if Jim's full name is Jim Hardy, the naming expression in each of the following sentences could be abstracted to "*a*":

Jim is six feet tall.
Jim Hardy is six feet tall.

Now consider this pair of sentences:

John believes that Jim is six feet tall.
John believes that Jim Hardy is six feet tall.

Here the underlying facts are John's beliefs. It is quite possible that John knows Jim only as "Jim," and believes "Jim

Hardy" to be someone else. John may then respond to the question "Is Jim six feet tall" affirmatively, while refusing to answer the question "Is Jim Hardy six feet tall," or giving a negative response. "Jim" and "Jim Hardy" are not interchangeable in this latter pair of sentences while preserving truth-value no matter what the underlying facts. We have shown how the truth-value could change when the naming expression is varied. A naming expression for which any other naming expression with the same referent can be substituted without the pair of involved sentences differing in truth-value, no matter what the underlying facts, is known as a *transparent* naming expression. In PL analysis, we can replace *only* transparent naming expressions with PL constants. Although this is a severe restriction in analyzing many arguments in everyday contexts, most naming expressions occurring in statements of scientific or mathematical fact occur transparently.

Even for very simple sentences, there is no convenient separate expression for the *claim* which a statement makes about the objects which are referred to transparently by its naming expressions. An expression for the claim did not develop in traditional grammar because grammarians were more interested in the meaning of single sentences than in the structure of arguments containing several sentences. Logicians have therefore had to find symbolic expressions to abstract such claims from the statements which are used to make them. These expressions abstracting claims will be known as *predicate expressions*. In the case of the sentence "Jim has red hair," a one-place predicate expression is abstracted by replacing the naming expression "Jim" with a PL variable and enclosing the result in parentheses. A PL *variable* is any small letter of the alphabet occurring after "*r*" (sometimes with primes or subscripts). The parentheses are used to indicate that some PL abstraction has taken place, and that we no longer have an English sentence. Replacing "Jim" with the variable "*x*," we obtain the predicate expression "(*x* has red hair)" from the previously considered sentence. A one-place predicate expression like this is not a

sentence, nor does it abstract a sentence, but we can turn it
into a sentence by dropping parentheses and replacing the
variable with a suitable naming expression. It is thus useful
for abstracting the claim which a sentence may make about
some definite object. When a sentence is formed from a one-
place predicate expression by replacing its variable with a
naming expression and omitting the surrounding parentheses, we will say that the predicate expression has been *instantiated*. We can also say that a one-place predicate expression is *true of* some object if the instantiation of that predicate
expression by any naming expression for the object is a true
sentence.

If a statement contains a naming expression which refers
to a single object which is fully identified in the context, we
will say that the statement has *specific reference*. But statements may also make claims about *all* objects or individuals
of some kind, and they may make claims about at least one
individual who or which is not sufficiently identified to be
referred to by a naming expression. A statement about all
objects of some kind will be said to have *general reference*,
and a statement about at least one object not fully identified in
a context will be said to have *indefinite reference*.

We will use PL constants to set down expressions to be
called *hybrid sentences* which will be considered to have a
truth value just like English sentences making statements
except that a PL constant will appear in one or more places
where a naming expression would appear in an English sentence. For convenience, we will add to the class of PL constants all those symbols which can be obtained from PL
variables by circling them. Circled variables, like "ⓧ," "ⓨ,"
etc., are PL constants and *not* PL variables. In a given context, a hybrid sentence such as "ⓧ has red hair" will be
treated just like the sentence "Jim has red hair," except for
the different naming expressions. We will often write down
hybrid sentences in order to be able to cite conveniently an
English sentence from which some one-place predicate expression could have been abstracted. Hybrid sentences are
merely an expository device which we will use to introduce

various one-place predicate expressions without constructing elaborate contexts for their justification.

The hybrid sentence "ⓧ has weight" has specific reference. By contrast, the sentence "Everything has weight" has general reference. It should be clear that "everything," while the grammatical subject of the sentence, is not a naming expression. The markedly different treatment of statements of general reference from statements of specific reference marks a divergence between traditional grammar and PL analysis, although this difference in no way clashes with traditional grammar. Using the one-place predicate expression "(x has weight)," which can be obtained from the hybrid sentence, we abstract "Everything has weight" to the following PL expression:

$$(\forall x)(x \text{ has weight})$$

This expression is to be read "For any x, x has weight," and it makes the claim that every instantiation of the one-place predicate expression "(x has weight)" is a true statement of specific reference. The PL expression is called the *universal quantification* of the one-place predicate expression "(x has weight)." To universally quantify a one-place predicate expression, we prefix to that predicate expression the universal quantifier obtained from the following expression by filling in the blank with the variable occurring in the predicate expression:

$$(\forall \_)$$

The universal quantification of a one-place predicate expression abstracts any statement which is equivalent to claiming that every instantiation of the one-place predicate expression is a true statement of specific reference.

The difficulty with universal quantification that must be watched very carefully in abstracting arguments is that we must be able to specify *which* instantiations are meant to be counted when we speak of all of the instantiations of a one-place predicate expression. To specify the range of intended instantiations, we describe a *universe of discourse* for every statement of general reference. A universe of discourse is a well-defined set of individuals or objects each of which can be identified and referred to by a naming expression if we care to take the trouble to define all of the naming expressions. In describing a universe of discourse, we cannot *list* the naming expressions involved in every case, since at least sometimes we want to talk about a universe of discourse in which there are an infinite number of individuals, for example, certain sets of numbers. But in this case, we must be able to specify a means of finding a name for any particular individual that we might want to talk about in a statement which is an instantiation of the one-place predicate expressions that we are considering. Once a universe of discourse has been specified, we sometimes need to complicate the PL expression abstracting a statement of general reference in order to avoid certain anomalies. This is hardly ever the case when we are considering a single statement, but when quantifiers are used to abstract different statements within the same argument, various difficulties arise which can be suitably illustrated by an example. Suppose that we have already abstracted a statement of general reference in the context of some scientific argument whose quantifier must range over the integers. Now when we abstract "Everything has weight" later on in the course of the same argument, we may get the PL expression we have already used to abstract this statement. But now one instantiation of the one-place predicate expression results in the sentence "4 has weight," which is patently nonsensical. Clearly, in the context of the argument, the sentence "Everything has weight" is being used to make a statement which might better be advanced through the use of this sentence:

Every physical object has weight.

How can we abstract this slightly more complex claim? For simplicity, suppose that the universe of discourse for the entire argument consists of the integers plus all physical objects of some determinate kind. We now introduce two one-place predicate expressions, "(x is an integer)" and "(x is a physical object)," which we can imagine have been abstracted from suitably chosen hybrid sentences. Now, if the one-place predicate expression "(x has weight)" results in a true statement for each instantiation when the universe of discourse consists of physical objects only, then the more complex one-place predicate expression "(x is not a physical object or x has weight)" results in a true statement for each instantiation when the universe of discourse consists of physical objects and integers. This is not quite straightforward, but we can defend it as follows. The instantiation for "4" looks like this: "4 is not a physical object or 4 has weight." We can call this disjunction true because the disjunct "4 is not a physical object" is true. On the other hand, the remaining disjunct is still apparently nonsensical. Since we are not asserting it here, it hardly matters how we view it, but the usual attitude of logicians is to stretch credibility slightly by calling this disjunct false on the grounds that a number could not be put through any of the operational tests for weight. Returning to the complex one-place predicate expression, we see that any instantiation of it for a physical object is true because the second disjunct is true in a straightforward sense while the first is false if we must decide on a truth-value for it. The manufactured one-place predicate expression thus enables us to find a PL expression to abstract the original sentence when the universe of discourse must be enlarged. Taking care that all quantifiers can be thought to range over the same universe of discourse when more than two quantifiers must be used to abstract all of the sentences in some argument is an annoying but important detail of PL analysis.

Let us look again at the one-place predicate expression "(x is not a physical object or x has weight)." Any instantiation of this one-place predicate expression will either be a sentence or a hybrid sentence. A convenient way to discuss an instantiation is to form the instantiation which is the hybrid sentence obtained by circling the variable in the predicate expression. Doing this, we obtain:

ⓧ is not a physical object or ⓧ has weight.

This sentence has truth-functional structure, and we may analyze it to obtain an extended SL form as follows:

∼ (ⓧ is a physical object) ∨ ⓧ has weight.

If a hybrid sentence is obtained from a one-place predicate expression by circling its variable, and an SL form is then obtained from it by abstracting as much truth-functional structure as possible, and if this SL form is such that no negation sign negates a disjunctive or conjunctive SL form, then we will call the SL form so obtained the *related hybrid sentence* of the one-place predicate expression. We know from SL analysis that negation can always be distributed so as to obtain such a form. From the related hybrid sentence we may obtain an expression which is equivalent to a one-place predicate expression by uncircling all of the variables circled to obtain the hybrid sentence, and adding parentheses where necessary. This expression is equivalent to the original one-place predicate expression in this sense: Replacement of the variables of both by the same naming expression results in a pair of sentences which are equivalent in the sense that one is an SL abstraction of the other, so that if one is used to make a true statement, the other abstracts that true statement. A quantification of one predicate expression will clearly be equivalent to a quantification of the other. The following pair of PL expressions is thus equivalent:

($\forall x$)(x is not a physical object or x has weight)
($\forall x$)($\sim$ (x is a physical object) ∨ (x has weight))

The one-place predicate expression in this last PL expression uses SL logical symbols in a new way to give truth-functional structure for a predicate expression rather than for a sentence.

Without further explanation, this use of SL symbolism is not justified. It is justified because of the significance of the whole PL expression, which is that any instantiation of "($\sim$ (x is a physical object) $\lor$ (x has weight))" abstracts a true statement if and only if the same instantiation of "(x is not a physical object or x has weight)" is a true statement. These instantiations, of course, must be taken relative to a fixed universe of discourse and a fixed argumentative context. From now on, we will always use extended SL analysis to expose any truth-functional structure in a one-place predicate expression by this means. We will call the one-place predicate expressions appearing in the PL expression with no truth-functional structure the *simplest constituent predicate expressions* of the PL expression. In our example, "(x is a physical object)" and "(x has weight)" are the simplest constituent predicate expressions of

$$(\forall x)(\sim (x \text{ is a physical object}) \lor (x \text{ has weight}))$$

One more point can be gleaned from this past example. In the universe of discourse consisting of integers and physical objects, we have seen that the statement advanced by the sentence "Everything has weight" is more accurately expressed by the sentence "Every physical object has weight." This last sentence is obviously equivalent to "All physical objects have weight." This sentence has the informal significance of claiming that all objects of one kind are objects of another kind. Technically, such a statement is known as a generalization. If we could not express generalizations, we could not capture the dependencies which make the PL test for validity a useful extension of the SL test for validity. Nearly every valid argument of scientific or mathematical interest which is invalid by the SL test but is valid by the PL test will contain at least one generalization indicating a dependency between different predicate expressions. Further, this dependency is nearly always of the simple kind of generalization which we have already introduced. If we can find a one-place predicate expression "(x is of kind A)" and another "(x is of kind B)," the generalization that all individuals of kind A are also individuals of kind B may be abstracted to a PL expression like this:

$$(\forall x)(\sim(x \text{ is of kind A}) \lor (x \text{ is of kind B}))$$

The PL expression we have used to abstract "All physical objects have weight" is an example of this kind of PL expression. Looking back to the illustrative argument beginning this chapter, we see that the first premise, "All men are mammals," is also of this general description. We can therefore abstract it to this PL expression:

$$(\forall x)(\sim (x \text{ is a man}) \lor (x \text{ is a mammal}))$$

In doing this, we are skipping over the elaborate justification provided for the PL expression abstracting "All physical objects have weight," but it should be clear that this justification could easily be provided in this case. Occasionally, instead of expressing dependence between objects of kind A and objects of kind B, we wish to express their complete independence, that is, the fact that *no* objects of kind A are of kind B. For example, consider the sentence "No Republicans are Democrats." This can be abstracted to the following PL expression:

$$(\forall y)(\sim (y \text{ is a Republican}) \lor \sim (y \text{ is a Democrat}))$$

Suppose that this claim is true. Then any instantiation will be true because the referent of the naming expression is said to be either *not* a Republican or *not* a Democrat. This is sufficient to capture the claim that no individual can be both. For practice, we may consider the complication introduced by supposing that the universe of discourse for some argument containing this sentence includes some men who are not U.S. citizens (the universe of discourse implicitly suggested by the sentence). Using our previous strategy, we would need to complicate the abstracting PL expression to this:

$(\forall y) (\sim (y$ is a U.S. citizen$) \lor (\sim (y$ is a Republican$) \lor (y$ is a Democrat$)))$

We now turn to sentences with indefinite reference. "Something is biting Jim" has indefinite reference, since it makes the claim that at least one instantiation of the one-place predicate expression "$(x$ is biting Jim$)$" is true. We abstract this to the following PL expression:

$(\exists x) (x$ is biting Jim$)$

This expression is to be read "There is at least one x such that x is biting Jim." The PL expression is called the *existential quantification* of the one-place predicate expression "$(x$ is biting Jim$)$." To existentially quantify a one-place predicate expression, we prefix to that predicate expression the *existential quantifier* obtained from the following expression by filling in the blank with the variable occurring in the predicate expression:

$(\exists \_)$

The existential quantifier of a one-place predicate expression abstracts any statement which is equivalent to claiming that at least one instantiation of the one-place predicate expression is a true statement of specific reference.

As in the case of universal quantification, care must be taken with respect to the universe of discourse and the quantifier. A recipient of an unsigned valentine may assert "Somebody loves me." The obvious abstraction, "$(\exists x) (x$ loves me$)$," abstracts exactly the claim that something or other in the universe of discourse loves the person in question. We may get closer to the intended meaning by restricting the source of this love to a human being as follows:

$(\exists x) ((x$ is a person$) \land (x$ loves me$))$

Usually, an existentially quantified PL expression may re-

quire additional restricting predicate expressions to narrow
down the intended objects of instantiation. Notice that in this
example we have exposed truth-functional structure in the one-
place predicate expression by extended SL analysis. The way
in which this is done and the justification for the technique
can be taken over with only incidental terminological
changes from the justification which was given earlier for the
use of extended SL analysis in exposing the truth-functional
structure of universally quantified one-place predicate expressions.

A statement will be said to be of kind (1) if it may
be construed as having indefinite reference. As usual, this
terminology may also be applied to sentences which are
normally used to make statements. "Tom owns a horse" is of
kind (1) because it can be construed as a statement of indefinite reference about some object (a horse) which Tom
owns that is neither named nor identified in the statement. If
the statement were true (we assume this in abstracting the
PL expression for it) and Tom owned only one horse, we
might consider it identified, but the statement is compatible
with Tom's owning several horses, in which case we would
require further information before we could be said to have
identified the horse in question. Statements of kind (1) will
be abstracted to existential quantifications of some appropriate one-place predicate expression. Our example may
be abstracted to this PL expression:

$$(\exists x)((x \text{ is a horse}) \land (\text{Tom owns } x))$$

A statement will be said to be of kind (2) if it is not of kind
(1) but may be construed as a claim with general reference.
Statements of kind (2) will always be abstracted to the universal quantification of some appropriate one-place predicate expression. "There is no greatest prime number" is a
statement of kind (2) that may be abstracted as follows:

$$(\forall y)(\sim (y \text{ is a prime number}) \lor (\text{there is a prime number} \text{ greater than } y))$$

The restriction that a sentence is of kind (2) provided that it is not of kind (1) is important. Consider the following sentence:

Somebody loves everybody.

If we don't first consider whether this sentence is of kind (1), we would certainly consider it to be of kind (2), since it does say something about everybody. It will turn out that we need to examine whether this sentence is of kind (1) first in order to distinguish it from other sentences, for example,

Everybody is loved by somebody.

The two sentences can differ in truth-value on certain underlying facts. Let us suppose the first sentence to be false because everyone has somebody that he doesn't love. (This will, of course, not be true given certain religious convictions.) The falsity of the first sentence under these circumstances is quite compatible with everyone loving himself. But in this case, the second sentence would be true. Now, even though both sentences say something about everybody, only the first sentence has indefinite reference. The two sentences are distinguished at least by the fact that the former is of kind (1) while the latter is of kind (2). A statement is of kind (3) if it is neither of kind (1) nor of kind (2). "Dobbin is a horse" is about an object identified in the statement as Dobbin. This statement is therefore of kind (3). It might be supposed that this statement is really equivalent to the following statement:

There is a horse named Dobbin.

This appears to be of kind (1), but strictly it is not. It does not refer to an object not identified in the statement, since we know which horse is being referred to, namely Dobbin. A simple test is this. If the words "identical with" can be placed between the "is" and the "a" of such a sentence, then the sentence is really the expression of an identifying reference, and does not make a substantive claim about an unidentified object. Our sentence is equivalent to "Dobbin is identical with a horse," indicating that it is not genuinely of kind (1). By comparison, "Dobbin is too old to race" has no difficulties, and is obviously of kind (3).

In deciding the kind of a given sentence, we usually make the simplifying assumption that, in a suitable context, proper names will have definite reference. If we had a sentence like "Hamlet is the prince of Denmark" and knew that "Hamlet" referred to no person, living or dead, there would be no straightforward way of abstracting a PL expression. Temporarily, this is a useful breakdown, since fictional reference is a topic of considerable controversy that requires delicate treatment. We will assume that naming expressions refer to actual objects. or individuals for the time being. For most arguments of mathematics and science, this position will create no difficulties unless one is attached to some philosophical ontology that requires special exposition in abstracting to logical form.

To summarize, we find a PL expression abstracting a statement by first attempting construal of the statement as of kind (1), then attempting a construal as of kind (2). If neither construal is possible, we leave the sentence as of kind (3). This order of search is important if appropriate PL expressions are to be abstracted from given sentences.

We have seen how a sufficiently simple sentence of kind (1) or kind (2) may be abstracted to a PL expression which is either the universal or existential quantification of some one-place predicate expression derived from the original sentence. The difficulty with PL analysis is that the simplest constituent predicate expressions of PL expressions may themselves conceal further PL quantificational structure. We obviously want to find PL expressions abstracting sentences which express as much quantificational structure as we possibly can.

To illustrate the problem, we may attempt abstraction of the sentence "Somebody loves everybody," where we will assume for simplicity that the universe of discourse is that of human beings. (It does not matter that the statement it makes would probably be false.) Since this sentence is of kind (1), we can quickly find this PL expression to abstract it:

(∃ x) (x loves everybody)

If this abstracts a true statement, then some instantiation of the predicate expression which occurs in it is a true statement. Suppose this instantiation to be the following:

ⓧ loves everybody.

To make sense of this, we can suppose ourselves reserving the PL constant "ⓧ" for an individual making this sentence true, should there be one. We now apply PL analysis to this hybrid sentence, which is clearly of kind (2), and abstract this PL expression:

(∀ y) (ⓧ loves y)

Since this PL expression abstracts a sentence, if we replace the naming expression "ⓧ" by a variable, the resulting expression can be construed as a one-place predicate expression, since when it is quantified, it will abstract a sentence. In this case, we find the one-place predicate expression by uncircling the variable "x," and then quantification with the quantifier used earlier will clearly give us a PL expression abstracting the original sentence:

(∃ x) (∀ y) (x loves y)

We introduced circled variables as PL constants primarily to keep track of prior quantifications in the process of abstracting a multiply quantified PL expression. In quantifying a one-place predicate expression which begins with a quantifier, we omit any outer enclosing parentheses for convenience. Quantifications of quantified one-place predicate expressions obtained by an extension of this technique are clearly required to abstract sentences with complex quantificational structure.

Suppose we have a PL expression abstracting a sentence of kind (1) or kind (2) satisfying the restriction that negation signs must not negate disjunctive or conjunctive expressions. We can easily construct the related hybrid sentence for each simplest constituent predicate expression in the PL expression to see if it is in turn of kind (1) or kind (2). All hybrid sentences which are of kind (1) or kind (2) are then abstracted to PL expressions. The hybrid sentences formed from the simplest constituent predicate expressions appearing in these new predicate expressions are then examined to see whether they are of kind (1) or kind (2). If they are, appropriate PL expressions are abstracted. This cycle can be repeated until no related hybrid sentences of kind (1) or kind (2) are found for the simplest constituent predicate expressions at some level of analysis. Then the last abstracted PL expressions replace the hybrid sentences from which they were abstracted, and these hybrid sentences, with appropriate variables uncircled, then replace the predicate expressions from which they were derived. The original quantifiers are reintroduced at the appropriate steps in this process until a most sophisticated PL expression is synthesized to abstract the original sentence.

We are now ready to begin discussion of the abstraction of an entire argument to what we will call a *most sophisticated PL argument consistency expression form* for that argument. The first step is to abstract a most sophisticated SL argument consistency form in which no negation sign precedes a negated SL form and in which no negation sign negates a conjunctive or disjunctive SL form. The next step is to find a most sophisticated PL expression to abstract each statement in the argument of kind (1) or kind (2) which is abstracted to either an SL capital letter or the negation of an SL capital letter in the most sophisticated SL argument consistency form. We must abstract the *entire* statement abstracted to the negation of an SL capital letter which is of kind (1) or kind (2) since we do not yet recognize any significance attached to the negation of a quantified PL expression. In abstracting, we keep track of each variable used in finding a one-place predicate expression, using a different variable each time a one-place predicate expression is abstracted from any variable used earlier in an abstractive step in the analysis of the given argument. The PL expressions found then replace the corresponding capital letters (or negations thereof) in the most sophisticated SL argument consistency form. The result is a most sophisticated PL argument consistency expression form.

We will illustrate the abstraction of a most sophisticated PL argument consistency expression form by finding one for this argument:

All horses are animals.
Therefore, all heads of horses are heads of animals.

To find a most sophisticated PL argument consistency expression form, we take the premise and the negation of the conclusion as two lines, and then we may abstract to obtain this most sophisticated SL argument consistency form:

(1) P
(2) $\sim Q$ $\sim$(CON)

We start PL analysis by abstracting a PL expression for the statement here abstracted to the SL capital letter "P." The sentence so abstracted is clearly of kind (2), and we may abstract the following PL expression for it in view of our remarks earlier in the chapter:

$(\forall x)(\sim(x$ is a horse$) \lor (x$ is an animal$))$

The related hybrid sentences for this PL expression are "ⓧ is a horse" and "ⓧ is an animal," neither of which is either of kind (1) or kind (2). Therefore, this PL expression is suitable to abstract line (1).

The abstraction of a most sophisticated PL expression for

line (2) at this stage is about as difficult an abstractive problem as one is likely to encounter in practice. The sentence
to be abstracted is "It is not the case that all heads of horses
are heads of animals," abstracted to the negation of a capital
letter in the most sophisticated SL argument consistency
form. This sentence is of kind (1), since it is equivalent to
"There is some head of a horse which is not the head of an
animal." It might be thought that since "All heads of horses
are heads of animals" can be abstracted to the following
PL expression by the techniques introduced earlier,

$(\forall y)(\sim (y$ is the head of a horse$) \lor (y$ is the head of an
animal$))$,

and this would abstract the sentence abstracted to "Q," we
could abstract line (2) as the following PL expression:

$\sim((\forall y)(\sim (y$ is the head of a horse$)) \lor (y$ is the head
of an animal$))$

Indeed, this abstraction is equivalent to the one we will introduce, but the difficulty in giving rules for handling the
negations of quantified PL expressions is such that we will
avoid such abstractions for the present. We will, instead,
paraphrase a sentence abstracted to the negation of a capital
letter in the most sophisticated SL argument form until we
can abstract it directly as a sentence of kind (1) or kind (2).
The ability to do this must be acquired if PL analysis is to
make intuitive sense. Our paraphrase of line (2) can be
abstracted as follows:

$(\exists y)((y$ is the head of a horse$) \land (y$ is not the head of an
animal$))$

The related hybrid sentences for the simplest constituent predicate expressions of this PL expression are both of kind (1).
One of them can easily be abstracted to this PL expression:

$(\exists z)((z$ is a horse$) \land (\mathcal{Y}$ is the head of $z))$

The related hybrid sentences are "Ⓩ is a horse" and "Ⓨ is the head of Ⓩ." Since both are of kind (3), no further analysis is required. The other hybrid sentence derived from the paraphrase is "Ⓨ is not the head of an animal." It is easy to make a mistake with this, since it appears superficially to be quite like some sentences of kind (1). But the sentence does not claim that Ⓨ is the head of an otherwise unidentified animal; it claims that Ⓨ is not the head of *any* animal. This is equivalent to asserting "No animal is such that Ⓨ is its head," a sentence of kind (2), which may be abstracted to this PL expression:

$$(\forall s)(\sim (s \text{ is an animal}) \lor \sim (Ⓨ \text{ is the head of } s))$$

Once again, the related hybrid sentences are of kind (3), and no further analysis is required. We now replace the related hybrid sentences of the first abstracted PL expression by the PL expressions just abstracted from them. Uncircling the variables of these PL expressions, we obtain this pair of predicate expressions:

$$(\exists z)((z \text{ is a horse}) \land (y \text{ is the head of } z))$$
$$(\forall s)(\sim (s \text{ is an animal}) \lor \sim (y \text{ is the head of } s))$$

Replacing the simplest constituent predicate expressions in the PL expression first abstracted by these new one-place predicate expressions, we obtain this most sophisticated PL expression for abstracting line (2):

$$(\exists y)((\exists z)((z \text{ is a horse}) \land (y \text{ is the head of } z)) \land (\forall s)$$
$$(\sim (s \text{ is an animal}) \lor \sim (y \text{ is the head of } s)))$$

The most sophisticated PL argument consistency expression form for the argument we have been considering may thus be given as follows:

(1) $(\forall x)(\sim (x \text{ is a horse}) \lor (x \text{ is an animal}))$
(2) $(\exists y)((\exists z)((z \text{ is a horse}) \land (y \text{ is the head of } z)) \land$
       $(\forall s)(\sim (s \text{ is an animal}) \lor \sim (y \text{ is the head of } s)))$
                                 $\sim (\text{CON})$

What about the universe of discourse? It is messy, as it must contain horses, animals, and heads of both, but we can construe these as distinct objects, giving each a name, so that all instantiations will be true or false in this universe of discourse.

In the discussion of abstraction to a most sophisticated PL argument consistency expression form for an argument, we have been utilizing only the intuition that one-place predicate expressions abstract simple claims common to many sentences, and the idea that we can understand instantiations, universal quantifications, and existential quantifications of one-place predicate expressions. But the most sophisticated PL argument consistency expression form that we abstract in analyzing an argument still contains English phrases with substantive content. This means that our techniques for PL abstraction have not reached a point of abstraction comparable to that attained by a most sophisticated SL argument consistency form before the test for validity by proof.

To obtain a most sophisticated PL argument consistency form at the same level of abstraction as a most sophisticated SL argument consistency form, we abstract the fragments of English remaining in the most sophisticated PL argument consistency expression form for an argument to what we will call *predicate letters*. Then the process of PL abstraction will be complete. The fragments to be abstracted to predicate letters must never contain quantifiers, or the symbols for negation, disjunction, or conjunction. What will be abstracted to predicate letters will be those phrases containing some words of English, and perhaps some PL variables and constants, but neither of the SL symbols "$\lor$" or "$\land$." The expressions to be abstracted will not always be identical with predicate expressions used to abstract some PL expression, for the following reason: In order to justify our method of abstracting a most sophisticated PL argument consistency expression form, we are supposing at each step of analysis that it makes good sense to abstract only a one-place predicate expression, that is, a predicate expression that could be turned into a sentence by a single instantiation of the variable occurring in it. Some of these fragments, like "(y is the head of z)," contain more than a single variable. Now, we may regard this particular fragment as a two-place, rather than a one-place, predicate expression. For two operations of instantiation, one for one of the variables, and the subsequent one for the other, will turn this expression into a sentence (a hybrid sentence if PL constants are used to instantiate). The notion of an n-place predicate expression ($n = 1, 2, 3, \ldots$) is easily given by extension. It is the n-place predicate expressions in a most sophisticated PL argument consistency expression form for some argument that will basically be abstracted to predicate letters. The major exception is that any *sentences* in the most sophisticated PL argument consistency expression form which can be seen to be instantiations of n-place predicate expressions occurring elsewhere in the most sophisticated PL argument consistency expression form may also be abstracted to predicate letters after the initial abstraction of the n-place predicate expressions.

A *predicate letter* is a capital letter of the alphabet which is followed by one or more variables or PL constants and which may be preceded by a negation sign. "*Pxy*," "*~ Pyx*," "*Pyx*," "*Pxa*," and "*Pxx*" are distinct predicate letters. The first variable or constant following the capital letter is called the *first member* of the predicate letter, the second variable or constant, the *second member*, and so on. We use n-membered predicate letters to abstract the claims made by n-place predicate expressions. Two n-place predicate expressions containing the same variables make the same claim if any instantiation of the variables of one predicate expression makes the same claim as the instantiation of the other predicate expression in which the same naming expressions replace the same variables. The two-place predicate expression "(x loves y)" makes the same claim as the two-place predicate expression "(y is loved by x)" in nearly every argumentative context. These two-place predicate expressions could thus be abstracted to the same predicate letter, say "*Lxy*." Two n-place predicate expressions abstracting the same claim using identical variables are called *identical*, and the justification for their abstraction to the same predicate letter is obvious. Two n-place predicate expressions may be such that they make the same claim if their variables are correlated in such a fashion that any instantiation of one would be equivalent to the instantiation of the other when naming expressions are used to replace the correlated variables. We will call such a pair of n-place predicate expressions *similar*. Similar n-place predicate expressions will be abstracted to different predicate letters, but predicate letters with the same initial capital letters both followed by n variables, the order of the variables indicating the appropriate correlation. For example, if "$(x$ loves $y)$" is abstracted to "Lxy," then the similar predicate expression "$(y$ loves $z)$" would be abstracted to "Lyz." Again, the justification for the abstraction of similar predicate expressions to such pairs of predicate letters is quite straightforward.

A predicate expression of fewer than n places may be *restrictive* of an n-place predicate expression if the n-place predicate expression is such that when *some* of its variables are replaced by naming expressions, a predicate expression of less than n places results, which is similar to the first predicate expression. For example, "$(Jim$ loves $z)$" is restrictive of "$(x$ loves $y)$" when "Jim" replaces "x." PL constants must be used to abstract restrictive predicate expressions. If "$(x$ loves $y)$" is abstracted to "Lxy," the restrictive predicate letter "Laz" may abstract "$(Jim$ loves $z)$" under the stipulation that the PL constant "a" be used as abstracting the naming expression "Jim." The method of forming restrictive predicate letters should be clear from this example. A predicate expression of fewer than n places may be a *degenerate* case of an n-place predicate expression if it is similar to a predicate expression which results from the n-place predicate expression by replacing one or more variables in the predicate expression by other variables already occurring in the predicate expression. Degenerate predicate expressions are occasionally of importance. If "$(\forall x)(\exists y)(Lxy)$" abstracts "Everything is larger than something," so that "Lxy" abstracts the predicate expression "$(x$ is larger than $y)$," then "Nothing is larger than itself" could be abstracted as "$(\forall z)(\sim Lzz)$," where "Lzz" is a degenerate predicate letter abstracting "(*z* is larger than *z*)." The occurrence of the same capital letter as the first symbol in predicate letters with the same number of members in a most sophisticated PL argument consistency form indicates non-independence between the predicate expressions which these predicate letters abstract. In the example given, "(∀*z*)(~ *Lzz*)" and "(∀*z*) (~ (*Lzz*))" are equivalent. We can omit parentheses which enclose a single predicate letter only.

There is one last difficulty in abstracting to predicate letters caused by choice in abstracting negation to the SL symbol "~" which may arise at various points in abstracting a most sophisticated PL argument expression form. Two *n*-place predicate expressions are complementary if their variables and constants may be correlated so that when both are instantiated by naming expressions replacing corresponding variables, sentences result which are such that one is the negation of the other. If two predicate expressions are complementary, and one is abstracted to a given predicate letter, the other is abstracted to a similar predicate letter or an identical predicate letter preceded by a negation sign. For example, if "(*x* loves *a*)" is abstracted to "*Lxa*," then "(*a* is not loved by *z*)" would be abstracted to "~ *Lza*."

To abstract a most sophisticated PL argument consistency form directly from a most sophisticated PL argument consistency expression form, one begins with a predicate expression with as many distinct variables as any in the most sophisticated PL argument consistency expression form. An appropriate predicate letter is used to abstract it. Other predicate expressions which are identical, complementary, restrictive, or degenerate predicate expressions by comparison to the abstracted predicate expression are then abstracted to related predicate letters as indicated above. The predicate expressions in the most sophisticated PL argument consistency expression form which are so abstracted are then replaced by the predicate letters which abstract them. Then some other predicate expression with as many distinct variables as any left in the most sophisticated PL argument consistency expression form is abstracted to a predicate letter not previously used. If the predicate expression is of a different number of places than any yet abstracted, any appropriate predicate letter will do. Otherwise, a predicate letter with an initial capital letter not yet used is chosen to abstract the predicate expression. Again, any predicate expressions related to this predicate expression in one of the ways we have discussed are abstracted to related predicate letters. This process is continued until all of the predicate expressions in the most sophisticated PL argument expression form are replaced by predicate letters. The result is a most sophisticated PL argument consistency form.

It is possible that a most sophisticated PL argument consistency form as we have described it will contain SL capital letters which are never replaced by PL expressions or PL forms because they are of kind (3). To cover this case, we will suppose that a most sophisticated PL argument consistency form is not finally obtained until this situation is handled along the following lines, where it exists. If any sentences abstracted to SL capital letters are such that they can be construed as complete instantiations of one of the predicate expressions abstracted to a predicate letter, then they should be abstracted to restricted predicate letters which contain only PL constants as members. For example, the sentence "John loves Mary" may survive analysis abstracted to a capital letter. Should a predicate expression like "$(x$ loves $y)$" or "$(John loves z)$" occur somewhere in the most sophisticated PL argument consistency expression form, then "John loves Mary" can be abstracted to a predicate letter. More specifically, let "$(x$ loves $y)$" occur and be abstracted to the predicate letter "Lxy." Then "John loves Mary" could be abstracted to "Lcd," where "c" and "d" are used to abstract the appropriate naming expressions. These PL constants must either be introduced or found identical with PL constants previously introduced during the abstractive process. When this additional step is completed where applicable, the result will be a most sophisticated PL argument consistency form without qualification.

It is possible that SL capital letters may remain in a most

sophisticated PL argument consistency form as we have defined it. Indeed, we can view most sophisticated SL argument consistency forms as identical with a certain class of most sophisticated PL argument consistency forms in which no quantificational structure is shown because all SL capital letters in the most sophisticated SL argument consistency forms which constitute the most sophisticated PL argument consistency form abstract statements of kind (3). On this basis, we can see quite naturally that SL is a part of PL, and that PL is an elaboration or extension of SL.

Using *"Tyz"* to abstract "(*y* is the head of *z*)," *"Hx"* to abstract "(*x* is a horse)," and *"Ax"* to abstract "(*x* is an animal)" at appropriate steps in the process we have just described, we can find a most sophisticated PL argument consistency form for the argument discussed earlier as follows:

(1) $(\forall x)(\sim Hx \lor Ax)$
(2) $(\exists y)((\exists z)(Hz \land Tyz) \land (\forall s)(\sim As \lor \sim Tys))$
$\sim (\text{CON})$

For convenience, we have omitted outer parentheses around single predicate letters which are part of a more complex PL form.

Exercises

1. Let a universe of discourse consist of five rectangular wooden blocks colored red, blue, or yellow, and labeled "*a*," "*b*," "*c*," "*d*," and "*e*." We can make statements about these blocks which might occur in various arguments. Using "*Cx*" to abstract the one-place predicate expression "(*x* is cubical)," "*Rx*" to abstract "(*x* is red)," "*Bx*" to abstract "(*x* is blue)," "*Yx*" to abstract "(*x* is yellow)," "*Lxy*" to abstract "(*x* is larger than *y*)," and "*Sxy*" to abstract "(*x* weighs the same as *y*)," find PL forms to abstract the following statements:

   a. All of the blocks are yellow.
   b. Some of the blocks are yellow and some are red.
   c. Every yellow block is cubical.
   d. Some red blocks are not cubical.
   e. At least one of the blocks is either red or cubical.
   f. Some block is red or some block is cubical.
   g. All of the blocks are red and all are cubical.
   h. All of the blocks are red and cubical.
   i. A block is either cubical and blue or neither.
   j. All of the blocks are blue or all are cubical.
   k. All of the blocks are blue or cubical.
   l. All of the blue blocks are cubical.
   m. All of the blue and all of the red blocks are cubical.
   n. There is a block which is cubical and blue.
   o. All of the non-cubical blocks are yellow or red.
   p. Each block is larger than some other.
   q. Each block weighs the same as some block.

    r. If one block is larger than another, then it doesn't weigh the same as the other.

    s. No block weighs the same as itself.

    t. Some block is larger than all of the others.

    u. Two blocks the same size weigh the same.

    v. Larger blocks weigh more than smaller blocks.

                     (See Answer No. 52.)

2. We can describe a definite universe of discourse consisting of five blocks by listing the characteristics of each block. "Larger" is ambiguous, but we will define it in terms of the number of cubic inches of volume. Let "$a =$ <red, cubical, 6, 12>" mean that block a is red, cubical, of six cubic inches volume, and of twelve ounces weight. We now describe a set of five blocks using this code:

$a =$ <blue, cubical, 6, 12>
$b =$ <blue, not cubical, 6, 10>
$c =$ <blue, not cubical, 10, 10>
$d =$ <blue, not cubical, 6, 12>
$e =$ <blue, not cubical, 6, 12>

Which of the statements abstracted in Exercise 1 are true if this set of blocks is the universe of discourse?

                     (See Answer No. 31.)

3. Here is another universe of discourse:

$a =$ <blue, not cubical, 6, 12>
$b =$ <red, cubical, 6, 12>
$c =$ <blue, not cubical, 6, 10>
$d =$ <yellow, cubical, 6, 10>
$e =$ <yellow, cubical, 6, 12>

Which of the statements abstracted in Exercise 1 are true if this set of blocks is the universe of discourse?

                     (See Answer No. 64.)

4. Can you describe a set of blocks such that statements e. and f. would differ in truth-value?

                     (See Answer No. 15.)

5. Can you describe a set of blocks such that statements g. and h. would differ in truth-value?

                     (See Answer No. 79.)

6. Can you describe a set of blocks such that statements j. and k. would differ in truth-value?

                     (See Answer No. 47.)

7. Can you describe a set of blocks such that statements a., c., f., j., k., l., m., o., q., and r. would make jointly true statements about them?   (See Answer No. 5.)

8. Can you describe a set of blocks such that statement p. would make a true statement about them?

(See Answer No. 24.)

9. Is the following argument valid:
   Each block is larger than some other.
   Therefore, if one block is larger than another, then it doesn't weigh the same as the other.

(See Answer No. 42.)

10. Let a universe of discourse consist of some indeterminate number of wooden or metal blocks which are either cubical or spherical, and either red or blue. For this universe, let "*Wx*," "*~ Wx*," "*Cx*," "*~ Cx*," "*Rx*," and "*~ Rx*" abstract "(*x* is wooden)," "(*x* is metal)," "(*x* is spherical)," "(*x* is cubical)," "(*x* is red)," and "(*x* is blue)," respectively. Find most sophisticated PL argument consistency forms for these arguments:

   a. All wooden blocks are red.
      All cubical blocks are wooden.
      Therefore, all cubical blocks are red.
   b. No blue blocks are cubical.
      Some metal blocks are blue.
      Therefore, some metal blocks are not cubical.
   c. No cubical blocks are red.
      All metal blocks are cubical.
      Therefore, no metal blocks are red.
   d. All metal blocks are red.
      Some metal blocks are cubical.
      Therefore, some cubical blocks are red.
   e. Some cubical blocks are wooden.
      Some metal blocks are not cubical.
      Therefore, some metal blocks are not wooden.

(See Answer No. 83.)

11. Using the symbolism and universe of discourse of Exercise 10, and using "*Lxy*" and "*Sxy*" as in Exercise 1, abstract the following arguments to most sophisticated PL argument consistency forms:

   a. If one block is larger than a second, then the second is not larger than the first.

Therefore, no block is larger than itself.

b. If one block weighs the same as a second, then the second weighs the same as the first.
Therefore, no block weighs the same as itself.

c. Block *a* is metal and cubical.
Block *b* is larger than any block which is cubical.
Therefore, block *b* is larger than block *a*.

d. Some blue blocks are larger than any wooden blocks.
No blue blocks are larger than any cubical blocks.
Therefore, no wooden blocks are cubical.

e. Every cubical block weighs the same as any red block.
Some wooden blocks weigh the same as no red block.
Therefore, some wooden blocks weigh the same as all cubical blocks.

f. All blue, cubical blocks are larger than every red block.
Some blue blocks weigh the same as block *c*.
Therefore, block *c* is larger than every red block.

(See Answer No. 7.)

8. Testing for PL Validity

It may seem that the argument whose most sophisticated PL argument consistency form was developed in the last chapter must be valid since no possible world could be such that "All heads of horses are heads of animals" would be false. Although we can perhaps not conceive of such a world, this failure of conception is not conclusive, as we can see by returning to fundamental questions about validity. We would not, for example, consider the following argument SL valid even though its conclusion is true:

Jeeves is a good butler.
Therefore, Paris is the capital of France.

The *de facto* truth of a conclusion does not make an argu-ment valid even though it does show that no false conclusion is being drawn from the premise or premises in the normal interpretation of the argument. In SL, the test for validity is to abstract to SL forms, and then to treat the SL capital letters as abstracting independent statements. The given argument, along with the following patently invalid argument, can both be abstracted to the same most sophisticated SL argument consistency form by an appropriate choice of SL capital letters in the abstractive process:

$2 + 2 = 4$
Therefore, $5 + 3 = 9$

In the most sophisticated SL argument consistency form which may abstract both arguments, the SL capital letters are taken as standing simply for statements of the original argument with no internal truth-functional structure which can be assumed to be independent of one another. In other words, the substantive content of the original argument has disappeared, and only its (truth-functional) *form* as analyzed by SL techniques remains. The form is useful precisely because it enables us systematically and mechanically to survey the relevant possible worlds without getting hung up on various conceptual problems.

Returning to the argument we have been analyzing by PL techniques, we can paraphrase it as follows:

All horses are animals.
Therefore, if anything is related to a horse by virtue of being its head, then it is also related to an animal by virtue of being its head.

The conclusion now makes a claim that anything bearing a certain relationship to an object of one kind also bears the same relationship to an object of another kind. Such a statement is not, in general, true. Compare "All tailpipes of automobiles are tailpipes of airplanes," which makes a false claim of the same structure. What makes the statement about horses' heads true is that each horse is, in fact, also an animal by virtue of certain biological facts and the way in which we express them. So we then may think (implicitly) that if anything is the head of a horse, then it must also be the head of an animal (namely, the same horse). On the other hand, automobiles are not airplanes, and so the statement about tailpipes is false. Consider this argument:

All automobiles are airplanes.
Therefore, all tailpipes of automobiles are tailpipes of airplanes.

This argument has the same logical structure as the argument

about horses' heads, and both should be valid or invalid together, even though this argument has a false premise. (In-
cidentally, this argument shows why the premise is required
in the argument about horses' heads.) In fact, it is easy to see
that the most sophisticated PL argument consistency form
which was abstracted for the argument about horses' heads
can also be found as the most sophisticated PL argument consistency form for this latter argument, with "*Tyz*" abstracting
"(*y* is the tailpipe of *z*)," "*Hx*" abstracting "(*x* is an auto-
mobile)," and "*Ax*" abstracting "(*x* is an airplane)." Similarly to the case in SL, we can treat the most sophisticated PL
argument consistency form for an argument as giving the
argument's form in abstraction from the substantive content of its naming expressions and claims. But to complete
a comparison with the SL test, we need to find a method of
searching systematically for a possible world in which the PL
forms of the most sophisticated argument consistency form
abstracted from a given argument jointly abstract true statements.

We proceed to develop a concept of proof for PL which is
an extension of the concept of SL proof. To begin with, we
write down as the first *n* numbered lines of a proof the *n* PL
forms corresponding to the most sophisticated PL argument
consistency form that we have abstracted for the argument
whose validity we are testing. This is equivalent to assuming
that these PL forms jointly abstract true statements, as in
SL proofs. We now define, for convenience, the kinds of PL
forms. Any expression in a most sophisticated PL argument
consistency form which can be obtained from a PL expression
abstracted during the process of finding a most sophisticated
PL argument consistency form for the argument by replacing
predicate expressions with the predicate letters abstracting
them will be known as a *sentential* PL form. In other words,
a sentential PL form is always the abstraction of a sentence or
statement. So far, we have used "PL form" as though it were
equivalent to "sentential PL form," and we will continue to
do so. A sentential PL form will be said to be a *descriptive*
PL form if it contains no quantifiers. A descriptive PL form

is always a predicate letter all of whose members are PL constants, or a truth-function of such predicate letters. We now extend the SL rules of proof to PL rules of proof as follows: A new line may be added to a PL proof provided that it may be justified by the substitution of PL forms for the lower-case letters of an SL rule of proof. The justification for the addition of such a new line on the right-hand side of the line is given just as it was in SL proof. The auxiliary rule D may also be used in PL proof to add a line which is one disjunct of a previous disjunction of PL forms, justification being provided in the same manner. We thus take the techniques of SL proof over entirely into techniques of PL proof, and SL proofs become merely special cases of PL proofs.

By using the extended SL techniques, we can obviously add lines to a PL proof until each line is either an SL capital letter, or a PL form. Since descriptive PL forms abstract sentences of kind (3), we can treat them all as though they were SL capital letters, that is, as abstracting simplest constituent statements which are independent of the other simplest constituent statements. The problems with PL proof thus resolve to finding some means for simplifying lines of a proof which are PL forms beginning with a universal quantifier or an existential quantifier and which are not truth-functions of such a PL form with another PL form. We will call such lines *universally quantified* PL forms and *existentially quantified* PL forms, respectively. When the quantifier is omitted from such a line, the remaining expression clearly abstracts what was or could have been a one-place predicate expression at some point in the process of abstracting the most sophisticated PL argument consistency form for the argument being tested. Our clue to simplification lies in the original observation that a universally quantified one-place predicate expression abstracts a true statement if and only if every instantiation of that one-place predicate expression abstracts a true statement or is a true statement, while an existentially quantified one-place predicate expression abstracts a true statement if and only if at least one instantiation of that one-place predicate expression abstracts a true statement or is a true statement. Now we can easily define a *formal one-place predicate expression* as the expression which results from the omission of the initial quantifier from a universally or existentially quantified PL form. We now need to discuss how to instantiate such a formal one-place predicate expression. Originally, one-place predicate expressions were said to be instantiated in terms of naming expressions or PL constants. Now, if PL constants appear in a most sophisticated PL argument consistency form, we could instantiate the formal one-place predicate expressions in terms of these constants. But there are two difficulties. The first is that no PL constants may appear in a most sophisticated PL argument consistency form. (The most sophisticated PL argument consistency form we abstracted in the last chapter as an example illustrates this possibility.) The second difficulty is that there are no doubt always possible instantiations of formal one-place predicate expressions in terms of PL constants related to the universe of discourse which do not appear explicitly in the most sophisticated PL argument consistency form, even if some PL constants do so appear. (*A fortiori*, our example illustrates this possibility as well.) In view of these difficulties, we need a way of treating the universe of discourse in order to define the class of permissible instantiations of a universally or existentially quantified PL form which appears as a line of a PL proof.

In the PL test for validity, we are not interested in the particular individuals which were members of the universe of discourse of the abstracted argument. What is important is simply their number. A PL argument, to be valid, must be such that the premises and the negation of the conclusion cannot be jointly true in *any* non-empty possible world. So, to begin with, we assume that a possible world always contains at least one individual. Actually, although the philosophical possibility confronts us that nothing exists, we can reasonably enough propose for logical purposes that at least one individual exists in every possible world so that the notion of instantiation will make sense in every PL test of validity. Since we are interested only in the number of distinct individuals in any possible world, we will speak of possible worlds in terms of domains, which are simple sets of integers describing the number of distinct individuals to which PL constants might be assigned as abstracting naming expressions in any conceivable non-empty universe of discourse. (From now on, we will omit the inessential adjective "non-empty.") A finite domain of m members will consist of the set D_m ($D_m = \{1, 2, \ldots, m\}$), whose elements are the first m positive integers. Only one infinite domain is relevant, the infinite domain which has a denumerable, or enumerably infinite, number of members. This domain will consist of the set D_ω of all positive integers ($D_\omega = \{1, 2, \ldots\}$). In advanced work, a universe of discourse may be associated with an argument which has more individuals in it than the number in D_ω, for example, the set of all real numbers. This is not an embarrassment to PL, but it does expose a feature of PL which is often referred to as the Löwenheim Theorem. One way of putting this theorem is to say that there is no most sophisticated PL argument consistency form whose constituent PL forms can abstract jointly true statements in some infinite universe of discourse, but cannot jointly abstract true statements in the domain D_ω. We cannot prove this here, but it should not be surprising in view of the significance of PL notation that if the PL forms in a most sophisticated PL argument consistency form can jointly abstract true statements, there will be some way of letting them abstract statements about the domain D_ω which are jointly true. For the sole problem is the interpretation of quantified PL forms, and we have seen that these PL forms have significance because of their instantiations, that is, the class of their possible instantiations. But the size of the class of instantiations we can actually make is limited to the number of distinct PL constants which may be used to form instantiations. Now, the PL constants, abstracting naming expressions, can be at most denumerable in number. Names or naming expressions, even though they may be generated by some function or process, can always be put down in a list (those that we have already assigned in a finite list) one after another, and hence are at most denumerable because they may be correlated one-to-one with the positive integers. We are to find that the development of a PL proof will find a set of instantiations justifying the assumption that the first n lines of a proof abstract jointly true statements just in the cases where that assumption is true, and that there will be at most a denumerably infinite set of instantiations found during this process. A PL proof will thus always exhibit a set of instantiations illustrating the Löwenheim Theorem for the most sophisticated PL argument consistency form.

We regard the domains as giving the individuals for every possible world relevant to a determination of PL validity. The usual numerals ("1," "2," etc.) for the positive integers will be regarded as the PL constants for these possible worlds, and we include the numerals for the integers among the PL constants. The numerals of the first n positive integers can be regarded as a mere relabeling of the PL constants already abstracted from naming expressions for the individuals of some universe of discourse associated with a given argument.

All instantiations of quantified PL forms in a proof will be in terms of positive integers, and we will use the ordinary numerals as PL constants for the purposes of instantiation. What we will try to do in a PL proof is to use instantiation to simplify quantified PL forms by eliminating their quantifiers (along with the extended SL rules of proof to eliminate truth-functional structure), until a proof blocks, or a proof is completely simplified to descriptive PL forms and SL capital letters from which we can read off the description of a possible world satisfying the original assumption that the PL forms constituting the most sophisticated PL argument consistency form for the argument being tested jointly abstract true statements.

First, we eliminate any PL constants appearing in the first n lines of the proof which are the PL forms of the most sophisticated PL argument consistency form by replacing them with numerals. Suppose there are l distinct (that is, different) PL constants in the most sophisticated PL argument consistency form. We replace all of the occurrences of each of these constants with some unique numeral chosen from the standard way of representing the domain D_l with the first l positive integers as its elements. Every occurrence of one PL constant is replaced by "1," and every occurrence of some other by "2," and so on. The justification for this is provided by the significance of the PL constants. Part of the claim embodied in the assumption that the first n lines of the proof jointly abstract true statements is that each distinct PL constant refers to some unique individual in the universe of discourse associated with the argument. To mirror this claim, we use the first l numerals to relabel these PL constants. It does not matter in which order we do this, since only the number of distinguishable individuals matters to validity. With the PL constants relabeled in this fashion, we need worry only about simplifying quantified PL forms.

A universal quantifier may be removed by the following rule ($\forall$ - elimination):

> If any line of a proof is a universally quantified PL form, a line may be added which is the instantiation of the formal one-place predicate expression following the quantifier in terms of any numeral already appearing in the proof, or of the first numeral *not* already appearing in the proof. The new line is justified on the far right by citing " $\forall$ - elimination."

$\forall$ - elimination is quite clearly a rule of proof, since if a universally quantified PL form abstracts a true statement, every instantiation of it must either abstract a true statement, or be a true statement. As $\forall$ - elimination is always accompanied by instantiation in terms of a positive integer, the instantiation will abstract a true statement if the original line does, as integers are taking the place of the objects of the original universe of discourse. Since *every* instantiation of a universally quantified PL form must abstract a true claim if the universally quantified PL form does, we can apply $\forall$ - elimination as often as we wish to a single line. In this respect, it is different from any rule of proof we have had so far. But to avoid needless repetition, we will not use $\forall$ - elimination to add a line identi-

cal to some line already in the proof, and if at least one numeral already appears in some line of the proof which has not
previously been used in ∀-elimination on the PL form in
question, we will restrict instantiations justified by ∀-elimina-
tion to instantiations in terms of such numerals already appearing in the proof.

The elimination of existential quantifiers is somewhat more
troublesome. An existentially quantified PL form abstracts a
true statement if and only if at least one of its instantiations
does. The difficulty is that we do not know *exactly* which
one, and we do not know whether there is more than one. In
eliminating existential quantifiers, we do not want to add a
line which is equivalent to claiming that we know *exactly*
which instantiation is true, and we do not want to add a line
which is equivalent to claiming that more than one instantiation is true. When we instantiate the formal one-place predicate expression following an existential quantifier, we will
do so only *once*. This will prevent our adding a line equivalent
to claiming that two or more instantiations of an existentially
quantified line are true. Further, the numeral used to instantiate the formal one-place predicate expression following an
existential quantifier will always be the next one not already
appearing in the proof. For if we instantiated in terms of a
numeral already appearing in the proof, we would be claiming to know exactly which instantiation was true. In addition
to these two restrictions on ∃-elimination, there is one
further source of difficulty which may be traced to a kind of
redundancy. Suppose that "(∃x)(Fx)" and "(∃y)(Fy)"
appear as two lines of a proof. One of these lines merely
repeats the claim made by the other, and together they say
no more than that at least one individual can truly have a
certain claim made about it. Now suppose we eliminate
quantifiers so as to add both of the lines "F4" and "F5," say,
by virtue of two applications of ∃-elimination in developing
the proof from the previously cited pair of lines. Then we
have added an extra claim that two distinct individuals can
have the relevant claim made about them. To avoid this, we
will cross out any existentially quantified line in a proof which

is such that some line of the proof is already equivalent to *an instantiation* of its formal one-place predicate expression. If the rest of the lines of the proof can jointly abstract true statements, then the statement abstracted by the line crossed out can be added to abstract a true statement along with the others, yet nothing is deducible from it which is not deducible from its earlier instantiation. A line crossed out on this basis will have "RED" cited to the far right. We will examine each existentially quantified PL form which is a line of a proof to make sure that RED will not justify its being crossed out before ∃-elimination is applied. We take this as understood in citing ∃-elimination:

> If any line of a proof is an existentially quantified PL form (to which RED cannot be applied), a line may be added to the proof which is the instantiation of the formal one-place predicate expression following the quantifier in terms of the next numeral not already appearing in the proof. The new line is justified by citing "∃-elimination" on the far right.

Since ∃-elimination can only be applied once, the existentially quantified PL form which is simplified by an application of ∃-elimination may be crossed out for convenience (provided, of course, that it does not occur after a line prefixed with an asterisk). The status of ∃-elimination as a rule of proof may seem suspect, and requires discussion. What we know is that an existentially quantified PL form abstracts a true statement if and only if some instantiation of it abstracts a true statement. The step of ∃-elimination corresponds metaphorically to finding the right instantiation, and then providing a PL constant (the next numeral) in order to set it down formally. But since we are not looking through a fixed set of individuals, we cannot really speak of "finding" the right instantiation. Here we must fall back on our strategy. We are looking for a possible world in which all of the PL forms in the most sophisticated PL argument consistency form for the argument we are testing jointly abstract true statements. If we can find this possible world, the argument being assessed is invalid. To follow our conservative strategy, we must try to find an instantiation which will abstract a true statement if any instantiation will. This strategy is satisfied, in general, only if we choose a new individual for the instantiation, since we can let the claim abstracted by the formal one-place predicate expression be true of this new individual if it can be true of any individual, that is, if there is no generalization to the effect that no individual can have this claim attributed to it which appears abstracted in another line of the proof. If we don't choose a new individual, we always run the risk of choosing an instantiation which does not abstract a true statement jointly with the other lines of the proof for quite accidental reasons. For let our line to be instantiated be "$(\exists x)(Fx)$," and let the numeral "3" already appear in the proof. If we instantiate and add the line "$F3$," this may block the proof unnecessarily because "$\sim F3$" is either another line of the proof, or can be added as a line of proof during the development of the proof from other lines. Now, "$\sim F3$," to which we would be committed in any case, can abstract a true statement jointly with "$F6$," if "6" appears as yet nowhere in the previous lines of proof, so that choosing a new individual will always permit us to avoid unnecessarily blocking the proof due to the properties that some individual already introduced into the proof happens to have by virtue of claims already embodied in previous lines of the proof. Consequently, we can justify $\exists$ - elimination as a rule of proof, since it will help to describe a possible world in which the first n lines of the proof jointly abstract true statements if there is one to be described.

In the interest of theoretical completeness, it is necessary to say something more about the rule RED. RED directs us to cross out any existentially quantified line some instantiation of which is equivalent to a line already appearing in the proof. For simple examples, equivalence and non-equivalence are sufficiently obvious to enable us to apply RED correctly. It would be possible to develop some formal tests to provide rigorous conditions for equivalence and non-equivalence. The difficulty is that these tests cannot be made sufficiently comprehensive. They will not determine the equivalence or non-equivalence of any arbitrary pair of possible lines of a PL proof. To complete a discussion of RED, we need to decide what to do when we are not sure whether RED applies. Proofs should always be developed according to the following strategy: *Whenever it is not clear whether RED applies, assume that it does not apply and proceed with ∃ - elimination.* This strategy will never lead to an incorrect assessment of validity. The complete justification for this claim cannot be given in an elementary textbook, but we can indicate why this strategy is successful. In the first case, suppose the assumption of the strategy is correct. Then RED does not apply and the proof is developed entirely within the limits of the justification we have already provided. In the only remaining case, RED does apply but we assume that it does not. Where this is the case, we have mistakenly instantiated equivalent lines as though they were non-equivalent. For every line of the proof containing the numeral used in the one instantiation, there is another (possible) equivalent line of the proof containing the other numeral. The argument for the strategy is to show that this makes no difference to the assessment of validity, and that a proof containing such redundancies is always equivalent in outcome to a proof using RED correctly, a proof which could be obtained by crossing out all the members of the set of lines containing the higher numeral, and then rewriting any lines containing numerals higher than the one crossed out by replacing all such numerals by the next lower numeral in systematic fashion. Crossing out for redundancy and rewriting numerals might have to be done more than once to show equivalence between a given pair of proofs. Suppose the first numerals involved in a misuse of RED are "5" and "6." If the proof blocks, it may do so either because of lines derived from the line instantiated with "5" or because of lines derived from the line instantiated with "6." Since they both abstract the same claim, both lines cannot be required to establish blockage. We take the proof to block because of the line instantiated with "5." If the proof blocks from this line, it is obvious. Otherwise, the blockage traced from the line instantiated by "6" is repeated by development from the other line, appropriate redundancies being omitted. Then all of the lines containing "6" could be crossed out, the original existentially quantified line crossed out by RED, and a rewriting of numerals carried out. On the other hand, if the proof does not block on the assumption that RED has been misused, we can justify a similar rewriting procedure. All of the lines containing "6" could be crossed out and the proof still wouldn't block. (This is, of course, trivial.) Therefore the proof could be rewritten as one in which RED was used correctly without change in the assessment of validity. Our strategy is therefore successful: a proof carried out using the strategy always results in the same assessment of validity as some proof using RED correctly. This does not mean that RED can be eliminated from our description of proof procedures. We need to use RED and an assumed omniscience about equivalence and non-equivalence of possible lines of proof to justify the correctness of our proof procedure. As a theoretical stratagem, this is perfectly sound, since each pair of lines either is or is not equivalent. But it is a relief to learn that we do not need to be omniscient in practice, but can rest content that the procedure we follow yields an assessment of validity which is correct and which is the same as that provided by some proof in which RED is used correctly, even though we may not know whether RED has been used correctly at each point in any given proof. In sufficiently simple proofs, intuition is an adequate substitute for omniscience. By the time the student of logic attempts complicated mathematical proof, he can absorb the complete technical justification for more advanced proof techniques.

With ∀ - elimination, ∃ - elimination, and RED, the rules of PL proof are complete in the sense that we can simplify any line of the proof which can be further simplified by the use of one of these rules or by extended SL rules of proof. First, let us consider the case where a proof blocks (and D has been used optimally). A blocked proof is one in which an SL capital letter and the negation of that SL capital letter stand as two

lines of the proof, or one in which a PL form and the negation of that PL form stand as two lines of the proof. This
situation shows that some statement and its negation must
both abstract true statements in any possible world in which
all of the constituent PL forms of the most sophisticated PL
argument consistency form for the argument being tested abstract jointly true statements. Since this is absurd, not all of the
constituent PL forms can abstract true statements, and the
original argument is PL valid, or valid. Of course, if a proof
appears to block and D is not used optimally, DS is used in
the same manner as in SL proofs to search for a proof which
does exhibit an optimal use of D.

If a proof does not block when D is used optimally, it may
completely simplify the PL forms of the first n lines so that no
new lines can be added. Here we must enforce the informal
restriction limiting the instantiations by ∀ - elimination, or
redundant lines could be added over and over. Should this
situation occur, we can read off a description of a possible
world in which all of the PL forms of the first n lines abstract
true statements, and the original argument is then shown to be
invalid. For example, suppose an argument to be abstracted to
this most sophisticated PL argument consistency form:

(1) $(\exists x)(Fx)$
(2) $(\exists y)(\sim Fy)$ $\sim$ (CON)

The original argument was to the effect that since some individual in some universe of discourse could have a certain
claim made about it, every individual in that universe could
have the same claim made about it. Clearly, if there are two
or more individuals in the universe of discourse, one possible
world is that in which one individual can have the claim
truly made about it and the other cannot. This possible world
shows the argument to be invalid. We show this by a PL proof
of two additional lines:

(1) ~~$(\exists x)(Fx)$~~
(2) ~~$(\exists y)(\sim Fy)$~~ $\sim$ (CON)

(3)	$F1$	(1)	$\exists$ - elimination
(4)	$\sim F2$	(2)	$\exists$ - elimination

Here the proof is completely simplified and we can read off a description of a universe in which the PL forms of the most sophisticated PL argument consistency form are jointly true.

An SL proof will either block (with D used optimally) or completely simplify after a finite number of steps provided that we enforce the restrictions avoiding repetition of lines. The reason for this is that the only steps involving choice are justified by rule D, which allows only two alternatives. By using DS, we can test all possible alternative proofs. In PL, however, there is no guarantee that a proof will either block or completely simplify in a finite number of steps. This can be illustrated by the following PL form:

$$(\forall x)(\exists y)(Lxy)$$

Suppose this is the first line of a proof and we proceed to try to simplify it, assuming for convenience that no numerals (replacing PL constants) appear anywhere in the first n lines of the proof:

$(n+1)$	$(\exists y)(L1y)$	(1)	$\forall$ - elimination
$(n+2)$	$L12$	$(n+1)$	$\exists$ - elimination
$(n+3)$	$(\exists y)(L2y)$	(1)	$\forall$ - elimination
$(n+4)$	$L23$	$(n+3)$	$\exists$ - elimination

Clearly, each use of $\exists$ - elimination introduces a new numeral which may then be used in $\forall$ - elimination on (1), so new lines can constantly be added to this proof. Of course, such a proof may block if we simplify lines other than line (1).

We now exhibit a proof which fails to block or completely simplify in any finite number of lines. The reason is that the PL forms in the most sophisticated PL argument consistency form of the first n lines can jointly abstract true statements only in D_ω, that is, only if there are an infinite number of instantiations of the quantifiers. This proof demonstrates the possibility raised in the last paragraph. The first four lines constitute the most sophisticated PL argument consistency form:

(1) $(\exists x)(\exists y)(Fxy)$
(2) $(\forall z)(\exists w)(Fzw)$
(3) $(\forall s)(\forall t)(\forall u)(\sim Fst \vee \sim Ftu \vee Fsu)$
(4) $(\forall v)(\sim Fvv)$ $\qquad$ $\sim$(CON)

We develop the proof in this fashion:

(5) $(\exists y)(F1y)$

$\qquad\qquad$ (1) $\exists$-elimination

(6) $F12$

$\qquad\qquad$ (5) $\exists$-elimination

(7) $(\exists w)(F2w)$

$\qquad\qquad$ (2) $\forall$-elimination

(8) $F23$

$\qquad\qquad$ (7) $\exists$-elimination

(9) $(\forall t)(\forall u)(\sim F1t \vee \sim Ftu \vee F1u)$

$\qquad\qquad$ (3) $\forall$-elimination

(10) $(\forall u)(\sim F12 \vee \sim F2u \vee F1u)$

$\qquad\qquad$ (9) $\forall$-elimination

(11) $\sim F12 \vee \sim F23 \vee F13$

$\qquad\qquad$ (10) $\forall$-elimination

(12) $\sim F23 \vee F13$

$\qquad\qquad$ (11), (6) DS_1

(13) $F13$

$\qquad\qquad$ (12), (8) DS_1

It becomes clear that the first three lines of the proof jointly abstract true statements if and only if a kind of chain can be built up in the sequence "1," "2," "3," . . . such that each instantiation of "Fxy" where the numeral replacing "x" comes before that replacing "y" in the sequence is a line of the proof and abstracts a true statement. Line (2) insures that the chain of instantiations is endless, but this may happen either because the chain is infinitely long, or because the chain is circular. Line (4) can abstract a true statement if and only if the chain is infinitely long. For, let the chain be circular, that is, suppose "$Fz1$" abstracts a true statement for some numeral

z. Since "$F1z$" abstracts a true statement by further development of the proof, "$F11$" must abstract a true statement by line (3). But this contradicts line (4). Therefore, the chain must be infinitely long. Our example is sufficient to indicate both that a proof may neither block nor completely simplify in a finite number of steps. This is easily seen to be associated with the development of a proof in the domain D_ω by continuous use of $\exists$-elimination following $\forall$-elimination as illustrated in the last paragraph.

Suppose that we start to develop a proof and add any number of lines without the proof terminating in a blocked proof (D used optimally) or a completely simplified proof. In general, we cannot tell whether the proof will terminate at some later step or will simply fail to terminate, and hence we do not know when we have not terminated a proof whether the original argument is valid or invalid, or even necessarily whether we will find out by continuing to develop the proof. This makes the PL test for validity quite different from the SL test. We know that an SL test will terminate in a decision as to the validity of the original argument. In the PL test, we do not know whether the PL test will terminate, and hence we do not know if we shall be able to make a decision about the validity of the original argument. Occasionally we can see a pattern suggesting that the proof will not terminate. For example, we can see a pattern in the proof which was developed in the last paragraph which enables us to see that the proof will not terminate. Let the domain be D_ω, and let "Fxy" abstract the mathematical relationship "(x is less than y)," or "$x < y$." Then we could interpret the first four lines of the proof as mathematical statements in this fashion:

(1) $(\exists x)(\exists y)(x < y)$
(2) $(\forall z)(\exists w)(z < w)$
(3) $(\forall s)(\forall t)(\forall u)(\sim (s < t) \vee \sim (t < u) \vee (s < u))$
(4) $(\forall v)(\sim (v < v))$ $\sim$(CON)

Line (1) makes the claim that there are at least two positive integers such that one is larger than the other. Line (2) makes the claim that there is at least one positive integer larger than any given positive integer. Line (3) makes the claim that if one positive integer is larger than another, which is in turn larger than a third, then the first is larger than the third. Line (4) makes the claim that no positive integer is larger than itself. It is easy to see that all of these claims, expressed in a mixture of PL and mathematical symbolism, are true of the positive integers. We may use this interpretation to describe the possible world in which "*Tij*" is taken to abstract a true statement if and only if "$i < j$" abstracts a true statement about the positive integers. This is not completely constructing a possible world; it is merely showing by a mathematical interpretation of the PL symbolism that the construction of the possible world begun in the development of the PL proof can continue on indefinitely without blocking, so that the original argument is invalid. This method of showing invalidity is quite like giving an informal counterexample to the original argument. If we think of the mathematical interpretation showing that the proof will continue on indefinitely, we can convince ourselves of the PL invalidity of the original argument, even though we cannot force the proof to terminate. But this attack on the problem has every disadvantage of the method of counterexample: we have to think of a relevant mathematical interpretation. Some most sophisticated PL argument consistency forms are so complex that we cannot systematically find a mathematical interpretation for them even though all of their constituent PL forms can jointly abstract true statements. This may seem intuitively plausible, but it will be shown later that all of the jointly true claims about the positive integers cannot be systematically listed (Gödel's Theorem) so that there is no hope of trying all possible counterexamples to a given most sophisticated PL argument consistency form by some mechanical process. If a proof does not terminate at a given line, therefore, we cannot be sure at that point that the first n lines abstract jointly true statements.

We can summarize the facts about the PL test of validity in this way. If the first n lines of a proof cannot jointly abstract

true statements, the proof will eventually block with an
optimal use of D. The development of the proof gradually
traces out every consequence of the assumption that the first
n lines are jointly consistent. If they are not, two of these
consequences must sooner or later be inconsistent, and show
up in the proof as two lines, one of which is the negation of the
other. For if the proof can develop without terminating, there
is a domain (D_ω) in which a possible world can be described
satisfying the assumption that the first n lines of the proof
jointly abstract true statements. On the other hand, if the first
n lines of a proof can jointly abstract true statements, we
may discover this either if the proof terminates without blocking, or if we find a mathematical interpretation of the first
n lines demonstrating their consistency. But neither may
happen. The first n lines may jointly abstract true statements, but the proof may develop indefinitely without our
chancing on a suitable mathematical interpretation as an
indication that the proof will never block. The PL test for
validity will always show that a (PL) valid argument is
valid because it will eventually block. On the other hand, the
PL test for validity will not always show that a PL invalid argument is invalid, since as long as the proof continues to develop
in the absence of a suitable mathematical interpretation, we
do not know whether it will terminate or not. In this fact we
find the ultimate justification for the philosophy of conservatism. Since we are interested in locating valid arguments, it is
useful to note that the PL test will locate valid arguments,
that is, demonstrate their validity. On the other hand, the
fact that there is no demonstration of PL invalidity cannot
be remedied. An important general argument (Church's
Theorem) establishes that a demonstration of PL invalidity
cannot be provided by *any* method of systematically testing
most sophisticated PL argument consistency forms, so that this
defect is not a result of the way in which we have chosen to
develop proofs. What decisions have been supported by
conservatism have at least led to the strongest possible result:
a method of proving an argument PL valid if the argument is
in fact PL valid.

We will now give a proof for our illustrative argument from the last chapter, showing at long last that the argument is valid because a proof for it blocks with an optimal use of **D**:

(1) $(\forall x)(\sim Hx \vee Ax)$

(2) ~~$(\exists y)((\exists z)(Hz \wedge Tyz) \wedge (\forall s)(\sim As \vee \sim Tys))$~~ $\sim$ (CON)

(3) ~~$(\exists z)(Hz \wedge T1z) \wedge (\forall s)(\sim As \vee \sim T1s)$~~   (2) $\exists$-elimination

(4) ~~$(\exists z)(Hz \wedge T1z)$~~   (3) CS_1

(5) $(\forall s)(\sim As \vee \sim T1s)$ (3) CS_2

(6) $H2 \wedge T12$ (4) $\exists$-elimination

(7) $\sim A2 \vee \sim T12$ (5) $\forall$-elimination

(8) $\sim H2 \vee A2$ (1) $\forall$-elimination

(9) $H2$ (6) CS_1

(10) $A2$ (7), (9) DS_3

(11) $\sim T12$ (7), (10) DS_3

(12) $T12$ (6) CS_2

Exercises

1. Determine whether the argument in Exercise 9, Chapter 7, is PL valid or invalid by developing a PL proof.
   (See Answer No. 46.)

2. Develop PL proofs for the most sophisticated PL argument consistency forms abstracted in Exercise 10, Chapter 7. Which of the arguments in that exercise are PL valid? (See Answer No. 32.)

3. Develop PL proofs for the most sophisticated PL argument consistency forms abstracted in Exercise 11, Chapter 7. Which of the arguments in that exercise are PL valid? (See Answer No. 60.)

4. For appropriate arguments in the last exercise which are *not* PL valid, can you find mathematical interpretations for their most sophisticated PL argument consistency forms which indicate that the proof will develop without blocking? (See Answer No. 8.)

5. A two-place predicate expression is often called a *relation* in the literature. Let such a two-place predicate expression be abstracted to the predicate letter "Fxy." Given this abstraction, the relation is said to be *transitive* if and only if the following PL form abstracts a true statement:
   $$(\forall x)(\forall y)(\forall z)(\sim Fxy \lor \sim Fyz \lor Fxz)$$
   This PL form abstracts the claim that if the relation holds between one individual and a second, and between the second and a third, it also holds between the first and the third. A relation is *irreflexive*, given the abstraction, if

and only if the following PL form abstracts a true statement:

$(\forall u)(\sim Fuu)$

An irreflexive relation does not hold between some individual and itself. A relation is *asymmetric*, given the abstraction, if and only if this PL form abstracts a true statement:

$(\forall v)(\forall w)(\sim Fvw \lor \sim Fwv)$

An asymmetric relation either does not hold between two individuals, or it holds only in one way. Prove that the following arguments are valid where, in each, "*Fxy*" abstracts a relation in some specific context:

a. "*Fxy*" abstracts an asymmetric relation.
    Therefore, "*Fxy*" abstracts an irreflexive relation.
b. "*Fxy*" abstracts a relation which is transitive and irreflexive.
    Therefore, "*Fxy*" abstracts an asymmetric relation.
c. "*Fxy*" cannot abstract a relation that is transitive, asymmetric, and irreflexive.   (See Answer No. 76.)

6. Abstract most sophisticated PL argument consistency forms for the following arguments, and develop PL proofs:
    a. If the moon is inhabited, then every scientist is wrong about lunar evolution.
        But not every scientist can be wrong about lunar evolution.
        Therefore, the moon is not inhabited.
    b. St. Louis is west of New York, and Los Angeles is west of St. Louis.
        Therefore, Los Angeles is west of New York.
    c. Some Australians have not lost a match in the tournament, and Rod Laver is the best of the Australians.
        Therefore, Rod Laver has not yet lost a match.
    d. Students with the Ph.D. must previously have obtained the B.A. with honors.
        To obtain the B.A. with honors, one must take every course on the recommended major list.
        Harvey has not taken French I, which is on the recommended list.
        Therefore, Harvey does not have the Ph.D.
    e. There is a rare stamp sought by all stamp collectors who seek any rare stamps at all.

Some stamp collectors do not seek rare stamps.
Therefore, some stamp collectors do not seek that stamp.

f. Children are refused admittance unless they are over twelve years of age, or are accompanied by a parent. Henry's child was unaccompanied by a parent but was not refused admittance.
Therefore, Henry's child is over twelve years of age.

(See Answer No. 16.)

9. Appropriateness in PL Abstraction

In Chapter 5, we explored some of the difficulties in abstracting appropriate most sophisticated SL argument consistency forms caused by the assumption of SL that the different simplest constituent statements in an argument are independent in truth-value. Since SL capital letters may appear in a most sophisticated PL argument consistency form, the same difficulties can arise in connection with PL abstraction. We will concentrate our attention, however, on some general problems of abstraction which are raised by the special features of PL symbolism which do not overlap those already discussed in connection with SL symbolism.

We have seen that PL symbolism depends upon recognizing the significance of PL constants to be that of abstracting naming expressions which refer to some number of distinct and identifiable individuals in a fixed universe of discourse. This assumption is best met where the individuals involved do not undergo change, and are such that, once identified, they are easy to recognize again. A paradigm class of such individuals is given by the positive integers, and the positive integers, along with other classes of (unchanging) mathematical objects, provide universes of discourse claims about which are ideally suited to the techniques of PL abstraction. An advantage in the abstraction of PL forms here is that once a claim has been made about such an individual, it will continue to have the same truth-value. For example, once we

know that the number two is an even number, we can set this
down as a mathematical fact which can be used for later
computation without fear of revision.

Let us first see, in a quite general way, what happens when
individuals can undergo change. We imagine that such an
individual is referred to by a naming expression abstracted to
the PL constant "*a*." Now, reference to individuals changing may be made in at least two types of cases: one type in
which the *same* individual has at first one characteristic, and
then another, and another type in which one individual
changes into another individual. First, the problem. Suppose
that individual "*a*" changes in such a manner that "*Ra*" first
abstracts some true statement but later abstracts a false statement. This seems a quite general pattern underlying change.
But this means that "*Ra*" and "~ *Ra*" are both (at different
times) abstractions of true statements, but they are clearly
contradictory. To avoid contradiction, so that we can consistently abstract statements about individuals undergoing
change, two paths seem open. The first is to say that the same
individual has different characteristics at different times, and
then bring an explicit temporal reference into the statements
being abstracted. To do this, we use a two-place predicate
expression "*Rxy*," where "*x*" is to be instantiated by the
relevant individuals, and "*y*" is to be instantiated by temporal
individuals. "*Rxy*" can be read something like this: Individual "*x*" has characteristic "*R*" at time "*y*." Now, if "t_1" and
"t_2" are appropriate instants ("t_1" would have to come before "t_2"), we might formalize the change in "*a*" by using
"t_1" and "t_2" as PL constants for the instants, and abstract
the two statements that we are interested in to "Rat_1" and
"~ Rat_2." With this device, the PL forms are no longer contradictory, but this solution involves a considerable philosophical problem. For to abstract change we must import explicit reference to temporal individuals, and with that some
theory of time whose presence in the abstractions requires
some philosophical justification. Without going into details, it
should be obvious that such a theory would be required
to say whether or not there is a *first* instant at which "*a*" does

not have the characteristic "R," and so on. Any answer to such a question involves some deep controversies about the nature of time, so that our move to keep the PL forms consistent seems to involve some of the difficulties raised in connection with formalist attitudes in Chapter 5. We are taking the logical form of a sentence which does not mention time as having explicit reference to time, so that the logical form may well seem too precise as an abstraction for the statements with which we started. The other path for avoiding contradiction in the PL forms abstracting a change is that of saying that if "a" appears to remain the same and "Ra" first abstracts a true statement about it, and then "$\sim Ra$" does, "a" must surely have changed into a new individual, which we will call "b." The facts are then correctly abstracted to "Ra" and "$\sim Rb$," and contradiction vanishes. This approach avoids the development of a theory of time, but it has to pay the even more serious price that it usually flatly conflicts with our intuitions about the identity of individuals, since there are frequent cases in which we would claim that some individual can remain the same while undergoing change. It should be quite apparent that PL abstraction from arguments in which the individuals in the universe of discourse undergo change will not be easy, and will require in many cases supplementation of statements made about these individuals with considerable philosophical or logical explanation of divergencies between these statements and features of the PL forms used to abstract them. This is not to say that these explanations cannot be given, but that they must be given if we are to feel confident that our abstractions are appropriate to the argument being assessed. In some areas of science one can talk about particles which exhibit variations in their spatio-temporal relationships as a function of time. Such areas of science are capable of appropriate abstraction to PL forms when a suitable means of abstracting the theory of space and time contained in the scientific statements is developed. As the theory of space and time needs to be made explicit in scientific contexts, this need not involve an overly elaborate paraphrase. Richer scientific contexts and many everyday contexts are nearly hopeless in many cases, unless specific arguments deal with a temporal period of short enough duration that the individuals involved can be regarded as unchanging within the context of the argument. Where we must decide between the two paths for abstracting an argument about changing individuals, the road to inappropriateness is broad and easy.

The preceding considerations have shown difficulties in abstraction where individuals undergo change in time even though these individuals are capable of clear identification. Quantification becomes difficult to employ in any universe of discourse where individuals cannot be sharply distinguished by an objective criterion. We cannot explore the ensuing perplexities here, but merely indicate them. In order to have distinct individuals satisfying the assumptions involved in using PL constants, we should be able to *count* the number of individuals in the universe of discourse, or at least be able to count the number of individuals within a suitably restricted part of such a universe. For example, if we are talking about the black areas in some black surface, or the actions done by certain human beings, or the events which have taken place in some process, there are considerable philosophical difficulties to be faced before we can legitimately speak of identifying distinct individuals to which PL constants can refer.

There are further difficulties in abstracting to PL forms which are traceable to the fact that each *n*-place predicate letter in a PL form is regarded as abstracting a claim which is independent of the claim abstracted by any predicate letter of some other number of places, and which is also independent of the claim abstracted by any other *n*-place predicate letter with a different initial capital letter. Independence is, strictly, defined for statements, but the predicate letters can be regarded as independent in the sense that any full instantiation of one must be regarded as a descriptive PL form abstracting a statement which is independent of any full instantiation of the other. The difficulty here is analogous to the difficulty with the assumption of independence of simplest constituent statements in most sophisticated SL argument consistency forms. Independence of abstracted claims will often not be a feature of the abstracted argument. An interesting example is provided by Anthony Kenny's polyadicity problem. (See [K2], pp. 159–62.) This problem is conveniently illustrated by the following pair of sentences:

(A) Brutus murdered Caesar.
(B) Brutus murdered Caesar with a knife.

In any ordinary context, (B) cannot be used to make a true statement unless (A) makes a true statement as well. The following argument is therefore intuitively valid:

Brutus murdered Caesar with a knife.
Therefore, Brutus murdered Caesar.

But any attempt to abstract this argument to a most sophisticated PL argument consistency form results either in an assessment of the argument as invalid, or in some PL forms which are clearly not appropriate. About the best attempt to obtain a most sophisticated PL argument consistency form which will show the argument to be valid depends on constructing some predicate expressions so as to produce this:

(1) $Mbcd$
(2) $(\forall x)(\sim Mbcx)$ $\sim$ (CON)

To obtain this, we have to take "Brutus murdered Caesar" as equivalent to "Brutus murdered Caesar with something," an intuition that is not easily extended beyond this argument. If Brutus is direct, strangling Caesar with his bare hands, or suitably inventive, sending Caesar off on a doomed mission, we would need to locate some other equivalence to effect an abstraction. It seems doubtful that an appropriate abstraction can be found to conclude that Caesar was murdered by Brutus from any statement of his having been murdered by some means or other, or in some place or other, or in some manner. But we have not found an apparently invalid argument whose PL assessment indicates that the argument is valid, so that we could argue that conservatism is maintained, and suppose that a suitable test for validity might be found in some extension of PL. It might also be noted that this kind of inference is most common in ordinary contexts. A similar case involving mathematical or scientific predicate expressions is difficult to find. Inspection of examples indicates that existential quantification of *n*-place scientific and mathematical predicate expressions does not result in an expression equivalent to some *n* + 1-place predicate expression. Consider, to take a particular case, the three-place predicate expression "(*x* is between *y* and *z*)." The two-place predicate expression "(*x* is between *y* and someplace")" has no obvious use, and is not equivalent to any regular two-place predicate expression used in science or mathematics. In view of this situation, some method of expressing dependency between predicate expressions seems to be required if appropriate PL forms, or some extension of PL forms, are to be found for correctly assessing the validity of many arguments dealing with human agency.

In addition to problems relating to assumptions involved in the use of PL constants and PL predicate letters, abstractions involving the existential quantification of a one-place predicate expression sometimes raise various interpretive difficulties. We have just had an example where existential quantification of a three-place predicate expression was the locus of a failure of appropriateness. The significance of the existential quantifier is best understood by looking at its relationship to the universal quantifier. Consider, for example, this pair of PL forms:

$$(\forall x)(Fx) \text{ and } \sim(\exists x)(\sim Fx)$$

The first PL form abstracts a true statement if and only if *every* instantiation of "*Fx*" abstracts a true statement. The second abstracts a true statement if and only if it is not the case that there is at least one instantiation of the formal one-place predicate expression "$\sim Fx$" such that the instantiation abstracts a true statement. This is to say that the second PL form abstracts a true statement if and only if it is not the case that there is at least one instantiation of the formal one-place predicate expression "Fx" which abstracts a false statement. But if it is not the case that at least one instantiation of "Fx" abstracts a false statement, then every instantiation of "Fx" abstracts a true statement. Therefore, the pair of PL forms abstracts statements which are equivalent. A universal quantification of a one-place predicate expression can always be replaced by the negation of the existential quantification of the negation of the same one-place predicate expression. A similar argument would show that an existential quantification of a one-place predicate expression can always be replaced by the negation of the same one-place predicate expression. We have not been able to use these facts in developing proofs because we have not had rules for simplifying a PL form which was the negation of a quantified PL form. Instead, we have eliminated abstraction to such PL forms by adopting a strategy insuring abstraction to a PL form which was not a negation of a quantified PL form. Theoretically, this interdependence of the quantifiers is important, and must be preserved in the PL symbolism. But the argument to show the equivalence of the pair of PL forms given above will not work if "$(\exists x)(\sim Fx)$" has the significance that *exactly* one instantiation of "$\sim Fx$" abstracts a true statement. For if it is not the case that *exactly* one instantiation of "Fx" abstracts a false statement, this may be because *two* instantiations abstract false statements, and it does not follow that every instantiation of "Fx" abstracts a true statement. There are important reasons, therefore, why we must never abstract a claim that some unique instantiation of a one-place predicate expression is a true statement to the existential quantification of that one-place predicate expression. Consider the following pair of sentences:

John knows a politician.
There is a politician whom John knows.

In an appropriate context, the latter, but not the former, may suggest a unique instantiation. It is therefore not appropriate to abstract the latter sentence to an existentially quantified PL form, although the former might be abstracted to this:

$$(\exists x)(Kcx)$$

The fact that we can draw this distinction will enable us to avoid making incorrect equivalences in the course of an abstraction if we are careful to watch for its application.

When problems of temporality are combined with care in using the quantifier, we can avoid the mistake of mishandling a sentence like the following:

John wishes to carve a statue.

If we satisfy ourselves that John does not have a unique statue in mind, we cannot immediately abstract to a PL form as follows:

$$(\exists x)(Bdx)$$

This abstraction suggests that there is at least one statue which John wishes to build, and which exists now, and this is patently wrong. For the sense of the statement is such that no statue exists now which can be referred to by a PL constant. We cannot refer to what John wishes to create as an individual in the right manner until he has brought it into being.

As we have noted earlier, the individuals referred to by PL constants must be said to exist, not to be such that they may exist, or will exist. In doing this, we brushed over such problems as whether fictional entities can be said to exist in the appropriate sense. One of the difficulties here is that as creatures of human invention, they may fail to show the consistency which science (and users of PL symbolism) expect to find in real objects and individuals. For example, we may logically conclude from various premises asserted in some piece of fiction that the murder knife must not be in the drawer, only to have the detective find it there. In a fictional context, we may conclude that the author has made a mistake. In a real life situation, we would know that at least one of the premises was false if events proved some valid conclusion incorrect. For this reason alone, it is difficult to find a use for abstracting from arguments within a fictional context to any logical symbolism because the notion of validity for fictional contexts does not seem grounded in underlying fact.

This same difficulty goes over into other areas in which the beliefs, wants, wishes, doubts, intentions, and so forth, of human beings are involved. Here again, a human being may construct an imaginary world reflecting these various interests and attitudes, an imaginary world which is either inconsistent with fact, or internally inconsistent. As in the fictional case, we take the failure of logical consequence from given premises in such a world to indicate a failure in construction on the part of its human author, and not a proof that one or more premises are actually false.

A much discussed example of this is provided by human belief. It is a not unusual fact of life that a man who holds various beliefs fails to hold a belief which is a logical consequence of these, or holds some further belief that is actually inconsistent when held jointly with the former. For a man may simply not notice the relevant valid inference. This fact is quite decisive against any easy method of abstracting a man's beliefs as a relationship between him and various objects, the strategy that seems suggested by a simple grammatical analysis of the sentences expressing such belief. Consider these examples:

(A)   John believes that the president is not well.
(B)   John believes that Peter Wendling is not well.
(C)   John believes that Peter Wendling is well.
(D)   Jim believes that the president is not well.

We may conveniently imagine these as given in a common context, a context in which the president and Peter Wendling are one and the same person. As we have seen earlier, since

(A) may be true while (B) is false, perhaps because John does not know or suspect or believe that the president is identical with Peter Wendling, we cannot use PL constants to abstract (in general) from naming expressions occurring as part of a reported belief, and it follows from our methods that we cannot (in general) form a one-place predicate expression like "(John believes that x is not well)" and quantify it. An alternative seems to be that of taking the portion of each belief sentence after "believes that" in our examples as a complex naming expression. Consider the example "the president is not well" from (D). This is, by itself, a sentence. The problem is to see what a sentence might be taken to refer to. If it referred to its truth-value, then (A) and (B) would be equivalent, and we have begun by supposing that the nature of belief contravenes this conclusion. The only apparent alternative is to take the sentence, in context, as referring to a statement. The difficulty is now that of determining to which statement it might refer. But even if this could be determined, there are considerable philosophical difficulties in finding a criterion for determining whether two statements are identical, since statements are not individuals easily open to inspection of their properties. But the failure of inference would persist anyway, since a human being may not believe both of a pair of equivalent statements whose equivalence eludes his understanding. It appears that no simple relational view of belief will easily attain an appropriate abstraction of belief sentences.

In the face of difficulties with the relational approach, many logicians have proposed that belief sentences be regarded as only pseudo-relational, having in actual analysis the status of claims ascribing some complicated belief property to a single individual. Sentence (A) above is then phrased somewhat as follows:

(A') John believes-that-the-president-is-not-well.

The hyphenated part of the sentence is simply a description

of a complex property which is not to be further analyzed.
We can abstract A') to this PL form:

Wa

This method of logical phrasing of belief sentences can be
partially defended by the philosophy of conservatism. Since
it allows no inference about belief, it cannot be used to mistakenly assess some invalid argument about beliefs as valid.

Are there *any* arguments about beliefs that we can think
valid in spite of a human agent's liability to construct inconsistent belief structures? Two possibilities arise given the
sentences (A)–(D) above. It would seem to follow from (A)
and (D) that John and Jim have the same belief, and it would
seem to follow from (B) and (C) that John's beliefs are inconsistent. Neither of these arguments can be abstracted to
valid most sophisticated PL argument consistency forms that
are in any sense appropriate to the sentences involved. What
attitude are we to take toward the existence of apparently valid
arguments whose validity cannot be demonstrated by PL
techniques as they have been developed so far? The obvious
attitude is one of expecting extensions of PL which will expose additional arguments as valid which are invalid on the PL
test, just as PL exposes valid arguments whose validity eludes
the test of SL. For various purposes, logicians have found
extensions of PL which will expose additional arguments as
valid which are not correctly assessed by PL techniques.

In order to make an intelligent extension of PL, we need
some clearer view of the relationship between PL forms
and ordinary language. For the most part, we have been discussing the relationship of logical form to language by
reference to conservatism, that is, insuring that the logical
form abstracted never permits the false step of assessing an
invalid argument as valid. But this is an insufficient point of
view by itself, since it could be satisfied by the Procrustean
technique of uniformly assessing every argument as invalid.
The support for the philosophy of conservatism actually used
in abstracting SL and PL forms has been the suggestion that

these forms expose a pattern of underlying fact which can provide the basis for a systematic search by proof procedure of the validity of an argument. If every extension of PL is to be compatible with this background, we might expect the extensions to be based on the suggestion that further factual pattern can be exposed by more complex forms. This is largely correct, but it still leaves room for considerable difference of opinion about the extensions which should be permitted. At the risk of oversimplification, we will sketch here two quite different attitudes toward the relevant characterization of underlying fact which seem to have prompted various extensions of PL proposed by contemporary logicians.

The first attitude is that logical form is properly considered a *regimentation* of sentences in ordinary language, sentences that may often be used to make confused and near meaningless statements. This attitude supposes that scientific fact should constitute the important notion of underlying fact, and it is an immediate consequence of this outlook that regimentation is to be considered successful if a concept of logical form is found which will expose the validity of every important scientific (and mathematical) argument. A more subtle consequence is a willingness to accept a few intuitively valid arguments assessed as invalid in a logical system, provided that the important arguments are assessed correctly and that the concept of logical form and the related test of validity have the scientific virtues of simplicity and elegance. A logician who adopts the attitude of regimentation takes logical form as exposing the theoretical structure of sentences which relates them to scientific or mathematical fact, and he does not demand that the abstracted logical form of a sentence conform very closely to the form of the sentence given in a grammar of the relevant language. Logical form is viewed as a *clarification* of the factual claims made by sentences in ordinary language, and the model for this clarification is that of any good scientific theory and its special symbolism.

In contrast to the attitude of regimentation on many issues of extending PL forms is an attitude toward logical form that may be called the phenomenological attitude. This attitude can be expressed as follows: If there is some argument which would (on reflection) be granted by everyone to be deductively sound in that it would not permit a false statement to follow from the expressed premises in any conceivable circumstances, then if the logical forms we can abstract and the related test for validity do not assess this argument as valid, we have not yet exposed a completely adequate notion of logical form and an adequate test of validity. The phenomenological attitude is subversive even with respect to PL, since there seems to be no general argument that an adequate notion of logical form in the phenomenological sense can be developed which will capture as valid just those simple arguments which intuition assesses as valid. In addition, there are differences of opinion about intuitive validity in nearly every area of discourse that has been closely examined. The obstacles to implementing the phenomenological attitude with a symbolic logic are so patent, and so numerous, that many logicians starting with the phenomenological attitude have abandoned any hope that a suitable logic fitting their requirements can be found by an extension of PL, and they have turned instead to the development of less symbolic tests for validity. But there is plenty of contemporary activity designed to extend PL symbolism, or to replace it with another symbolism, that can be regarded as an attempt to work out the phenomenological attitude in terms of a concept of abstracted logical form and a related systematic test of validity.

To show how these attitudes can lead to divergent opinions about the justification for extending PL symbolism, we will look at two simple cases where they conflict. Both of these attitudes can be supported by intelligent philosophical and methodological argument, so that these conflicts are not intended to suggest a right and a wrong approach. This discussion is included to suggest some of the interesting problems which exist for logicians who are interested both in the techniques of logical systems and in philosophical problems about language.

We can look first at the arguments about belief which were suggested as valid on the basis of the sentences (A)–(D).

These arguments are of no conceivable importance to science or mathematics, and it is quite difficult to replace them with any argument about beliefs which would have this kind of importance. In scientific or mathematical argument, the fact that such and such a person holds certain beliefs is not usually important. The beliefs themselves are important and they are simply asserted as though they were true, various consequences then being drawn from them by arguments whose validity may be successfully tested by the usual PL techniques. In the face of this situation, the attitude of regimentation leads naturally to the view that these few arguments about belief be set aside as harmless anomalies in the interests of simplicity of logical theory, and the pseudo-relational analysis used where belief attributions need abstraction. A logician with the phenomenological attitude is more likely to feel that these arguments are not anomalies, but are symptomatic of deep-seated misunderstandings about the nature of belief, its relationship to knowledge, and so on, which are fostered by the use of PL symbolism. Such a logician will be interested in the development of special symbolism to illuminate our understanding of belief sentences.

A much more difficult case is presented by the existence of ethical arguments which appear to be valid. Consider this argument:

John ought to pay his debts.
John owes the corner grocer ten dollars.
Therefore, John ought to pay the corner grocer ten dollars.

The point is not in the detail of this argument, since some background information may require explicit mention if validity is to become sufficiently obvious, but in the patent fact that there are many arguments about duties, obligations, and so forth, which seem intuitively to be valid to most of us. A logician with the attitude of regimentation may hold that this intuition is mistaken, arguing that claims about obligations and duties are not properly regarded as *statements*, since there are no scientific facts which would allow us to conclusively establish their truth or falsity. Arguments about such claims should not be abstracted preparatory to assessing them as valid or invalid, but must be judged by some completely different criteria. A logician with the phenomenological attitude would almost certainly be interested in finding an extension of PL symbolism, or some alternative symbolism, which would appropriately abstract and assess such arguments. There can be no easy abstraction by PL technique, since obligations are not individuals in the right sense, and some special symbolism seems inevitable. It seems fair to claim that no entirely successful special symbolism has been found, but the problem itself has been attacked only recently.

Fortunately, the two attitudes about extension do not always conflict. We can close this chapter by describing an extension of PL which nearly all logicians agree is of considerable importance in various applications. This extension does not violate conservatism, and yet it exposes as valid many arguments whose validity is not correctly assessed by PL abstraction alone. To obtain this extension, we add "$=$" to the logical symbols of PL, and we may refer to this extension as PL($=$). (In the literature, it is often called Predicate Logic *with* identity.) The symbol "$=$" is used to abstract the concept of identity, and, like the other logical symbols, it will be treated as a fixed symbol for which various rules of manipulation will be introduced. In using PL, we assumed that each distinct individual in a universe of discourse was to be referred to by a unique PL constant in abstracting a most sophisticated PL argument consistency form. But language, whether scientific, mathematical, or ordinary, usually contains a number of naming expressions to refer to at least some individuals. In PL($=$), we abstract different naming expressions to different PL($=$) constants, and if we know that two of them refer to the same individual, we then also abstract a separate claim that an identity relation holds between these PL($=$) constants. PL($=$) constants will have the same symbols as PL constants; we will simply interpret them as though two PL($=$) constants could refer to the same individual if certain facts become known. All PL forms are also PL($=$) forms, but there are additional forms in PL($=$) which contain the symbol "$=$." "$(x = y)$" can be treated as a two-place predicate expression in that it abstracts a statement after two steps of instantiation or of quantification, or one of each. The important difference is that we do not further abstract claims about identity to predicate letters in obtaining a most sophisticated PL(=) argument consistency form. We can construct all PL(=) forms using this similarity, by *adding* to the set of all PL forms those forms which can be obtained by replacing one or more occurrences of any predicate letter of two members whose initial capital letter is "*F*" with "=," this latter symbol being preceded by the constant or variable which is the first member of the predicate letter, and being followed by the second member. "*Fab*" permits us to add "$a = b$" as a PL(=) form, "$(\forall x)(\forall y)(\sim (Fxy) \lor Fxy)$" permits us to add "$(\forall x)(\forall y)(\sim (Fxy) \lor (x = y))$" or "$(\forall x)(\forall y)(\sim (x = y) \lor (x = y))$," and so on. The set of PL(=) forms is thus easy to describe. We can also let the PL rules of proof become PL(=) rules of proof, applying to PL(=) forms rather than to PL forms.

We use PL(=) forms to abstract statements of identity, or statements about the *exact* number of individuals concerning which certain claims are said to be true. These statements cannot (in general) be appropriately abstracted by PL forms. Consider this patently valid argument:

The president and Peter Wendling are one and the same man.
The president is not well.
Therefore, Peter Wendling is not well.

The presidency is no doubt an office held by various persons over a period of time, but we can ignore this temporal feature in the usual context of argument. A most sophisticated PL argument consistency form for this argument will look like this:

(1)   *Gab*
(2) $\sim Wa$
(3)   *Wb* $\sim$ (CON)

No development is even needed. The argument is invalid by the PL test. This is due partly to the fact that "*Gab*" could abstract a claim that "*a*" and "*b*" were not identical, so that this argument consistency form is also that of an invalid argument.

Using PL(=) forms, we abstract to this most sophisticated PL(=) argument consistency form:

(1) $a = b$
(2) $\sim Wa$
(3) Wb $\sim$ (CON)

Although we no longer require in PL(=) that each different PL(=) constant refer to an individual distinct from that referred to by any other, we retain the PL restriction that naming expressions are not abstracted unless they are transparent. Clearly, if a claim may be made about some individual when referred to by one PL(=) constant, then an equivalent claim may be made when the same individual is referred to by another PL(=) constant. We therefore add the rule of proof ID to the rules of proof for PL(=):

ID: If a line of a proof is an identity of the form "$\alpha = \beta$" or "$\beta = \alpha$," and another line of the proof contains an occurrence of the expression "α," then we may add a new line to the proof like this line except that the expression "β" replaces "α." The numbers of the two lines and "ID" are cited on the far right of the new line.

In stating ID, we use the phrase "expression 'α'" rather than referring to PL constants, because in some uses of PL(=) such as that introduced in the next chapter, expressions other than PL constants which refer to individuals will be used in making identity statements. Using ID, our proof blocks in one line:

(4) Wa (1) , (3) ID

Rule of proof ID nearly completes the characterization of

PL($=$). One more addition is required to define a proof blocking. Suppose a line of proof is reached which is an instantiation of "$\sim (x = x)$." (We can also write "$\sim (x = x)$" as
"$x \neq x$.") Since each PL($=$) constant refers to the same
individual on each occurrence, any instantiation of this line
must abstract a false statement in any possible world. Therefore, a PL($=$) proof will be said to block either if such a line
is reached, or if some PL($=$) form and its negation occur as
two lines of a proof. With this addition, we now have complete
rules of proof for PL($=$).

Let us assess another argument by PL($=$) techniques:

There is at most one owner of the Hope Diamond.
Tom says that he is the owner of the Hope Diamond.
Bill says that he is the owner of the Hope Diamond.
Therefore, at least one of Tom and Bill is wrong.

We assume, in context, that Tom and Bill are not identical.
The argument may be abstracted along with this piece of
information to the following most sophisticated PL($=$) argument consistency form:

(1) $(\forall x)(\forall y)(\sim (Hx \wedge Hy) \vee (x = y))$
(2) Ha
(3) Hb
(4) $\sim (a = b)$
(5) $\sim (\sim Ha \vee \sim Hb)$ $\sim$ (CON)

Line (1) abstracts the claim that if two instantiations of
"Hx" and "Hy" jointly abstract true statements, then the
PL($=$) constants used must refer to the same individual.
This is easily seen to be equivalent to the first premise. The
proof is easily seen to block upon development. We first
replace "a" with "1" and "b" with "2." The proof may then
be developed as follows:

(1) $(\forall x)(\forall y)(\sim (Hx \wedge Hy) \vee (x = y))$
(2) $H1$
(3) $H2$

(4) $\sim (1 = 2)$

(5) $\sim (\sim H1 \vee \sim H2)$

$\sim$ (CON)

(6) $(\forall y)(\sim (H1 \wedge Hy) \vee (1 = y))$

(1) $\forall$ - elimination

(7) $\sim (H1 \wedge H2) \vee (1 = 2)$

(6) $\forall$ - elimination

(8) $(1 = 2)$

(7)   DS*

Given the extended rules of proof, lines (4) and (8) block the proof, and the original argument is valid. It would be a mistake to conclude that the proof blocks because line (8) is *false*. Construed as a statement of mathematics, line (8) *is* false, but it is not a statement of mathematics as a line of the proof. We use "1," "2," etc., as defining members of a domain in a proof, and line (8) reflects only the fact that the first two PL(=) constants assigned to individuals in the domain we are constructing must be regarded as referring to the same individual on the assumption that the PL(=) forms of the most sophisticated PL(=) argument consistency proof jointly abstract true statements.

The extension of PL to PL(=) has proven extremely valuable in scientific and mathematical contexts. It represents the one extension of PL whose importance is recognized both by logicians with the attitude of regimentation, and those with the phenomenological attitude. We will see an example of its usefulness in Chapter 10.

Exercises

1. In Chapter 9 it was shown that any line of proof which is the negation of the existential quantification of a one-place predicate expression is equivalent to a line of proof which is the universal quantification of the negated one-place predicate expression. Similarly, if a line of proof is the negation of the universal quantification of a one-place predicate expression, then this line is equivalent to the existential quantification of the negation of the one-place predicate expression. In developing proofs, we can use these equivalences to add new lines to a proof, citing "QN" on the far right of the added line along with the number of the equivalent line from which it is derived. By using QN, we can simplify those lines of a proof which are the negations of quantified PL or PL($=$) forms, by first adding the equivalent line by QN, and then using $\forall$-elimination or $\exists$-elimination. On the supposition that each of the following PL or PL($=$) forms occurs as a line in a proof, find equivalent PL or PL($=$) forms which can be added as lines to the proofs by QN in those cases where QN is applicable:

a. $\sim (\forall x)(\sim Rx \lor \sim Tx)$
b. $\sim\sim (\exists y)(Ry \land Ty)$
c. $\sim (\exists y)(\sim (Ry \land Ty))$
d. $\sim (\forall x)(\exists y)(\sim Rxy \lor Ty)$

(See Answer No. 68.)

2. The availability of QN makes abstraction to most sophisticated PL or PL($=$) argument consistency forms much

easier. Instead of finding a paraphrase for the negation of the conclusion of an argument before abstraction, one can abstract the conclusion directly to a PL or PL(=) form and then prefix this form with a negation sign, obtaining a PL or PL(=) form equivalent to that which would be obtained by the old method of paraphrase. Which of the following pairs of PL forms can be regarded as equivalent ways of abstracting the conclusion of some argument:

a. $(\exists y)(\exists z)(Fyz)$, $\sim (\forall y)(\forall z)(\sim Fyz)$

b. $(\forall x)(\exists y)(Fxy)$, $\sim (\exists x)(\forall y)(\sim Fxy)$

c. $\sim (\forall x)(\sim Fx)$, $(\exists x)(Fx)$

(See Answer No. 28.)

3. For the arguments of Exercise 10, Chapter 7, abstract most sophisticated PL argument consistency forms using the newer method for abstracting the negation of a conclusion, and then develop proofs for these forms.

(See Answer No. 39.)

4. In Chapter 4, Exercise 6, the notion of a tautology was introduced. It would seem that we can take this notion over into PL so as to define a tautology as any statement whose negation is abstracted to a PL form which, when taken as the sole premise of a proof, initiates a proof which blocks. For various historical reasons, the name *tautology* is not used to describe such statements in PL, but we refer to such statements as *logically valid statements*, or as *logical truths*. Which of the following abstract logical truths:

a. $(\forall x)(\sim Fx \lor Fa)$

b. $(\forall x)(\sim (Fx \lor Gx)) \lor ((\exists y)(Fy) \lor (\exists z)(Gz))$

c. $(\forall x)(\sim Fx) \lor ((\forall y)(\sim Gy) \lor (\exists z)(Fz \land Gz))$

d. $((\exists x)(\sim (P \lor Fx)) \lor P) \lor (\forall y)(Fy)$

e. $(\forall x)(\exists y)(\sim Fxy) \lor (\forall z)(\exists w)(Fzw)$

f. $(\exists x)(\forall y)(\sim Fxy) \lor (\forall z)(\exists w)(Fzw)$

(See Answer No. 66.)

5. The following are PL(=) forms. Which of these forms are logical truths which can be established using PL rules of proof only, and which become logical truths when PL(=) rules of proof are also employed:

a. $(\forall x)(\forall y)(\sim (x=y) \lor (x=y))$

b. $(\forall x)(\forall y)(\sim (x=y) \lor (y=x))$

   c. $(\forall y)(y = y)$
   d. $(\forall x)(\forall y)((x = y) \lor \sim (x = y) \lor \sim (x = x))$
   e. $(\forall y)(\forall x)(\sim (x = y) \lor \sim (x = x) \lor (y = x))$
   f. $(\forall y)(\forall x)(\sim (x = y) \lor (y = x) \lor (x = y))$
   g. $(\forall x)(\sim Gxx) \lor (\exists y)(\exists z)(Gzy \land \sim (z = y))$
                             (See Answer No. 10.)

6. Let a universe of discourse be as in Exercise 1, Chapter
    7, and abstract PL(=) forms for the following state-
    ments, using "*Rx*" to abstract "(*x* is red)":
    a. At least one block is red.
    b. At most one block is red.
    c. Exactly one block is red.
    d. At least two blocks are red.
    e. At most two blocks are red.
    f. Exactly two blocks are red.   (See Answer No. 21.)

7. Consider this argument:

> The composer of *King Porter Stomp* was a great pianist.
> Jelly Roll Morton was the composer of *King Porter
> Stomp.*
> Therefore, Jelly Roll Morton was a great pianist.

This argument seems valid, and we can demonstrate its
validity by using PL constants to abstract the naming
expressions "Jelly Roll Morton" and "the composer of
King Porter Stomp." The latter naming expression is
known in the literature as a *definite description,* for it
refers to an individual by describing him sufficiently to
identify him. Definite descriptions normally involve presuppositions which are, in general, too complicated to
discuss here. In our example, however, the description
succeeds in singling out a definite individual provided
only that *King Porter Stomp* is not a collaborative effort,
and is a clearly recognizable composition with a definite
composer. When definite descriptions do not appear in the
same form throughout an argument, they call for special
treatment rather different from simple abstraction to PL
constants. Consider this argument:

> The composer of *King Porter Stomp* was also the com-
> poser of *London Blues.*
> Therefore, somebody composed both the *King Porter
> Stomp* and *London Blues.*

This is a trivial argument, but not an easy one to abstract.

We need to "look inside" the descriptions involved to show validity, and we cannot therefore abstract them to PL constants. In such cases, statements claiming that some individual identified by a description has a certain characteristic are abstracted by complex PL(=) forms which abstract a claim that *exactly one* individual has the defining characteristic and also the other characteristic. The premise of the given argument can be abstracted on the basis of this clue to the following PL form:

$(\exists x)(\forall y)((Kx \wedge Lx) \wedge (\sim Ky \vee (x = y)))$

   a. Abstract a most sophisticated PL(=) argument consistency form for this argument and prove its validity.

   b. Abstract a most sophisticated PL(=) argument consistency form for the first argument cited in this exercise without using PL constants.

(See Answer No. 58.)

8. Suppose that John knows that the match will be played, and suppose that John knows that if it is played, Fulham will not lose. Does it follow that Fulham will not lose?

(See Answer No. 49.)

9. Which of the following are PL or PL(=) valid arguments:

   a. I have a right to sing the blues, and I have an obligation to do what is right.
Therefore, I have an obligation to sing the blues.

   b. Peter sailed slowly down the river in his white boat. Peter's white boat is identical with his new boat.
Therefore, Peter sailed down the river in his new boat.

   c. All the world loves a lover.
If two people are in love, then someone is a lover.
Therefore, if no one is a lover, no one loves a lover.

   d. All of our citizens have a right to freedom.
All of these prisoners are also citizens of ours.
Therefore, all of these prisoners have a right to freedom.

   e. This statue is made entirely of stone.
Therefore, every bit of this statue is made entirely of stone.

   f. Henry was fishing on the Hudson and he felt cold.
Therefore, Henry felt the cold while fishing on the Hudson.

   g. All fathers are sons.

Therefore, all fathers of fathers are fathers of sons.

h. If there are at least two different positive integers, there is a positive integer between them.

No positive integer is between two positive integers unless it is larger than one and smaller than the other.

Every positive integer other than the positive integer 1 is larger than the positive integer 1.

Therefore, there is a positive integer smaller than some other positive integer.   (See Answer No. 13.)

10. Let "α" and "β" stand for arbitrary PL expressions. If a PL expression of the form "$\sim (\alpha) \lor \beta$" occurs in a PL sentential form, we could always replace it by the expression "$\alpha \supset \beta$," and vice versa, much in the manner that the conditional was introduced into SL forms. To justify this, we could follow through the justification for any occurrence of "$\lor$," and construct a parallel justification for a corresponding occurrence of "$\supset$" by means of the allowed replacement. We have not used the conditional very much in order to avoid smuggling in its temporal suggestion by forgetting about the equivalence to disjunctive statements which is used to explain its significance as a logical symbol. This is good practice, but PL forms containing the conditional are often easier to read than equivalent PL forms containing negation and disjunction, much as in the case of equivalent SL forms. Express the most sophisticated PL argument consistency forms for a., b., and c., of Exercise 10, Chapter 7, and for a., b., d., and e., of Exercise 11, Chapter 7, using the conditional where possible.   (See Answer No. 43.)

10. Ordering Integers

In this chapter, we will see how various arguments concerned solely with certain mathematical statements about the positive integers can be appropriately tested for validity by using PL($=$) techniques. We will also see how PL($=$) techniques can be used to systematize these arguments so as to enable us to describe an infinite number of true statements about the integers by means of assuming a few such statements to be true and then utilizing the concept of the set of total logical consequences of these statements. The appropriateness of the use of PL($=$) in this connection follows from the fact that the integers and statements involved fit the presuppositions of PL($=$) symbolism exactly. For example, the integers are paradigm cases of distinct individuals which do not undergo change with time.

Informally, we can set down simple true statements about the relative size of integers in the manner of school mathematics. The following is an example:

If $x \leqq y$ and $y \leqq z$, then $x \leqq z$.

The use of variables here is somewhat different from their use in PL($=$). This expression could not abstract a statement in PL($=$), although it might abstract a three-place predicate expression. In a mathematical context, however, this expression can be used to make the statement that if one positive integer is less than or equal to another, and the second is less than or equal to a third, then the first is less than or equal to the third. This statement is true of all the integers as well, but we are concerned in this chapter with the positive integers, just those numbers normally named by the numerals we use in our proof techniques. It might also be noted that two integers are said to be *equal* in mathematical contexts just in case they are *identical* from the point of view of logic. We can paraphrase our claim as follows: "For any integers x, y, and z, if $x \leqslant y$ and $y \leqslant z$, then $x \leqslant z$." The mathematical statement then seems to involve the notion of universal quantification which we use in PL and PL$(=)$. The logician could therefore attempt abstraction of this statement as follows:

$$(\forall x)(\forall y)(\forall z)(((x \leqslant y) \wedge (y \leqslant z)) \supset (x \leqslant z))$$

Strictly, this is not a PL$(=)$ form, since it contains the symbol "$\leqslant$," which is not a symbol of PL$(=)$, but its intended meaning and the fact that it abstracts a statement is perfectly clear. It may seem strange to regard this expression as an *abstraction* from the informal mathematical statement with which we started, since we have *added to* the notation in which the original statement was expressed. A logician would defend this as an abstraction by pointing out that the informal mathematical statement had significance only in a well-defined context. For in some other contexts, variables are used in informal mathematical statements as though they should be existentially, and not universally, quantified in logical abstraction. For example, consider this informal statement:

$$x \leqslant 4$$

This can make a true statement in most contexts only if it means that some number is less than or equal to "4," and would be abstracted to something like this logical expression:

$$(\exists x)(x \leqslant 4)$$

The logician holds that the use of mathematical variables can be construed in every case as though these variables were universally or existentially quantified, the right quantification being indicated by the context. In *abstracting* to his notation, the logician is expressing the mathematical statement *and* the relevant context in one logical form.

We now consider PL(=) expressions abstracting mathematical statements about the relative sizes or ordering by relative size of the positive integers. The symbol "≦" will obviously occur in these PL(=) expressions. We can define a set of sentences containing this symbol, to be known as *ordering sentences* (for the positive integers). An ordering sentence is any expression which can be obtained from a PL(=) form containing no predicate letters and no PL(=) constants except one or more occurrences of predicate letters of two members whose initial capital letter is "*F*" by replacing all occurrences of these predicate letters with "≦," this symbol being preceded by the variable which is the first member of the predicate letter, and being followed by the other variable, with all three symbols being enclosed within a pair of parentheses. If "*F*" in the PL(=) form is preceded by a tilde as part of a complementary predicate letter, the tilde is now found prefixed to these surrounding parentheses. It should be noted that ordering sentences are *not* PL(=) forms.

Ordering sentences are examples of what are known as the sentences of a *formal language*. A formal language can be described as follows. The symbols of a formal language (its alphabet) can be regarded as given on the keys of a typewriter. Then any sequence of symbols punched out on the typewriter will be known as *strings* of the language. Among the strings of the language will be certain strings which will be regarded as making grammatical (or syntactical) sense. In particular, we are usually interested in a category of strings which can be thought of as abstracting sentences or statements. Our formal language will be known as OS, and we can set up a typewriter for producing its strings with the following symbols:

$$(,) , \sim , \wedge , \vee , \supset , \forall , \exists , x , y , z , * , = , \leqq$$

We use the symbol "*" to create additional variables beyond "*x*," "*y*," and "*z*" should they be required. Any of these variables followed by a finite number of occurrences of the symbol "*" will also be regarded as variables of OS. The strings of OS are every finite sequence of these symbols which could be produced by this special typewriter, so that symbols can be repeated as often as desired in a string. By virtue of our previous characterization of OS, we can recognize the strings that are variables, the strings that are ordering sentences, and so on. All of the meaningful strings of a formal language are usually referred to as well-formed-formulae (or *wffs*) of the language. A formal language should not be regarded as a special kind of language in the ordinary sense, since the wffs of a formal language need not have any particular significance; we can, if we like, regard them merely as sequences of symbols which have been arbitrarily distinguished from the rest by some criterion which allows us to tell whether any string is or is not among the wffs. The purpose of describing a formal language is to define a set of sentences which will abstract some range of statements in which one is interested entirely within the limits of a precise and finite alphabet of symbols.

Let us suppose that a set of sentences has been described within the context of a formal language. The next matter is to distinguish certain sentences from the remainder, much as the sentences themselves are distinguished from other wffs of the formal language, and the wffs are in turn distinguished from the remainder of the strings. The usual method of distinguishing a certain set of sentences from the remainder is to regard them as the *theorems* of an *axiomatic system*. An axiomatic system is defined when we select some of the sentences of a formal language as *axioms,* and then take the set of all of those remaining sentences which follow from the axioms by some concept of logical validity as the *theorems* of the axiomatic system. In this book we will assume that the axioms of an axiomatic system are always finite in number, and can consequently be cited by a complete list. Also, since every sentence will have (trivially) an infinite number of distinct logical consequences in every logical system we are interested in, we will assume that every axiomatic system has an infinite number of distinct theorems. An axiomatic system is completely characterized only when the related formal language and set of sentences of that language are given, when the axioms of the system are listed, and when the notion of logical consequence has been described. When an axiomatic system has been thus characterized, we can define its theorems as all of those sentences of the formal language which follow from the axioms by means of the logical system involved, but the theorems must be discovered one by one through the process of discovering proof that they are sentences following from the axioms by means of the logical system.

Since sentences follow trivially from themselves in the logical systems we have introduced, and we will use only these systems and some extensions of them in characterizing axiomatic systems, it should be clear that in the usual circumstances there are always alternative sets of axioms which may be chosen in order to yield the same total set of theorems in different axiomatic systems. Axioms are therefore usually *chosen* from the set of theorems to be defined because they are particularly simple and easy to remember, or because they are particularly few in number, or for various other reasons.

In practice, we usually choose axioms which we regard as true sentences, or as abstracting true statements, given the intended interpretation of the formal language in which they are expressed, and the purpose of an axiomatic system is to try to find sufficient axioms so that all and only the true sentences of the formal language will be provable as theorems of the axiomatic system. Two things should be pointed out about this usual practice. First, we can define axiomatic systems whose axioms are thought false on the intended interpretation, just to see what would follow from these sentences if they were true. And second, it is an important fact, to which we shall return in later chapters, that in many circumstances it is not possible to find an axiom set which permits all and only the true sentences on the intended interpretation of the formal language to be proven as theorems. In such cases, the true sentences are so numerous that they cannot be found among the denumerable consequences of any finite axiom set. We then look for axiomatic systems in which every theorem abstracts a true sentence, even though there are true sentences which are not theorems, hoping to find a system rich enough to include among its theorems all of the true sentences we are interested in for some purpose.

We now return to OS and proceed to characterize an axiomatic system of ordering sentences. For axioms, we select this pair of ordering sentences:

(Ax1) $(\forall x)(\forall y)(\forall z)(((x \leq y) \wedge (y \leq z)) \supset$
$(x \leq z))$

(Ax2) $(\forall x)(\forall y)((x \leq y) \vee (y \leq x))$

These ordering sentences are easily seen to abstract true statements about the relative size of the positive integers. The theorems of our axiomatic system will consist of all of those OS sentences which follow from these axioms using the test of consequence provided by PL(=).

The only non-logical symbol involved in the axioms and theorems of our axiomatic system from the viewpoint of PL(=) is "$\leq$." As we saw in Chapter 9, PL(=) can be regarded as an extension of PL obtained by adding the symbol "=" to the logical symbols of PL. Could we not just add "$\leq$" to the symbols of PL(=), and regard our axiomatic system as a new logical system obtained as an extension of PL(=)? To obtain PL(=), we added "=" to the symbols of PL, defined the notion of a PL(=) form, and then introduced rules of proof for simplifying lines of proofs containing PL(=) forms with one or more occurrences of "=." Here we have proceeded differently. We add the symbol "$\leq$," but instead of giving new rules of proof, we set down axioms containing the symbol and wish to use the old rules of proof with only slight alteration. But this actual difference in style does not prove that we couldn't introduce "$\leq$" as we introduced "=" earlier. Formally, both introductions could be managed in either style. The reason we do not introduce "$\leq$" as a logical symbol while we did so introduce "=" can only be supported by rather deep considerations in the philosophy of logic. Here we provide one simple consideration. Identity is a concept which seems applicable in theory to every possible world, even though some worlds are such that different names for the same object are not available to provide interesting inferences involving identity. The rule of proof ID and the additional blocking criterion of PL(=) seem to capture precisely all of the essential features of the concept of identity. The logical notion of identity and the symbolism for it seems to be an easy generalization of considerations involved in the way in which we use PL constants to abstract naming expressions for individuals. On the other hand, the symbol "≤" seems to abstract no concept which is common to every possible world and which is referred to by a familiar expression. This symbol is used to express a kind of weak ordering which is common to a great many order structures but which by itself is not very useful in making inferences. In this sense, (Ax1) and (Ax2) do not capture precisely the essential features of any easily recognizable concept, but they set down some features of an ordering concept which may or may not have application in some area of discourse. The symbol "≤" is used to abstract orderings of quite varied properties in different universes of discourse, and it is not used to abstract a single coherent notion common to all of them. We consequently regard its significance as context dependent, and do not introduce it as a logical symbol, but as a non-logical symbol which has precise meaning for us only in the context of OS. The symbol, of course, can well be used in other formal languages with a quite different significance.

From the standpoint of proof technique, the symbol "≤" is treated as is the initial capital letter of a two-member predicate letter. We use such special symbols in an axiomatic system to remind ourselves of the intended interpretation of the system. As far as the logical development of the axiomatic system is concerned, the sentences of the formal language are treated merely as strings of symbols, and it does not matter what they are about. To actually develop an axiomatic sys-

tem, however, some means of treating these strings as appropriate logical forms so that rules of proof can apply must
be found. In our axiomatic system, for example, occurrences
of OS sentences are treated as though they were the PL(=)
forms from which they are obtained by replacement of relevant occurrences of "*F*" by "≤." To be completely strict
about proof procedure, we might abstract all occurrences of
"≤" back to occurrences of "*F*," and carry out the proofs
entirely within the framework of PL(=) techniques, changing the relevant PL(=) forms back to occurrences of OS sentences after completion of the proof. By treating occurrences
of "≤" *as though they were* relevant occurrences of "*F*,"
therefore, we do not carry our proof development outside
the limits of the PL(=) rules of proof.

There is a change in our treatment of quantifiers in the
axiomatic system which is worth noting. We have been requiring that new variables be used to abstract each new
predicate expression in the course of obtaining most sophisticated PL(=) argument consistency forms. Strictly speaking,
this multiplicity of quantifiers is not required. Two quantified
PL(=) forms are equivalent if and only if the same descriptive PL(=) forms can be added from them as lines of a proof.
When this condition is met, the two PL(=) forms will obviously have the same significance in any possible world.
(These remarks are easily seen to be true of quantified PL
forms as well.) Because the instantiations permitted in steps
justified by ∀ - elimination and ∃ - elimination are not dependent on the variable used in the quantifier or on the variable
in the relevant one-place predicate expression, replacement of
a single variable throughout a quantified PL(=) form results
in an equivalent PL(=) form provided that the replacement
does not use a variable occurring in some other quantifier of
the PL(=) form. In this last case, confusion as to the one-
place predicate expression quantified is likely to result. The
suggested replacement always allows the *n* variables in a
quantified PL(=) form to be interchanged in any way, since
n other variables could be used to replace them, and then
these variables in turn could be replaced by the original

variables in some new order. To illustrate, using the variables
of PL(=) rather than those of OS, the following pair of
PL(=) forms are equivalent:

$$(\forall x)(\exists y)(Fxy)$$
$$\text{and}$$
$$(\forall y)(\exists x)(Fyx)$$

The first could be changed to the equivalent "$(\forall z)(\exists y)$
(Fzy)" and then "$(\forall z)(\exists u)(Fzu)$" by replacing "$x$" with
"z," and then "y" with "u," throughout. Next, replacing "z"
with "y" and "u" with "x," we could obtain the second
PL(=) form. If we had replaced "x" with "y" directly in the
first PL(=) form of the exhibited pair, we would have obtained this PL(=) form:

$$(\forall y)(\exists y)(Fyy)$$

This form has no clear meaning. It is to avoid forms like this
that can arise during the process of abstraction that we have
been using different variables at each step of quantification
during the abstraction of a most sophisticated PL(=) argument consistency form. Once the axioms and formal language
of an axiomatic system have been established, however, the
abstractive process for the axiomatic system is largely complete. We can then use the same variables in stating the axioms
and theorems of the axiomatic system without fear that meaningless sentences will appear. This explains why our axioms
and theorems all use the same variables in different OS sentences with the same number of quantifiers. This technique
can be taken back to the abstractive process for PL and
PL(=), so that we take care to use different variables only
for the abstraction of each single sentence which corresponds
to a premise or to the conclusion of the argument being considered.

We now develop our axiomatic system by proving that the
following OS sentence is a theorem of the system:

$$(\forall x)(x \leqq x)$$

A proof that this OS sentence follows from the axioms can be given in this way:

(1) $(\forall x)(\forall y)(\forall z)(((x \leqslant y) \wedge (y \leqslant z)) \supset (x \leqslant z))$
(Ax1)

(2) $(\forall x)(\forall y)((x \leqslant y) \vee (y \leqslant x))$
(Ax2)

(3) $\sim (\forall x)(x \leqslant x)$
$\sim$ (CON)

(4) $(\exists x)(\sim (x \leqslant x))$
(3) QN

(5) $\sim (1 \leqslant 1)$
(4) $\exists$ - elimination

(6) $(\forall y)((1 \leqslant y) \vee (y \leqslant 1))$
(2) $\forall$ - elimination

(7) $(1 \leqslant 1) \vee (1 \leqslant 1)$
(6) $\forall$ - elimination

(8) $(1 \leqslant 1)$
(5), (7) DS_1

We will call "$(\forall x)(x \leqslant x)$" *Theorem 1* (THM 1, for short) of our axiomatic system.

Exercises

1. Establish that the following are theorems of our axiomatic system:
   a. $(\forall x)(\forall y)(\sim(x \leqslant y) \supset (y \leqslant x))$ (THM 2)
   b. $(\forall x)(\forall y)(\forall z)((\sim(x \leqslant y) \wedge \sim(y \leqslant z)) \supset$
      $\sim(x \leqslant z))$ (THM 3)
   c. $(\forall x)(\forall y)(\forall z)((\sim(y \leqslant x) \wedge \sim(z \leqslant y)) \supset$
      $\sim(z \leqslant x))$ (THM 4)
   d. $(\forall x)(\forall y)(\forall z)((\sim(y \leqslant x) \wedge (y \leqslant z)) \supset$
      $\sim(z \leqslant x))$ (THM 5)
   e. $(\forall x)(\forall y)(\forall z)(((x = y) \wedge \sim(z \leqslant y)) \supset$
      $\sim(z \leqslant x))$ (THM 6)
   f. $(\forall x)(\forall y)(x = y) \supset ((x \leqslant y) \wedge (y \leqslant x))$
          (THM 7)   (See Answer No. 84.)

2. None of the theorems proved in Exercise 1 contained any variable other than "x," "y," or "z." Should an OS variable like "x^*" appear in a theorem, can the resulting proof be considered as taking place within the limits of PL(=) proof techniques?   (See Answer No. 26.)

3. An axiomatic system is said to be (*simply*) *consistent* if and only if it does not allow *all* of the sentences of its formal language to be proved as theorems. In the usual case, an axiomatic system can be said to be (simply) consistent if and only if each of its theorems is a true sentence on the intended interpretation. Clearly, given the significance of negation, every sentence of the formal language could be proved as a theorem in an inconsistent axiomatic system, and the axiomatic system could not be used to

distinguish true sentences from false sentences. Show that
if some sentence of OS and its negation are both provable
as theorems in our axiomatic system, then every sentence
of OS is also a theorem.   (See Answer No. 11.)

4. Since the theorems of an axiomatic system are infinite
in number, the (simple) consistency of an axiomatic
system cannot be established by actually looking at all
of the theorems of the system to see if a sentence and its
negation both appear among them. One method of showing (simple) consistency where negation is given in the
formal language is to find an interpretation for the axioms
which shows that they can be jointly true, or jointly abstract true statements, in some possible world. We can
then conclude that none of the false sentences can be
theorems, since we know that the logical system is conservative. But, strictly speaking, this shows that the axioms
are jointly true only if we can independently show that
our interpretation describes a consistent possible world.
Normally, we might not question this, but a logician
would be doubtful about proving the consistency of
axioms by interpreting them in a mathematical system
whose consistency could only be assumed. (Simple) consistency is therefore often shown not by reference to the
intended interpretation of the axiomatic system, but by
constructing a particularly simple interpretation in which
the truth of the axioms and the falsity of some sentence of
the formal language are easy to determine. A sentence
could be true in the interpretation used to prove consistency without necessarily being a theorem of the axiomatic system, because the axioms and rules of proof were
not powerful enough to show that the sentence must be
true in *any* interpretation in which the axioms are true.
This is discussed more fully in subsequent chapters. We
will now sketch an interpretation which will show the
(simple) consistency of our axiomatic system. Consider
this OS ordering sentence:

$(\exists x)(\exists y)(\sim (y \leqq x))$

In the intended interpretation, this abstracts the claim
that there are at least two integers which are not identical.
If we can show that this OS sentence does not follow from
(Ax1) and (Ax2) by constructing an interpretation in

which (Ax1) and (Ax2) are true and this sentence is false, then we can conclude that our axiomatic system is consistent.

a. Satisfy yourself that any attempt to prove this sentence in the axiomatic system results in a proof which cannot block.

b. Construct an interpretation of the axioms and of this sentence in the universe of discourse consisting solely of the integer "1" on the basis of which (Ax1) and (Ax2) make true statements while the OS sentence we are considering is false.   (See Answer No. 37.)

5. The theorems of an axiomatic system are said to be (*simply*) *complete* with respect to the sentences of a formal language if and only if either each sentence of the formal language or its negation is a theorem of the axiomatic system. The adjective *simply* is used here, as in the definition of consistency, to indicate that this is only one kind of completeness and one kind of consistency that can be defined for relatively simple axiomatic systems using PL as their related logical system. These are the only notions of consistency and completeness that are required at this level. An axiomatic system is shown to be (simply) incomplete if we can find a sentence of its formal language such that neither the sentence nor its negation is a theorem of the axiomatic system.

What is the relationship between (simple) completeness and (simple) consistency?   (See Answer No. 65.)

6. Describe what an axiomatic system is like which is *both* (simply) consistent and (simply) complete. If an axiomatic system could not be both, is it likely that a complete system would be preferred to a consistent system?
                    (See Answer No. 20.)

7. Find a sentence of OS which, when added to the axioms of our system, defines a new axiomatic system which is consistent, and which shows that the previous axiomatic system is incomplete.   (See Answer No. 50.)

8. A set of axioms for an axiomatic system is said to be *independent* if none of them could be deleted without changing the set of theorems of the axiomatic system. If an axiom set is not independent, then the same set of theorems can be proved when one or more axioms are

deleted from the axiom set. The failure of an axiom set to be independent is *not* as disturbing a feature of an axiomatic system as inconsistency. Sometimes we explicitly choose dependent axioms because they are elegant in form and easy to remember, or because they state intuitively "basic" principles from among the statements to be axiomatized. On the other hand, if we know that our axioms are independent, we know that in a certain sense the axioms embody no "superfluous" assumptions. To show a given axiom independent of the others, we need to show that it does not follow from them.

Find suitable interpretations to show that (Ax1) and (Ax2) are independent of each other.

(See Answer No. 27.)

9. It should be clear that an axiomatic system with a single non-logical symbol is likely to be pretty trivial. Most interesting axiomatic systems are obtained by relating several non-logical symbols to each other in the axioms. We will now sketch a way in which the axiomatic system of Chapter 10 might be enlarged by adding a new symbol and extending the formal language OS appropriately. The symbol "$+$" (intended in the usual way to express addition of numbers) to be introduced differs from the symbol "$\leqq$" in that when the latter is flanked by two variables, a predicate expression results which can be quantified to abstract a sentence, while when "$+$" is flanked by two variables, a naming expression rather than a predicate expression results. More carefully, we would say that when "$+$" is flanked by two variables, an expression results which becomes a naming expression for a number when it is instantiated. For example, "$x + y$" becomes "$4 + 1$," a naming expression referring to the integer "5," when "x" is replaced by "4" and "y" is replaced by "1."

We will now describe a class of expressions to be known as OS$+$ *sums*. The result of flanking the symbol "$+$" by two variables and enclosing the result in a pair of parentheses is known as a *simple sum*. The result of replacing any variable in a simple sum with a simple sum is also a simple sum. All of the following are simple sums:

$(x + y)$

$$(x + (y + z))$$
$$((x + x) + (y + z))$$

We call an ordering sentence of OS *simple* if it is not a truth function of an ordering sentence or sentences and has all of its quantifiers occurring as the initial segment of the string of OS symbols constituting it. (All of the OS sentences we have cited have been simple.) An ordering sentence of OS+ will be any sentence of OS+ identical with a sentence of OS or any expression which can be obtained from a simple ordering sentence of OS as follows:

(1) Delete the quantifiers.
(2) Replace one or more occurrences of any variable with an OS+ sum.
(3) Repeat (2) in the resulting string of OS+ as often as desired.
(4) Prefix to the resulting string one quantifier containing each variable occurring in the string.

We then take these OS+ ordering sentences as additional axioms for a new and larger axiomatic system:

(Ax3) $(\forall x)(\forall y)((x = y) \supset (x \leqq y))$

(Ax4) $(\forall x)(\forall y)(((x \leqq y) \wedge (y \leqq x)) \supset (x = y))$

(Ax5) $(\forall x)(\forall y)(\forall z)(((x + y) + z) \leqq (x + (y + z)))$

(Ax6) $(\forall x)(\forall y)(\forall z)((x \leqq y) \supset ((x + z) \leqq (y + z)))$

(Ax7) $(\forall x)(\forall y)(\forall z)(((x + y) = (y + z)) \supset (x = z))$

Before we can prove theorems, we need to look once more at the PL($=$) proof techniques in order to handle lines of proof containing the symbol "$+$." We call any fully instantiated OS+ sum a definite sum. Since definite sums are like other naming expressions, we treat every definite sum appearing in some line of a proof at a given point in its development as though it were a distinct numeral, with the possibility that they may be shown identical to other distinct numerals in the course of developing the proof. $\exists$- elimination proceeds as usual, with the introduction of a new numeral (not the instantiation of an OS+ sum) to instantiate the relevant one-place predicate expression. On the other hand, a line which is a universally quantified one-place predicate expression can be

true if and only if every instantiation of the one-place
predicate expression in terms of an introduced naming
expression is true. Therefore, we permit ∀ - elimination
to proceed by replacing the variable of the relevant one-
place predicate expression with "1," or any numeral or
definite sum already appearing in the proof. This modifica-
tion of ∀ - elimination is clearly in conformity with the
original justification for the rule once the significance of
sums is understood. It is possible to show in advanced
logic that this extension is entirely trivial, and can be regarded as within the limits of PL(=) proof technique,
but we cannot demonstrate that fact here.

The new axiomatic system should provide some indication of how axiomatic systems can be defined using
PL(=) and various formal languages for quite advanced
areas of mathematics.

a. Prove the following theorems in the axiomatic system which has just been described.
   (i) $(\forall x)(\forall y)((x+y) \leqq (y+x))$
   (ii) $(\forall x)(\forall y)((x=y) \supset ((x+z) \leqq (y+z)))$
   (iii) $(\forall x)(\forall y)(\forall z)(((x+z) \leqq (y+z)) \supset$
         $(x \leqq y))$
   (iv) $(\forall x)(\forall y)(\forall z)((x+(y+z)) \leqq$
         $((x+y)+z))$
   (v) $(\forall x)(\forall y)(\forall z)(\forall x^*)(((x=y) \wedge$
         $(z \leqq x^*)) \supset ((x+z) \leqq (y+x^*)))$
b. Is the new axiomatic system (simply) consistent?
c. Is the new axiomatic system (simply) complete?
d. Are (Ax1)–(Ax7) independent?
e. If you add "$(\forall x)(\forall y)(\exists z)(x=(y+z))$" as
   (Ax8), can the intended interpretation be kept for the
   new axiomatic system?   (See Answer No. 71.)

PART FOUR
FORMAL SYSTEMS

11. Axioms and Machines

We have said in preceding chapters that an important motivation in abstracting logical forms is to provide the basis for a test of validity which can be regarded as mechanical. In these last chapters, we will be discussing whether there are any grounds for supposing that the tests of validity embodied in our logical systems do not really achieve the objective of a mechanical test. It will be found that "mechanical" is a somewhat vague term as measured against the theoretical possibilities of testing procedures. But for the moment we may ask whether proofs can be carried out without dependence upon the significance of the symbolism in which the proofs are expressed. In other words, we are asking whether in developing proofs we need to depend implicitly upon the significance of the symbolism to guide the process of proof development. The test for this is to determine whether an appropriate machine could be devised which could carry out the various proof procedures used to test for validity in the various logical systems. One may argue that machine computation cannot depend upon insight, or upon an understanding of the symbolism, in just the appropriate sense to answer our question. The full expression of the philosophy of conservatism which underlies modern deductive logic is to identify the operations which can be programmed for machine computation with the logical operations. A major problem of advanced logic is consequently to determine exactly the nature and extent of logical operations by investigating the limits of machine computation under this assumed identification.

This problem of advanced logic could probably not have been formulated except for the development of the modern high-speed digital computer. Such computers are the model for machine computations which interest the logician, but the logician does not consider himself to be a computer scientist. The reason for this is that computer science must deal with actual computers and their mechanical problems, while the logician is interested in ideal computers which have no mechanical problems. An actual computer will have limitations on the speed of its operation, on the size of the calculations it can perform, and on its freedom from error which are a consequence of the number and reliability of its mechanical parts. These limitations restrict the kinds of problems that a given computer can solve. The logician is interested in discussing computers which have no mechanically imperfect parts, and which may contain an arbitrarily high number of component parts for the solution of a given problem. Since such a computer costs nothing to operate, the logician is quite willing to ignore time and expense when his computers operate, and is interested only in distinguishing the case where an ideal computer will (in principle) stop in a state defining the correct answer to the problem with which it started (no matter how many steps this may take) from failure of computer operation to locate the answer. This attitude provides a method for finding the limits of mechanical processes of a certain type. Clearly, the logician's interests and the interests of some computer scientists overlap considerably, since ideal computers are often used to provide a theory for the operation of actual computers.

For our purposes, we will restrict ourselves to considering ideal computers which can be put into a fixed state in which they are presented with certain linear instructions which can be represented as a string of symbols in some formal language. The computer then goes through a certain sequence of steps, each step being determined for the computer by its structure and the instructions with which it was presented. Computers which are determined in this way will repeat the same process exactly when given the same instructions several times, a feature that is important for the logician's purpose in looking to mechanical procedures. The computer is said to *solve* the problem represented by the instructions if it reaches a last step after which the answer to the problem can be read off from some feature of the computer's structure when it stops.

There are two sorts of such computers which it is useful to distinguish. One kind we will call a reading machine. A reading machine will be such that when certain linear instructions are given to it, it will sooner or later stop and give some agreed signal if and only if the linear instructions belong to a specified list of linear instructions. We can regard a reading machine as a computer programmed to recognize any well-formed-formula of a certain category from an arbitrary formal language. The other kind of computer we will call a computing machine. A computing machine is designed to solve problems represented by the linear instructions presented to it, and it may stop in a state which represents the answer to the problem if the answer can be obtained within the limits of its operations. The typical computer is usually a computing machine in this sense. A computing machine may stop with an answer which is a function of the instructions presented to it, and this answer might be different for each possible instruction. Clearly, a reading machine may be regarded as a particularly limited computing machine which can return only one answer to instructions when it stops. Reading machines, because of their relative simplicity, have been very prominent in discussions by logicians of the limits of machine and logical operations.

Let us look more closely at a reading machine. Such a machine may receive its instructions on a tape ruled into squares, which we may represent in this fashion:

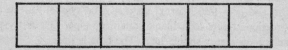

To give the machine instructions, we write a sequence of n symbols constituting a string of some formal language from left to right into the first n squares of the tape. The machine can then be started on the left-most square when it is in some internal state s_0, which we call the starting state. We will say that the machine *recognizes* this string of symbols if and only if, when the machine is started in the manner indicated, it later stops in some specified internal state after a finite number of computing steps. We also stipulate that the machine cannot run off the tape. (This is an instance of idealizing a computer.) If the machine is about to run off the tape originally inserted into it, we add on some blank squares at either end of the tape in order to keep the machine attached to some definite square of the tape at every step of its computation.

We now construct a very simple reading machine. Let the alphabet of the formal language contain the single numeral "1." From the set of all possible sequences of this symbol repeated a finite number of times, the sentences of the formal language, we are interested in distinguishing the subset of sequences containing an even number of occurrences of the symbol. A machine to recognize these sequences can be described by these symbols giving instructions for the various computational steps which the machine is permitted:

$(s_0, 1, R, s_1)$
$(s_1, 1, R, s_0)$
(s_0, B, R, s_2)
(s_1, B, R, s_1)

It will be sufficient to explain the first such symbol which describes one step of the machine operation as follows: If the machine is in internal state s_0 and is scanning a square of tape containing the symbol "1," then it moves one square to the right, and goes into internal state s_1. The symbol "B" in the instructions refers to a blank square of tape. Let us try the machine on a very simple tape. The tape is this:

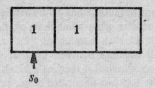

s_0

The arrow indicates the square scanned and the internal state of the machine as it starts. After one step of operation, the situation is this:

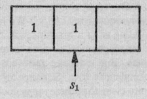

s_1

One more step brings us to this:

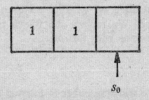

s_0

The machine stops at the next step, for which we add on one blank square on the right:

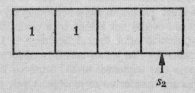

s_2

The machine stops because it has no instructions for an internal state s_2 no matter what symbol is on the square being scanned. Now, if an even number of "1's" are on the tape, the machine will oscillate between internal states s_0 and s_1 as it reads left to right until it reaches a blank square, when it will stop as in the last two illustrated steps, provided that one imagines a tape with the appropriate number of "1's" added on to the left. Suppose that there is an odd number of "1's" on the tape. Then the machine encounters a blank square while in internal state s_1, and by the fourth instruction, it simply computes endlessly, moving on indefinitely through the blank squares to the right. Our ideal simple machine then recognizes all and only the even sequences of "1's." We have not actually given plans for building such a machine, which would involve describing circuits or mechanical devices to realize the appropriate internal states. But we have reduced the problem of recognizing even sequences to a sequence of steps so simple that it becomes quite clear that these steps could be performed mechanically if we chose to build a reading machine for the purpose described.

We can also arrange a machine to stop in either of two internal states depending on whether an even or an odd sequence is inserted. We replace the fourth instruction characterizing the machine with this one:

$$(s_1, B, R, s_3)$$

This new machine will stop either in internal state s_2 or internal state s_3 after reading through the sequence from left to right, and the state of the machine will then tell us whether the sequence inserted had an odd or even number of symbols in it. A reading machine which will stop in either of two states after a finite number of steps depending on whether the tape inserted did or did not belong to a distinguished set of well-formed-formulae of a formal language is known as a *decision machine* for that set of well-formed-formulae.

Now suppose that sequences of SL forms or PL forms or PL($=$) forms are transferred to machine tapes, using a spe-

cial symbol to mark the space between any two forms in the
sequence. These sequences would correspond to most sophisticated argument consistency forms for the appropriate
logical system. We might then be interested in whether reading machines could be built that would recognize just the
sequences corresponding to valid original arguments. This
question would correspond quite closely to the general question of whether tests of validity can be made entirely mechanical for the logical systems we have introduced. The answer
to the question is that reading machines can be built in each
case. But, as might now be anticipated, a decision machine
can only be built for recognizing most sophisticated SL argument consistency forms corresponding to valid original
arguments.

It should not be difficult to convince oneself that reading
machines can be built whose operation parallels quite closely
the general lines of the proof procedures for SL, PL, and
PL(=) that have been discussed. These machines would not
simply read a sequence from left to right as did our sample
reading machine. The machines, much as the human following the procedures, must perform certain calculations before
recognizing a sequence, or failing to stop. Such machines
would have to move left as well as right, and would have to
change symbols on certain squares in order to put down
markers as an aid in keeping track of the calculations. These
steps would be required in order to handle such rules as D,
with the asterisk of the rule corresponding to a marker on
the tape. With these additional operations, machines can be
constructed which will systematically examine all possible pairs
of SL forms on their tapes to see if any pair is identical, or
to see if any pair consists of an SL form and the negation of
that same SL form. Further, such machines can determine
whether any SL form or pair of SL forms on the tape can be
regarded as substitutions into the left-hand side of any rule of
proof. A machine could always determine, first, whether its
tape was blocked, and if so, whether any form had been
marked with an asterisk, and then determine if any new line
could be added by working through the rules of proof in some

fixed order to see if any form or forms on the tape could
justify adding a form not identical with any existing form occurring as a separate form on the tape. Rule D could be used
without choice by always choosing the left-hand disjunct in
any of its applications. If a proof then blocked, the right-hand
disjunct could always be used with DS. Quantifier elimination
can also be brought within the scope of machine operation. To
be completely mechanical, the machine operation could not
utilize any of our rules for convenience in handling parentheses, repeated conjunctions, and so on. The details are simply
too complicated to give within the compass of this book, but
the student's experience in working out proofs may have
convinced him that proof development is well within the
limits of mechanization.

Let us consider a reading machine for sequences of SL
forms which correspond to valid original arguments. Clearly,
we can arrange the machine to stop in either of two internal
states depending on whether the proof blocks with optimal
use of D, or completely simplifies without blocking. This follows from the fact that there are only a finite number of conjunctive or disjunctive symbols in a most sophisticated SL
argument consistency form, and the SL form in which each
occurs can be simplified in a finite number of steps. An SL
reading machine can be converted into a decision machine
which will enable us to arrange all most sophisticated SL
argument consistency forms in a *systematic* fashion as follows. Let a most sophisticated SL argument consistency form
be abstracted as a sequence of SL forms. For convenience,
we imagine the SL capital letters put into a sequence so that
if n distinct capital letters appear in a most sophisticated SL
argument consistency form, we use the first n letters of the
sequence as the n capital letters of the most sophisticated SL
argument consistency form. We can imagine the argument
actually abstracted to this equivalent form, or we could even
construct a machine to turn most sophisticated SL argument
consistency forms into their equivalents before using the decision machine. We can then call the number of SL symbols
in the sequence of SL forms constituting a most sophisticated

SL argument consistency form (that is, the number including repetitions of the same symbol) the *length* of the sequence. All sequences of a given length are finite in number. We can see this by describing the way in which they could all be typed out on a typewriter containing the appropriate symbols. By inserting in some order described as alphabetical all of the most sophisticated SL argument consistency forms of length 1 (if any), length 2 (if any), and so on, we could gradually develop a systematic list of all of the most sophisticated SL argument consistency forms abstracting valid arguments from a single machine. If this list were printed from time to time as it got longer, we could simply check any most sophisticated SL argument consistency form that we abstracted (or its equivalent using the first n capital letters of the agreed sequence for abstraction) against this list to see whether it abstracted a valid argument. Even if the list did not yet contain most sophisticated SL argument consistency forms of an appropriate length, we could wait until such forms were added to the list, and then we would know whether the form was that of a valid argument or not.

The difference between having just a reading machine and having a decision machine for a logical system is partly clarified by the fact that no systematic list of valid most sophisticated PL (or PL(=)) argument consistency forms can be developed, even though a reading machine for most sophisticated PL (or PL(=)) argument consistency forms which abstract valid arguments can be constructed. It is sufficient to discuss this for PL. Suppose we order the PL symbols (including variables and predicate letters) in some appropriate way, attempting to use a scheme like that described for SL. Now, when we insert a sequence which is a most sophisticated PL argument consistency form into a reading machine for such forms, we know that the machine will stop if the form is that of a valid argument, but may compute endlessly if the form is that of an invalid argument. In the general case, where we do not know whether the form is that of a valid or an invalid argument, we do not know whether the machine will stop or not. As we have seen, the proof procedure on which the machine is based may fail to terminate if each use of ∀-elimination is followed by a use of ∃-elimination leading in turn to a new use of ∀-elimination. Therefore, the first time that we insert a most sophisticated PL argument consistency form not abstracting a valid argument for which the machine computation does not end, the machine is tied up for good and cannot be used to continue the list. We never know, no matter how long the machine continues to compute, whether it will suddenly stop, or keep on going. Therefore, to continue development of the list, we need to make more and more copies of the reading machine in order to insert new sequences corresponding to most sophisticated PL argument consistency forms if we want to develop the list on the basis of such a reading machine. Whenever a machine in use stops, we insert a new sequence, and add the sequence just recognized to our list of most sophisticated PL argument consistency forms abstracting valid arguments. Therefore, although we can pursue a strategy which will insure that we can constantly expand our list of valid PL argument consistency forms, there will be an absence of order in the list corresponding to our inability to guess whether a given machine is going to stop or not. We cannot therefore arrange the list systematically so as to determine after some time whether or not a most sophisticated PL argument consistency form of a fixed length is that of a valid argument. The difference between having a reading machine only and having a decision machine is thus far from trivial.

Every set of sentences of some formal language which can be given as the theorems of an axiomatic system with SL, PL, or PL(=) as its associated logical system will have a reading machine. For we can introduce into reading machines for the logical system sequences of forms consisting of the axioms of the system followed by single sentences in an effort to determine whether those sentences are theorems of the axiomatic system. In doing this, of course, the non-logical symbols of the axiomatic system would have to be re-abstracted to logical symbols of the same syntactical type as mentioned in Chapter 10. By continuing to duplicate the reading machine when current machines are still running, and by introducing new sequences into stopped machines, we can gradually produce a list of theorems of the system which will sooner or later include any sentence that we are interested in provided that it is a theorem of the system.

There is a connection between reading and decision machines for axiomatic systems which may be expressed in the following way. Suppose the set of sentences of some formal language to be given. Let S be a subset of these sentences identical with the theorems of an axiomatic system, and let $\bar{S}$ be the complement of S, namely, those sentences of the formal language which are not theorems of the axiomatic system, and hence do not belong to S. We can have a decision machine for S if and only if we can have a reading machine for $\bar{S}$.

We have a reading machine for S by virtue of its being identical with the theorems of an axiomatic system. Now suppose that we also have a reading machine for $\bar{S}$. The pair of reading machines together constitute a decision machine for S. Let some sequence consisting of the axioms of the axiomatic system for the set S followed by a sentence of the formal language be duplicated (a mechanical operation) and inserted into both reading machines. *One* of the reading machines will stop after a finite length of time, and we will be able to determine from the machine which stops whether or not the sentence is in set S. If the reading machines do not stop when any sentence (or sequence) which they do not read is inserted, we can determine whether the sentence inserted as part of such a sequence is or is not in set S by merely noting *which* machine stops. By a similar argument, the same pair of reading machines is also a decision machine for the set $\bar{S}$, and the set $\bar{S}$ can be gradually built up by the decision machine. It does not follow that the sentences in $\bar{S}$ can be given as the theorems of an axiomatic system in the sense introduced here. If a reading machine can be constructed to recognize just those sentences of the formal language belonging to $\bar{S}$ (those which do *not* follow from the finite set of axioms for S), the existence of this machine does not guarantee that some other finite set of axioms can be stated from which the sentences in $\overline{S}$ will follow as theorems using some logical system. This should indicate that some reading machines required for discussion in advanced logic differ considerably from our projected reading machines for valid SL, PL, and PL(=) argument sequences. The details of such machines are simply beyond the scope of this discussion. Returning to the converse of the relationship we have been considering, it is easily seen that if we have a decision machine for S (or $\overline{S}$), we can construct reading machines for S and $\overline{S}$. We can systematically introduce sequences into the decision machine, and then place the sentences we are interested in in lists for S or $\overline{S}$ depending on the decision which the machine provides. Indeed, we can duplicate the decision machine and arrange for it to keep computing if it does not find the sentence to belong to one of the two lists, so that the decision machine can be turned exactly into a reading machine for either S or $\overline{S}$ with the appropriate characteristics.

With reference to our initial concern with the mechanical nature of the tests of validity provided by our logical systems, these developments have the following consequences:

(1) For SL, a formal language can be defined whose sentences correspond to most sophisticated SL argument consistency forms. The set of such sentences corresponding to valid original arguments can be distinguished from the rest as the theorems of an axiomatic system. This axiomatic system is both (simply) consistent and (simply) complete. There is a decision machine for the sentences which are theorems of the axiomatic system.

(2) For PL and PL(=), a formal language can be defined whose sentences correspond to most sophisticated PL (or PL(=)) argument consistency forms. The set of such sentences corresponding to valid original arguments in either system can be distinguished from the rest as the theorems of an axiomatic system. This axiomatic system is (simply) consistent, but it is *not* (simply) complete. There is a reading ma-

chine for the sentences of the axiomatic system, but no decision machine. Consequently, no reading machine can be constructed for the set of sentences corresponding to invalid PL (or PL(=)) arguments.

The reason why PL (and PL(=)) are not (simply) complete when developed as axiomatic systems is that we can add to the axioms without causing inconsistency various forms which abstract claims that express some information about the number of individuals in the universe. No such statement can follow from any set of sentences abstracting the valid most sophisticated PL (or PL(=)) argument consistency forms since the valid forms are those whose validity is defined in terms of possible worlds of any non-empty size.

Another notion of completeness other than (simple) completeness is sometimes invoked. If we are interested in a set of statements which we can define exactly, we may say that an axiomatic system is *complete with respect to that set* if and only if its theorems are sentences expressing all and only the statements in the set. In PL and PL(=), we are interested in the valid most sophisticated argument consistency forms. The axiomatic systems whose sentences express valid most sophisticated PL (or PL(=)) argument consistency forms as theorems can be shown to be *complete with respect to the set of valid most sophisticated PL* (or PL(=)) *argument consistency forms*. This means that a sentence of the associated formal language is a theorem of the axiomatic system if and only if it abstracts a valid most sophisticated PL (or PL(=)) argument consistency form. This is what is meant when it is sometimes said that PL and PL(=) are complete.

From the point of view of our original concern, the detailed proof of these facts (available in more advanced texts) is sufficient to establish that the logical tests for validity which we have introduced are mechanical in the relevant sense that deterministic reading machines can be constructed to test validity. Appropriateness of abstraction remains an art, but it is possible to show that the test of validity of an abstracted argument depends upon no human insight, and is as complete as the underlying principles and any mechanical embodiment can permit it to be.

12. Logical Systems

In earlier chapters, we described the set of PL forms, and we defined certain sequences of PL forms as most sophisticated PL argument consistency forms. These sequences were thought of as abstracting valid arguments if and only if the proofs which were developed from them blocked. A similar strategy was followed in presenting the other logical systems. Now, there are two interesting and distinct notions actually involved, a fact which we have not explicitly noted so far. One is the notion of implication. We can say that the premises of an argument *imply* its conclusion if and only if the premises cannot be jointly true in any possible world in which the conclusion is false. This notion of implication as a relationship between premises and conclusion of certain arguments is simply another way of looking at the property of validity which we attribute to certain arguments, and it was this notion that provided the grounds for the development of a logical symbolism. After a symbolism has been constructed and abstraction to it clarified, we can say that implication holds between the premises and the conclusion of an argument if and only if the symbolic forms $"P_1,"$ $"P_2,"$ . . . , $"P_n"$ appropriately abstracting the n premises cannot all abstract true statements in some possible world while the form appropriately abstracting the conclusion abstracts a false statement. Given our earlier discussion, it should be obvious that an argument is valid if and only if this relation of implication holds between its abstracted premises and its abstracted conclusion. We express the relationship of implication holding as follows:

$$P_1, P_2, \ldots, P_n \models C$$

Once the symbolism has been developed, however, another notion also comes into play. We can say that a wff, "C," of a formal language is derived from other wffs, "P_1," "P_2," . . . , "P_n," of the same formal language if and only if "C" may be obtained from "P_1," "P_2," . . . , "P_n" by means of certain rules for the manipulation of the symbolic forms of the formal language. Thus we can discuss *derivations* of wffs of a formal language from other wffs entirely without reference to the notions of truth or validity. We express the relationship of derivability holding as follows:

$$P_1, P_2, \ldots, P_n \vdash C$$

In practice, we try to find rules of derivation which so correspond to the notion of validity that once an argument has been abstracted, the derivation expressed by a proof can be performed mechanically if and only if the conclusion is implied by the premises. Expressing this more formally, we can say that we want the following condition to hold for a suitable logical symbolism and related logical system:

$$P_1, P_2, \ldots, P_n \models C \text{ if and only if } P_1, P_2, \ldots, P_n \vdash C$$

Note carefully that a symbol like "C" does not have the same significance on both sides of this statement. After "$\models$," it stands for a statement which is *true* under certain conditions, and after "$\vdash$" it stands for a symbol which can be derived from other symbols in a system.

The method of finding SL, PL, and PL(=) proofs that we have used in this book does not carefully distinguish implication from derivation. We have allowed our intuition about the significance of the symbolism to help us in applying rules of proof. In the last chapter, we claimed that valid most sophisticated SL, PL, and PL(=) argument consistency forms could be recognized by an appropriate reading machine, so that the application of the rules of proof need not depend upon our understanding of the symbolism. Nonetheless, we did not even begin to prove this. Our rules of ∀-elimination and ∃-elimination, for example, are stated in English, and can be followed only by a human logician. The plausibility of the claim has to be given at this stage of development in terms of an intuition that there is nothing about the steps the human logician follows that could not be transformed into machine operations.

In advanced logic, explicit proofs of the claims made in Chapter 11 are provided by the explicit construction of duplicate systems of implication and derivation. On the one hand, the logician develops a system of derivation which is regarded as devoid of significance. This system contains only concatenations of symbols and rules for manipulating them which can be carefully set out as a program of instructions for mechanical computation. It is the system of derivation which is mechanized. Another system is developed at the same time in which the same symbols are regarded as significant, and as abstracting true or false statements in possible worlds. The concept of implication is then carefully worked out in terms of the possible worlds. Discussions of the two kinds of systems are often called *proof theory* (for the derivational system) and *model theory* (for the implicational system) with respect to a particular logical system. It is not always the case that the symbols of the two theories are identical, although the forms called *sentences* in the two systems must be identical if the condition given earlier is to be carefully stated. In many systems, the derivational system may contain auxiliary symbols (such as the numerals and asterisks of our proof procedure for PL) which are used for technical purposes during intermediate steps of a proof. A system of derivation for a logical system will always be tested against the related implicational system, since the system of implication defines the intuitive notion (validity) that we look to a logical system

to clarify under certain assumptions. Systems of derivation will
be said to be *adequate* if the previously cited condition holds
for explicitly constructed systems. We cite this condition once
more:

$$P_1, P_2, \ldots, P_n \models C \text{ if and only if } P_1, P_2, \ldots, P_n \vdash C$$

To prove that this condition holds for specific derivational and
implicational systems requires the use of a language (for
example, a supplemented portion of English) in which
the relevant features of the two systems can be discussed.
The details of such a proof for systems as complicated as
PL are obviously extensive, and difficult to manage. They may
be found by pursuing the references given in the section
Further Reading at the end of the book.

It may be useful to return once again to some very simple
considerations to see why two systems of derivation and
justification are required at all. In principle, an adequacy
proof would seem to suggest that the two systems are actually
equivalent when the condition holds, so that either, by itself,
could provide clarification of a sound argument under certain
assumptions. The introduction of a *pair* of systems is related
to a practical, rather than to a theoretical, consideration.
We begin by considering truth, and developing a system of
implication. In SL, PL and PL(=), for example, we can
define the systems of implication by reference to assignments
of truth-values to SL capital letters and descriptive sentences
of PL or PL(=) in the relevant set of possible worlds. The
implication relation holds if no possible world is such that
"P_1," "P_2," . . . , "P_n" can all be assigned the truth-value
truth in some possible world in which "C" is assigned the
truth-value falsity. It is implicit in our description of these
possible worlds that they become too unwieldy to use as a *test*
of validity for very complicated arguments, since the number
of possible worlds to be considered becomes enormous. We
turn instead to proof development as a *test* of validity,
and proof development can be given entirely within the system
of derivation. The advantage of proofs is that they break

down the problem of testing for validity into a sequence of symbolic steps each of which is, by itself, easy to comprehend and check. So easy, in fact, that a machine could do it. In SL, the convenience of a derivational system in correspondence with an implicational system becomes obvious when more than five simplest constituent assertions appear in an argument. In PL and PL(=), considerations of convenience virtually require a derivational system, since the possible worlds involved in direct testing for implication are often infinite in number. Reflection on these matters in terms of the strategy for developing proofs outlined in this book should indicate that the distinction between implicational systems and derivational systems is required if any formal or symbolic logical system is to be justified as a practical tool for evaluating the correctness of argument.

We have discussed the justification of each of our rules of proof by immediate reference to its conservative implicational property of never allowing a line to be added which could abstract a false statement when the preceding lines of proof could jointly abstract true statements. We can consequently feel reasonably confident that every argument we assess as valid by these techniques is in fact valid, and that the implication relation holds between the premises and the conclusion, but we have not in any sense begun to establish that every valid argument which can be expressed appropriately in the symbolism will in fact be assessed as valid by our symbolic tests. This more complicated side of establishing the adequacy of a logical system is obviously of considerable interest to logicians. Had this question not been asked and solved by logicians in terms of the pair of systems involved in complete justification of the adequacy of a logical system, there would be no way of telling whether or not the kind of practical system developed in this book was adequate.

The method of proof proposed in this book has the advantage of being so closely tied to intuitive considerations of validity that its conservative properties seem intuitively obvious. The proof procedure is also relatively easy to use in the sense that it takes little insight to add lines of proof during proof development by means of its rules. We have used this fact to suggest how a machine to develop proofs might be constructed. On the whole, methods of this kind are quite satisfactory for testing the validity of given arguments (or original concern), and they may also be carefully justified by elementary considerations in advanced treatments of the adequacy of logical systems. There are, however, several points of view leading to logical systems whose rules of proof are somewhat different from those proposed in this book. These logical systems usually contain implicational systems so similar that the same logical system is simply regarded as being given different derivational characterizations by these alternative methods of proof. Our system has the property that each line added to a proof is a form which can abstract a true statement in any of the relevant possible worlds. It is this feature which makes it relatively easy to show that the rules of proof are conservative. But as a proof is developed in PL or PL(=), new symbols (the numerals) are introduced into some lines of the proof which do not always simply repeat symbols found in the most sophisticated PL or PL(=) argument consistency form which initiates the proof. A most sophisticated PL argument consistency form, for example, may contain existential quantification and no PL constants in such a manner that at least two numerals are introduced into lines of the proof developed from it. In our everyday style of argument, we do not usually introduce discussion of individuals not mentioned in the premises or conclusion in order to attempt proof that a given argument is correct. It may therefore be desirable to find a method of proof which corresponds to what we regard as the features of natural argumentation, that is, a method which starts from the premises of an argument (or forms abstracting them) and proceeds directly to the conclusion (or a form abstracting it) by means of a series of intermediate steps which do not introduce reference to individuals not referred to in any of the sentences of the argument. Such a method might also avoid assuming even temporarily that the negation of the conclusion might be true.

Another drawback of the method of proof used in this book

is that it is not as well suited to the development of axiomatic systems as it is to the determination of the validity of a given argument. To develop an axiomatic system on the basis of the proof techniques introduced in this book, we need to first guess at theorems, and then see whether these guesses can be substantiated by proof development. Again, it would seem more natural to have rules of proof allowing us to start just with the axioms (or forms abstracting them) and then proceed step by step to other forms, some of which could be recognized and labeled as theorems of the axiomatic system. The issue, however, is not entirely as simple as this may suggest. Suppose we are interested in whether a particular sentence is a theorem of some axiomatic system, and suppose that our suspicion that it is a theorem is correct. Given the concept of proof earlier introduced, this will be discovered in time. Using the direct method, however, we cannot be sure that a proof will be found even if there is one to be found, for direct proof procedures depend on choices and insight into the strategy of development, and they do not terminate mechanically in a correct answer unless optimal choices are made at certain points. In spite of the fact that direct methods cannot be readily mechanized, they have the rather subtle advantage that interesting theorems may turn up as a by-product of attempting to prove a theorem, or even of attempting to prove a non-theorem. Our method of proof cannot yield this advantage since its added lines typically involve symbols whose occurrence rules the lines out as theorems of the related axiomatic system.

There is one last consideration telling for the development of direct methods. In Chapter 11, a distinction between reading machines and computing machines was mentioned. It would be of obvious advantage to have a computing machine that could be given the axioms of an axiomatic system and a characterization of the relevant formal language with instructions to compute the theorems one by one. With our method, we could construct a kind of computing machine by coupling a reading machine with a machine producing sentences of the formal language to be mechanically inserted into the reading machine, but the first non-theorem would jam this machine if PL or PL(=) are the logical systems involved. This difficulty can be circumvented, but not easily. Computing machines based on direct methods need not jam, since, properly constructed, they will not test non-theorems, and they can consequently lead to the description of single machines which will compute the theorems of an axiomatic system.

Direct proof methods are numerous in the literature, and are most easily recognized in the so-called natural deduction systems. In natural deduction systems for PL, for example, $\forall$-elimination and $\exists$-elimination are carried out by allowing variables rather than constants to instantiate the relevant predicate expressions. In addition, rules permitting the *introduction* of quantifiers under various restrictions are then added, so that quantified PL forms may be derived directly from quantified PL forms. Here is an example:

(1)	$(\exists x)(\forall y)(Fxy)$		
(2)	$(\forall y)(Fxy)$	(1)	$\exists$ - elimination
(3)	Fxy	(2)	$\forall$ - elimination
(4)	$(\exists x)(Fxy)$	(3)	$\exists$ - introduction
(5)	$(\forall y)(\exists x)(Fxy)$	(4)	$\forall$ - introduction

"$(\forall y)(\exists x)(Fxy)$" is here derived directly from "$(\exists x)(\forall y)(Fxy)$," whereas in our method of proof, we would find "$(\forall y)(\exists x)(Fxy)$" to be a consequence of "$(\exists x)(\forall y)(Fxy)$" by showing that the proof whose premises consisted of the latter PL form and the negation of the former would block. Restrictions must obviously be placed on the steps of natural deduction proofs so as to insure that a proof of adequacy is possible. For example, we cannot simply reverse the direction of the derivation given above, as the converse derivation does not correspond to an implication. The restrictions required for adequate systems of natural deduction are quite complicated, and no attempt can be made here to outline a specific system of natural deduction rules. A derivation in a natural deduction system will typically contain lines which cannot abstract statements, as line (3) of our sample. This makes the conservative character of natural deduction systems more difficult to establish, although it is possible to prove the adequacy of natural deduction systems in more advanced work.

There is an interesting connection between valid argument and tautologies or logical truths in the systems SL, PL, and PL(=) which is summarized in a statement known as *The Deduction Theorem* which holds in a suitable interpretation for all of these systems. In any of the systems, let "*C*" be derived from "P_1," "P_2," . . . , "P_n" so that the derivation relationship holds for these forms:

$$P_1, P_2, \ldots, P_n \vdash C$$

The Deduction Theorem (in one form) then states that this relationship holds if and only if the following statement holds as well:

$$(P_1 \supset (P_2 \supset \ldots (P_n \supset C) \ldots))$$

To see this more clearly, suppose the argument has a single premise. (We could regard any argument as having a single premise by taking the repeated conjunction of all of its premises as the sole premise.) Then *The Deduction Theorem* is this:

$$P_1 \vdash C \text{ if and only if } \vdash P_1 \supset C$$

What is the significance of "$\vdash P_1 \supset C$"? Using the relationship between derivational and implicational systems once again, we can assert the following:

$$\vdash P_1 \supset C \text{ if and only if } \vDash P_1 \supset C$$

"$P_1 \supset C$" is a form which abstracts a true statement no matter what possible world is considered. "$P_1 \supset C$" is thus a tautology (of SL) or a logical truth (of PL or PL(=)) provided that "P_1" and "C" are forms of the appropriate logic, and not sentences from an interpreted formal language containing non-logical symbols. There is thus a very close connection between validity and logical truth. Adequate logical systems can be used to develop the set of all tautologies, or of all logical truths which can be expressed in the derivational system of the logic. The important role of the symbol "⊃" in formal logic is largely due to the illuminating way in which it can be used to state *The Deduction Theorem* in order to establish this result.

Suppose we regard the forms of a logical system as the sentences of a formal language. Then by *The Deduction Theorem*, we could distinguish the tautologies or logical truths from the other sentences by means of the derivational system. Since no axioms are required to do this using our method of proof or natural deduction systems, we can develop what is an axiomatic system *without explicit axioms*.

Many logicians have preferred to develop the set of tautologies or logical truths in a more classical fashion by setting down some tautologies or logical truths as explicit axioms, and then, using particularly stringent rules of proof, showing that the set of theorems so defined is identical with the set of tautologies or appropriate logical truths. Once this has been done, the idea embodied in *The Deduction Theorem* can be used to show that an argument "$P_1, P_2, \ldots, P_n, C$" is valid if and only if the form "$(P_1 \supset (P_2 \supset \ldots (P_n \supset C) \ldots))$" abstracting it is a tautology or logical truth.

As this chapter should indicate, there are a variety of approaches to the development and use of logical systems. The student who wishes to pursue logic must learn various approaches, since the equivalence in theory of the approaches does not affect the fact that each one of these general approaches is most suitable for solving a certain range of practical and theoretical problems in the most intuitively satisfactory manner.

13. Theories

In Chapters 11 and 12, we have asserted the important fact that decision machines cannot be constructed for PL and PL(=). This has an obvious consequence for axiomatic systems such as those discussed in Chapter 10. Let an axiomatic system be given by citing axioms involving certain non-logical constants, and by taking PL, PL(=), or PL(=) with symbols like "+" as the associated logic. We are now interested in discussing such axiomatic systems in general. It can be assumed that the only axiomatic systems of interest to us are (simply) consistent. We may then investigate the (simple) completeness of such axiomatic systems, and the question of whether or not decision machines can be constructed for them. Clearly, some (simply) consistent axiomatic systems are (simply) incomplete. We had some examples in Chapter 10. It is also clear that decision machines are not available for at least some axiomatic systems. To show this, we can imagine that each axiomatic system is re-abstracted to forms of the logical system with which it is associated. Then the question of whether a particular sentence is a theorem of the axiomatic system becomes equivalent to a question of whether a particular logical form is derivable from a set of other logical forms. Since this latter question is not capable of solution in every case by virtue of the fact that there are no decision machines for PL or PL(=) or PL(=) with symbols like "+," the former question is not capable of general solution either. In other words, decision machines cannot be built for some axiomatic systems because they cannot be built for the related logical systems. This is not a surprising result, and it is one that is to be expected on the basis of the discussion in the preceding chapters.

The negative general result about decision machines does not mean that specific axiomatic systems do not have decision machines. For example, it is easy to show that if an axiomatic system is (simply) complete, then a decision machine can be built for it. Should the axiomatic system be (simply) complete and (simply) inconsistent, then the decision machine is trivial, since every sentence of the formal language is a theorem of the axiomatic system. As usual, therefore, the only interesting case we can formulate here arises when the axiomatic system is (simply) complete and (simply) consistent. We have seen earlier that the theorems of an axiomatic system can be given on a gradually lengthening list, and any particular theorem we are interested in will appear on that list after a finite length of time. Suppose we are interested in knowing whether or not a sentence "*D*" of the formal language is or is not a theorem of the axiomatic system. As the list of theorems lengthens, we check each new entry to see whether it is the sentence "*D*" or the negation of the sentence "*D*." (We have to assume here that the equivalence of a sentence on the list to "*D*" or to its negation can be determined in a finite sequence of steps, but this assumption is easily satisfied in practice.) If "*D*" appears on the list, it is a theorem, and if the negation of "*D*" appears on the list, "*D*" is not a theorem. By the (simple) completeness of the axiomatic system, either "*D*" or its negation must appear on the list. After some finite length of time, therefore, we will know whether or not "*D*" is a theorem of the axiomatic system. This decision machine is not very practical, since we cannot necessarily tell after any length of time has passed in which it has failed to produce a decision about "*D*", just how soon it *will* produce a decision about "*D*." It *is* a decision machine, however, in the strict sense that we know that it will produce a solution after a finite length of time, even though we cannot know (in general) when it will stop. In practice one attempts to construct more practical decision machines which will stop within a period of time that can be calculated from the nature of the inserted instructions. Such machines can be constructed for many (simply) complete axiomatic systems.

The failure of PL and PL(=) to have decision machines is related to their (simple) incompleteness. As we saw, there are pairs of PL or PL(=) forms and their negations such that neither is a theorem of PL or PL(=) developed as an axiomatic system. In general, if we insert a PL or PL(=) form into a reading machine, we cannot be sure that the machine will stop precisely because the PL or PL(=) form might be a member of one of these pairs.

Although the existence of a decision machine for an axiomatic theory follows from the (simple) completeness of the axiomatic theory, the converse relationship does not hold. A decision machine may or may not exist for a (simply) incomplete axiomatic system. It might at first seem that the strategy to be employed, consequently, is to try to find a (simply) complete theory as some kind of extension of any theory we are interested in by adding further axioms so that a decision machine for the complete theory would provide a decision machine for the theorems that we are interested in. We have already seen one reason why this strategy will not always bring reasonable results. In order to extend an axiomatic system for PL to a complete theory, we would need to add an axiom restricting the number of possible worlds, and this axiom would be incompatible with the intended use of PL. It might still seem possible, of course, that axiomatic systems such as those in Chapter 10 with non-logical symbols could always be extended to (simply) complete axiomatic systems in order to find decision machines for them. A most exciting result of twentieth-century logic is that many such axiomatic systems are both *essentially incompletable* and *essentially undecidable*.

Let us call an axiomatic system whose axioms and theorems contain non-logical symbols a *theory*. Theories, like logical systems, can be regarded as having both implicational and derivational interpretations. On the one hand, the formal language, the axioms, and the derivations permitted by the logical system as adapted to the formal language define a class of theorems of the theory which can be regarded merely as a distinguished set of strings of symbols in the alphabet of the formal language which fit syntactical criteria for being called sentences. At the same time, the use of the non-logical symbols points to an intended interpretation, or at least to a set of intended interpretations, by reference to which the sentences of the formal language of the theory can be regarded as abstracting certain statements. Here again, we would like to be able to prove a certain adequacy condition. We would like to have a sentence derivable as a theorem if and only if it abstracted a true sentence in the intended interpretation. The essential undecidability of many theories can then be stated as follows: It is often possible to describe each sentence of the formal language of a theory as true or false in the intended interpretation of the theory even though no finite set of axioms can be found which will permit all and only the true sentences on this interpretation to be derivable as theorems of the formal part of the theory.

Investigations into essential undecidability in this sense have largely taken place within the context of mathematical theories. This is not only because the sentences of mathematical theories often fit the presuppositions of PL(=) symbolism so exactly, but because the required definition of the truth or falsity of all of the sentences of the formal language can be given precisely for such mathematical theories. The most famous case is the attempt to find a theory for the true statements of arithmetic. We assume from arithmetical experience that any way of adding two non-negative integers together, or of multiplying two non-negative integers together, produces a unique non-negative integer as the sum or product. Further, since any two non-negative integers are either equal or not, we expect a sentence expressing the equality of two non-negative integers expressed as sums, products, or numerals, to be either true or false. By means of these insights, we can define a set of arithmetical statements expressed as the sentences of a formal language, and we can also define exactly the sentences of the formal language which are true in the intended interpretation.

In a formal language, non-negative integers are usually represented as formal numerals developed from a formal numeral like "0" and a sign called the *successor sign,* which we will write as the symbol "*S.*" "*S*0" then represents the ordinary numeral "1," "*SS*0" represents the ordinary numeral "2," and so on. Constants for the infinite set of non-negative integers can thus be generated from just two symbols. A formal language whose sentences are capable of expressing these constants, as well as all sums and products of these constants which define new formal constants, and which also contains the normal apparatus for quantification and identity provided in the symbolism of PL(=), will be said to be adequate to express the sentences of ordinary arithmetic.

One of the most famous modern discoveries about theories is that the set of true sentences of a formal language adequate to express ordinary arithmetic cannot be distinguished as the set of theorems of a derivational system for a theory defined in terms of the formal language. This is an almost immediate consequence of what is known in the literature as *Goedel's Theorem.* The proof of Goedel's Theorem amounts to providing a set of instructions for constructing a sentence known as a *Goedel Sentence* for any set of axioms defining a derivational system which is (simply) consistent and all of whose derivable theorems are true sentences of arithmetic in the intended interpretation. The Goedel Sentence constructed from a given set of axioms is always such that it can be shown to be true in the intended interpretation, but can also be shown to be not derivable as a theorem from the axioms on the basis of which the sentence was constructed. Since the construction of the Goedel Sentence can be carried out for any relevant set of axioms, it follows that the construction of the Goedel Sentence shows that every axiom set which purports to distinguish exactly the set of sentences of ordinary arithmetic which are true in the intended interpretation is incomplete. By using the construction over and over, and adding the Goedel Sentence found in each construction to the set of axioms by reference to which it is constructed, one can produce a series of more and more powerful theories, each containing all of the sentences of the preceding theory as well as some new sentences as theorems which are true in the intended interpretation. But the construction shows also that such a series can never be completed, and theories of ordinary arithmetic can never be axiomatized so as to be both (simply) consistent and (simply) complete.

Given our previous discussion, the incompleteness of theories about arithmetic does not demonstrate that no decision machine can be constructed for them. But this fact can also be demonstrated for a wide class of theories attempting to abstract only true sentences of arithmetic. The demonstration is not completely general, for there are various impoverished axiomatic systems for which a decision machine can be constructed. Tarski (and others) have established that there is a theory of arithmetic which is not very strong and which is *essentially undecidable* in this sense: the theory itself is undecidable and every extension of this theory to a more powerful theory results in a theory which is also undecidable. The essential incompleteness and essential undecidability of these theories of ordinary arithmetic is sufficient to show that the wanted adequacy condition for axiomatic theories of arithmetic cannot be satisfied.

The general situation for theories is much more complex than it is for axiomatic logical systems. For logical systems, we were able to define the class of logically true sentences, and show that an axiomatic system could be constructed which was adequate in the sense that the set of theorems coincided exactly with the set of logically true sentences. Now, in ordinary arithmetic, we cannot define very many interesting sets of true arithmetical statements which include only some of the true statements of arithmetic on the intended interpretation. Thus there are few arithmetical theories which are even complete relative to a set of sentences which have an important mathematical role. Instead, axiomatic theories usually define sets of theorems which are not *natural* in terms of intuitive mathematics, although they are precisely defined.

This result has often been said to destroy the significance of theories and to end early hopes for an axiomatic system which would embrace the totality of mathematical and scientific truth. Before this result, it was indeed hoped that a decidable theory which was (simply) complete and (simply) consistent relative to a formal language adequate to express sentences of mathematics and science could be constructed. But the discoveries of essential undecidability and essential incompleteness have turned out to have no greater destructive consequences for axiomatic systems than the discovery of the impossibility of constructing a perpetual motion machine has had on the development of modern machine design. Such discoveries establish certain limits on the procedures which must be observed in the construction of theories, and of machines. For as we have said, the method of axiomatic theories remains *the only method* of precisely characterizing an infinite number of sentences as true, and of distinguishing them from false sentences in a common language. If, therefore, we wish to show that mathematical arguments in the sciences can be completely justified, the technique is not to turn to a master logical system, but to construct a theory powerful enough to include among its theorems a sentence abstracting every mathematical statement required for the presentation of the mathematical argument. A theory powerful enough is sufficient to establish that an argument is valid, that it has consistent premises, and that it contains no implicit assumptions relative to certain explicit assumptions stated in the axioms. The lasting and permanent achievement of modern deductive logic is that it can provide theories powerful enough to accomplish this for a wide and ever growing range of mathematical and scientific argument. Logic, like mathematics, receives its ultimate justification as a method for externalizing and isolating from certain other influences various mental processes of great value, and for embodying these in conservative mechanical systems which can check the reliability of human computation, and which can perform complicated computations that would defeat the computational powers of a single human logician. There can be no real question as to who is master.

Further Reading

This book is only an introduction to modern deductive logic. In making some recommendations about further reading, I have been able to mention only a few good books from among those easily available at the time when this book was to go to press. There are many other good books about logic which are suggested in turn in the bibliographies of these books, or which can be recommended by anyone teaching college-level logic. The pitfall to be avoided is that of reading too many books superficially. For example, any student who reads [J1], [K1], and [K3] in that order, and rather carefully, will know a great deal about modern deductive logic.

Philosophy students who rarely need to use logic except to test the validity of a given argument need know no more than the method of testing for validity given in this book. A more elaborate and interesting treatment of this kind of method is presented in [J1]. There are some notational differences. [J1] uses "&" instead of "∧," "→" instead of "⊃," "(x)" instead of "(∀x)," and lower-case letters instead of numerals for ∃-elimination and ∀-elimination. In simplifying disjunctions, [J1] uses a branching tree structure instead of our rule D and the technique of erasure. Beyond these somewhat superficial differences, [J1] not only presents a very similar system, but provides a useful and complete justification for claiming that such a system is correct, and in its last chapter presents in detail an interesting intuitive argument for

Goedel's Theorem. A very sophisticated discussion of methods like that employed in this book and [J1] is to be found in [S4].

Students who wish to investigate logic as a separate philosophical discipline will need to learn the intricacies of at least one other kind of approach to logical systems. The natural deduction approach to tests of validity for logical systems equivalent to SL, PL, and PL(=) is to be found in most recent textbooks. [L1], [K1], and [M1] are recent discussions which should be comprehensible to the reader of this book. All of these have numerous worked examples for the student, and each has some special appeal. Both [K1] and [M1] introduce further valuable discussion of axiomatic systems. A very thorough and classic exposition of natural deduction systems with explicit discussion of the significance of rules of proof is to be found in [Q1], a book which is not easily understood by the beginning student.

The axiomatic approach to the development of logical systems is also mentioned in our Chapter 11, and developed in detail in such places as [M2], Chapter 10. A classic development is to be found in [C6], in which careful rigor and precision in logic can be seen in beautiful display, and which contains in one form or another nearly everything that is known about questions surrounding such systems as SL, PL, and PL(=). It is not, however, a beginner's book.

Philosophical problems in the application of logical systems have been repeatedly raised in the chapters of this book. General problems in philosophical logic are reviewed in the papers of [I1] and [S6]. The philosophical attitude of regimentation discussed in Chapter 9 receives a definitive statement in [Q3]. A sharp counterattack appears in [W1], which unfortunately is not readily available. The phenomenological attitude can be seen very carefully exhibited in [D1], [G1], [H2], and [K2]. Other philosophical issues can be explored by looking at those titles listed on pp. 231–34 which contain obvious reference to philosophical issues.

The use of logical systems to provide axiomatic systems for mathematics is still an exciting area of research and development. [T1] is still a sound introduction to the topic, and

may be read after this book. Many interesting applications of
logical systems in areas of mathematics and science are
provided in [S8] and [B1]. A superb treatment of nearly
every major issue is to be found in [K3] or [M2], which
are not easy reading, but which introduce the student to advanced work in mathematical logic and machine theory and
which are not beyond comprehension by slow and careful
study. [D2] is a book on the limits of machines as discussed
in Chapter 11. This book is fascinating, and like the previous
books it can be grasped by perseverance on the part of a relative newcomer to the subject. It might be noted that in these
advanced treatments of theories, theories with an infinite
number of axioms are discussed, but these do not change
the basic results reported in Chapters 10, 11, 12, and 13.
Books like [Q2] and [S7], which are devoted to the major advanced topic of providing axiomatic systems of set theory,
are not easily grasped without a prior study of the relevant
mathematics. To some extent, this is also true of [K3], [M2],
and [D2], but the college reader is more likely to have some of
the knowledge of elementary number theory required to
understand the technicalities. Discussions of the essential
completeness and essential undecidability of theories branch
out from [T2] and material in its bibliography, but understanding of these sources is best undertaken after grounding in
a book like [K3].

Switching networks and their logic, introduced in Chapter
6, can be pursued in [C1], [H1], and [R2], where special
techniques for simplification are introduced. The axiomatic
systems of Chapter 10 receive more elaborate treatment and
considerable extension in [S8], [L3], and [L4]. Students
interested in finding out about non-standard logical systems
and logical systems designed to treat non-deductive inference
can usefully look at [A1], [A2], and [P4] to examine the
literature on such topics.

[A1] ACKERMANN, R. J. *An Introduction to Many-Valued Logics*
(London, 1967).

[A2]   ————. *Nondeductive Inference* (London, 1966).

[A3]   ADAMS, E. W. "The Logic of Conditionals," *Inquiry, 8* (1965), pp. 166–97.

[A4]   AYER, A. J. *Language, Truth, and Logic* (London, 1946).

[B1]   BETH, E. W. *The Foundations of Mathematics* (Amsterdam, 1964).

[C1]   CALDWELL, S. *Switching Circuits and Logic Design* (New York, 1958).

[C2]   CARNAP, R. "On Belief Sentences." Reprinted as pp. 230–32 of Carnap, R., *Meaning and Necessity* (Chicago, 1956).

[C3]   CARTWRIGHT, R. "Propositions." In Butler, R. S., (ed.), *Analytical Philosophy,* Vol. I (Oxford, 1962), pp. 81–103.

[C4]   CHISHOLM, R. "Intentionality and the Mental." In Feigl, H., Scriven, M., and Maxwell, G., (eds.), *Minnesota Studies in the Philosophy of Science,* Vol. III (Minneapolis, 1958), pp. 507–39.

[C5]   CHOMSKY, N. *Aspects of the Theory of Syntax* (Cambridge, Massachusetts, 1965).

[C6]   CHURCH, A. *Introduction to Mathematical Logic,* Vol. I (Princeton, 1956).

[C7]   ————. "On Carnap's Analysis of Assertion and Belief," *Analysis, 10* (1950), pp. 97–99.

[C8]   ————. Review of [A4], *The Journal of Symbolic Logic, 14* (1949), pp. 52–53.

[D1]   DAVIDSON, D. "The Logical Form of Action Sentences." In Rescher, N., (ed.), *The Logic of Decision and Action* (Pittsburgh, 1967), pp. 81–95.

[D2]   DAVIS, M. *Computability and Unsolvability* (New York, 1958).

[F1]   FARIS, J. A. *Truth-functional Logic* (London, 1962).

[F2]   FORDER, H. G. *The Foundations of Euclidean Geometry* (Cambridge, England, 1927).

[G1]   GEACH, P. *Reference and Generality* (Ithaca, N.Y., 1962).

[G2]   GODDARD, L. "The Exclusive 'Or,'" *Analysis, 20* (1960), pp. 97–105.

[G3]   GOODMAN, N. *Fact, Fiction, and Forecast* (Cambridge, Massachusetts, 1955).

[H1]   HEILWEIL, M. F., and HOERNES, G. E. *Introduction to Boolean Algebra and Logic Design* (New York, 1964). A programmed text.

[H2]   HINTIKKA, J. *Knowledge and Belief* (Ithaca, N.Y., 1962).

[I1] ISEMINGER, G. *Logic and Philosophy: Selected Readings* (New York, 1968).

[J1] JEFFREY, R. C. *Formal Logic: Its Scope and Limits* (New York, 1967).

[J2] JENNINGS, R. E. "Or," *Analysis, 26* (1966), pp. 181–84.

[K1] KALISH, D., and MONTAGUE, R. *Logic: Techniques of Formal Reasoning* (New York, 1964).

[K2] KENNY, A. *Action, Emotion, and Will* (London, 1963).

[K3] KLEENE, S. C. *Mathematical Logic* (New York, 1967).

[K4] KLIMA, E. "Negation in English." In Fodor, J. A., and Katz, J. J., (eds.), *The Structure of Language: Readings in the Philosophy of Language* (Englewood Cliffs, 1964), pp. 246–50.

[L1] LEMMON, E. J. *Beginning Logic* (London, 1965).

[L2] ——. "Sentences, Statements, and Propositions." In Williams, B., and Montefiore, A., (eds.), *British Analytical Philosophy* (London, 1966), pp. 87–108.

[L3] LIGHTSTONE, A. H. *Symbolic Logic and the Real Number System* (New York, 1965).

[L4] ——. *The Axiomatic Method* (Englewood Cliffs, 1964).

[L5] LINSKY, L. *Referring* (London, 1967).

[M1] MATES, B. *Elementary Logic* (Oxford, 1965).

[M2] MENDELSON, E. *Introduction to Mathematical Logic* (New York, 1964).

[M3] MITCHELL, D. *An Introduction to Logic* (London, 1964).

[N1] NIDDITCH, P. "A Defence of Ayer's Verifiability Principle Against Church's Criticism," *Mind, 70* (1961), pp. 88–89.

[N2] NELSON, J. O. "Is Material Implication Inferentially Harmless," *Mind, 75* (1966), pp. 542–51.

[P1] PAP, ARTHUR. Footnotes to article. In Feigl, H., Scriven, M., and Maxwell, G., (eds.), *Minnesota Studies in the Philosophy of Science*, Vol. II (Minneapolis, 1958), p. 224.

[P2] PATTON, T. E. "A System of Quantificational Logic," *The Notre Dame Journal of Formal Logic, 4* (1963), pp. 105–12.

[P3] PRIOR, A. *Formal Logic* (Oxford, 1962).

[P4] ——. *Past, Present, and Future* (Oxford, 1967).

[Q1] QUINE, W. V. O. *Methods of Logic* (London, 1952).

[Q2] ——. *Set Theory and Its Logic* (Cambridge, Massachusetts, 1963).

[Q3] ——. *Word and Object* (Cambridge, Massachusetts, 1960).

[R1] REICHENBACH, H. *Elements of Symbolic Logic* (New York, 1947). Especially "Analysis of Conversational Language," pp. 251–354.

[R2] RICHARDS, R. K. *Arithmetic Operations in Digital Computers* (New York, 1955).

[S1] SAYRE, K. M. "Propositional Logic in Plato's *Protagoras*," *The Notre Dame Journal of Formal Logic, 4* (1963), pp. 306–12.

[S2] SCHEFFLER, I. *The Anatomy of Inquiry* (London, 1964).

[S3] SELLARS, W. "Intentionality and the Mental." In Feigl, H., Scriven, M., and Maxwell, G., (eds.), *Minnesota Studies in the Philosophy of Science,* Vol. III (Minneapolis, 1958), pp. 507–39.

[S4] SMULLYAN, R. M. *First-Order Logic* (Berlin, 1968).

[S5] STRAWSON, P. F. *Introduction to Logical Theory* (London, 1952).

[S6] ———. *Philosophical Logic* (Oxford, 1967).

[S7] SUPPES, P. *Axiomatic Set Theory* (Princeton, 1960).

[S8] ———. *Introduction to Logic* (Princeton, 1964).

[T1] TARSKI, A. *Introduction to Logic and to the Methodology of Deductive Sciences* (Oxford, 1959).

[T2] ———. In collaboration with Mostowski, A., and Robinson, R. *Undecidable Theories* (Amsterdam, 1953).

[V1] VENDLER, Z. "Each and Every, Any and All," *Mind, 71* (1962), pp. 145–60.

[W1] WALLACE, J. R. *Philosophical Grammar: A Study of Classical Quantification Theory, the Theory of Sense and Reference, and the Logic of Sortal Predicates.* Stanford University, Ph.D. Dissertation, 1964. University Microfilms #64-13,652.

Answers to Exercises

1. a. (1) $A \vee E$
      (2) S $\sim$ (CON)
     *(3) A (1) D
   b. *(4) S (2) D
   c. (4) $\sim P$ (2) CS_1
      (5) $\sim F$ (2) CS_2
      (6) $\sim (I) \wedge C$ (1) DS
      (7) C (6) CS_2
   d. *(5) $\sim (M)$ (2) D
     *(6) $\sim (S)$ (1) D

   a., b., and d. are SL invalid; c. is valid.

2. If you abstract "He ate and he ate and he ate" as a conjunction, the argument is valid. Now exchange the premise and the conclusion. The argument so formed is also valid, which may seem odd. In retrospect, it seems more perspicuous to take "He ate and he ate and he ate" as making a statement roughly equivalent to that which could be made with "He stuffed himself."

3. a., b., d., e., and g. are true claims; c. and f. are false.

4. (4) $P \wedge Q$ (1) DS*
   (5) $\sim P$ (2) DS*
   (6) P (4) CS_1

   Line (4) is justified because we can see that the disjunct "$(R \wedge S)$" would block with line (3) after a use of CS_2. We can also see that line (4) and line (2) will block, justifying line (5). With experience, one would see that this proof would block without actually developing it.

   (See Answer No. 87.)

5. Yes. a = <yellow, cubical, 6, 10>

6. a.
(4) $\sim P \vee Q$	(1) MC
(5) $\sim \sim P \vee R$	(2) MC
(6) $\sim Q \wedge \sim R$	(3) DMC
(7) $\sim Q$	(6) CS_1
(8) $\sim P$	(4) , (7) DS_2
(9) $\sim R$	(6) CS_2
(10) $\sim \sim P$	(5) , (9) DS_2
(11) P	(10) DN

   (See Answer No. 69.)

7. a.
   (1) $(\forall x)(\forall y)(\sim Lxy \vee \sim Lyx)$
   (2) $(\exists z)(Lzz)$ $\sim$(CON)

   b.
   (1) $(\forall x)(\forall y)(\sim Sxy \vee Syx)$
   (2) $(\exists z)(Szz)$ $\sim$(CON)

   c. Hint: The first premise is neither of kind (1) nor of kind (2). Use a PL constant to abstract it.

   (See Answer No. 53.)

8. The invalid arguments are b., d., e., and f. In each case, the argument completely simplifies with our informal restriction on $\forall$-elimination, and we do not need a mathematical interpretation to show that the argument will not terminate. It is possible to give mathematical interpretations showing that all of the lines of the most sophisticated PL argument consistency form are true on the interpretation, showing by another method than that of proof that these arguments are invalid. For example:

   b.
   (1) $(\forall x)(\forall y)(\sim(x \leqq y) \vee (y \leqq x))$
   (2) $(\exists z)(z \leqq z)$ $\sim$(CON) ,

   where the universe is that of the positive integers. The others are considerably more difficult.

9. Your answers to this exercise are correct if they differ from those given only by using different SL capital letters. This corresponds to a different choice in abstracting:

   a.
   (1) $A \vee E$
   (2) S $\sim$(CON)

   b.
   (1) S
   (2) $\sim(I) \vee S$
   (3) $\sim(I)$ $\sim$(CON)

   Be sure that you are abstracting the negation of the conclusion. In looking at c., be sure to notice that the second premise can be paraphrased as a conjunction.

   (See Answer No. 57.)

10. a., d., and f. are PL logical truths, and a., b., c., d., e., and f. are PL(=) logical truths.

11. Suppose that "Θ" and "∼Θ" are the pair of sentences of OS provable as theorems. Then a proof developed from (Ax1) and (Ax2) blocks if "∼Θ" or "∼(∼Θ)" is taken as line (3). "Θ ∧ ∼Θ" is also a theorem, and the proof blocks with "∼(Θ ∧ ∼Θ)" or "∼Θ ∨ ∼(∼Θ)" as line (3), but this line is clearly a tautology. The contradiction must therefore be due to (Ax1) and (Ax2) alone, and it does not matter what OS sentence stands as line (3).

12. Yes. Trace the different ways in which the switch can be closed.   (See Answer No. 22.)

13. a. PL and PL(=) invalid.
    b. PL and PL(=) invalid. This result seems counterintuitive. Why?
    c. PL (hence PL(=)) valid.
    d. A careless abstraction results in the assessment that this argument is PL and PL(=) valid. In context, what statement is the first premise likely to be making?
    e. PL and PL(=) invalid, in agreement with intuition.
    f. PL and PL(=) invalid. Henry may feel cold when it isn't really cold, perhaps as a result of sickness.
    g. Hint: Let "*Fxy*" abstract "(*x* is the father of *y*)." Then "*a* is a son" could be abstracted to "(∃*x*)(*Fxa*)."
        (See Answer No. 56.)

14. Examples a. and b. could be added as derived rules of proof. In each case, the second disjunct of the first expression is incompatible with the second expression when the appropriate substitutions have been made. Example c. could *not* be added as a rule of proof. "*P* ∨ ∼*Q*," "*P*," and "∼(∼*Q*)" can be substitutions, and the first two abstract true assertions while the third abstracts a false assertion in a possible world in which "*P*" abstracts a true assertion while "*Q*" abstracts a false assertion.   (See Answer No. 75.)

15. No.

16. a. (1) ∼*H*1 ∨ (∀*x*)(∼*Sx* ∨ *Ex*)
        (2) (∃*y*)(*Sy* ∧ ∼*Ey*)
        (3) *H*1   ∼(CON)
        PL valid; proof can be developed in nine lines.
    b. (1) *W*12
        (2) *W*31

      (3) $W32$ $\sim$(CON)

      PL invalid.

  c.   (1) $(\exists x)(Ax \wedge \sim Lx)$

       (2) $B1$

       (3) $\sim L1$ $\sim$(CON)

      PL invalid. Rod Laver had tennis elbow.

  d.   (1) $(\forall x)(\sim Px \vee Hx)$

       (2) $(\forall x)(\sim Hx \vee Cx)$

       (3) $\sim C1$

       (4) $P1$ $\sim$(CON)

      PL valid. Notice that the abstraction of line (3) is probably all right in most contexts, but not in all.

  e.   (1) $R1 \wedge (\forall y)(\sim (Cy \wedge Ly) \vee (Sy1)$

       (2) $(\exists x)(Cx \wedge \sim Lx)$

       (3) $(\forall z)(\sim Cz \vee Sz1)$ $\sim$(CON)

      PL valid. Does it matter if the stamp being sought is unique, or merely any stamp from a certain stamp issue?

  f.   PL valid.

17. Sensationalism, no doubt, or possibly conscious distortion of the truth. The logical point made by the journalist is correct, but this is not a sufficient justification. We expect good journalism to reveal as much pertinent detail as is available so as to avoid misleading the reader.

18. a. Simplified from "$(\sim (P) \vee Q)$."

     b. Hint: Is this a conjunctive or a disjunctive SL form?

                       (See Answer No. 81.)

19. Δ is equivalent to the negation of Θ, that is, Δ is a contradictory SL form.

20. Such an axiomatic system contains exactly one sentence as a theorem for each sentence and its negation in the associated formal language. In such a system there are as many theorems as there could be unless the system were (simply) inconsistent. We will see later that there are systems which cannot be both consistent and complete, no matter how many axioms are added to the original axiom set. Here consistency is most important, since a complete system which is inconsistent is of no value. It cannot distinguish true from false statements.

21. a. $(\exists x)(Rx)$

     b. Hint: This is equivalent to saying that if two objects are both red, they are identical.   (See Answer No. 38.)

22. $(P \wedge \sim Q \wedge \sim R) \vee (Q \wedge \sim R) \vee (P \wedge R)$

23. In view of the history of theology, it would seem presumptu-

ous to find any truth-functional structure in a. For most contexts, b. would seem to be a conjunction. The normal use of c. is probably to ascribe the belief that being electrocuted is equivalent to being dead, but hardly the reverse. No conjunctive structure seems appropriate. Example d. is complex, since John may believe that a certain couple is guilty (so the statement would be true in context) even though he does not believe that Mary is one of the couple, or is guilty. In such a case, presumably, John would fail to recognize Mary as one of the couple. Turn "lean and hungry" around and you have a surprise not explicable in terms of temporality. Could Cassius be overweight and e. nonetheless true? f. seems not to be conjunctive even though the conjunctive test for contraction results in a true sentence, but one expressing a different proposition.

24. No, since this cannot be done with any actual set of blocks of the kind we have considered, since such a set must be finite. We could define an infinite set of idealized mathematical volumes in which there was no largest; then p. could be true, but the volumes could not be listed.

25. a., c., d., and f.

26. Although "x^*" is not a PL(=) variable, we stipulated that PL and PL(=) variables could have superscripts. Thus we can treat every variable of OS as a variable of PL(=) for the purpose of developing proofs.

27. a. To show (Ax2) independent of (Ax1), replace "$\leq$" with "$<$" everywhere. Then (Ax1) is true but (Ax2) is false, given the intended interpretation of the mathematical symbols, where the universe consists of the positive integers.

    b. To show (Ax1) independent of (Ax2), we introduce an artificial universe and interpretation in which just these three simple statements are true:

    $1 \dashv 2$
    $2 \dashv 3$
    $3 \dashv 1$

    Clearly, (Ax2) is then true while (Ax1) is false when "$\dashv$" replaces "$\leq$."

28. a., b., and c. are all equivalent ways of abstracting the conclusion.

29. $(P \wedge (Q \vee R)) \vee (Q \wedge (P \vee R))$ Note carefully the words "at least."

30. This kind of situation arises frequently. A human being may have either a positive or negative attitude toward some action, or no definite attitude at all. It is easy to forget this last possibility. In fact, the polarized possibility of either (but not both) of two attitudes is a kind of exclusion. The nearly trivial statement should really be abstracted to an SL form like "$D \lor E \lor F$" to represent the three possible states. Unfortunately, this SL form is not a tautology, so it fails in its intention. We cannot repair this by replacing "F" with "$\sim (D \lor E)$," since this is equivalent to "$\sim D \land \sim E$," but we would not say that a person with no definite attitude has both of the extreme attitudes.

31. c., e., f., j., k., n., q., and t. Be sure you see why each instantiation of c. is true.

32. All are PL valid. We give two proofs.

a.
(4)	$\sim C1 \land \sim R1$	(3) $\exists$ - elimination
(5)	$\sim (\sim C1) \lor W1$	(2) $\forall$ - elimination
(6)	$\sim W1 \lor R1$	(1) $\forall$ - elimination
(7)	$\sim R1$	(4) CS_2
(8)	$\sim W1$	(7) , (6) DS_2
(9)	$\sim (\sim C1)$	(8) , (5) DS_2
(10)	$\sim C1$	(4) CS_1

b.
(4)	$\sim W1 \land \sim R1$	(2) $\exists$ - elimination
(5)	$\sim W1$	(4) CS_1
(6)	$\sim R1$	(4) CS_2
(7)	$\sim (\sim R1) \lor \sim (\sim C1)$	(1) $\forall$ - elimination
(8)	$\sim (\sim C1)$	(6) , (7) DS_3
(9)	$\sim (\sim W1) \lor \sim C1$	(3) $\forall$ - elimination
(10)	$\sim C1$	(5) , (9) DS_3

33. If an SL form is neither a tautology nor a contradiction, then it abstracts a true assertion in some possible worlds, and a false assertion in others. Let the two SL forms in the SL argument consistency form have no capital letters in common. Then we choose a possible world for each SL form in which it is true. The possible world which is taken as the combination of these two possible worlds is one in which both SL forms are true, so the argument is shown to be invalid by counterexample. (Why can't we form this larger possible world in every case where the SL forms have letters in common?)

34. All of them.

35. I think we would say that the statement making the connection which is justified by other information and observations would be justified. If a man made the first statement, and then was able to show that on similar occasions when it rained cricket matches had always been called off, he would have established an excellent *prima facie* case for the truth of his statement. Some authors have proposed that a conditional abstracted to "$P \supset Q$" is true if and only if there are some true observations, laws, or whatever, which, in conjunction with "P" as a further premise, will lead to "Q" by valid argument. See, for example, [F1].

36. d. (1) $(\forall x)(\sim(\sim Wx) \lor Rx)$
    (2) $(\exists y)(\sim Wy \land \sim Cy)$
    (3) $(\forall z)(\sim(\sim Cz) \lor \sim Rz)$ $\qquad \sim(\text{CON})$
    e. (1) $(\exists x)(\sim Cx \land Wx)$
    (2) $(\exists y)(\sim Wy \land \sim(\sim Cy))$
    (3) $(\forall z)(\sim(\sim Wz) \lor Wz)$ $\qquad \sim(\text{CON})$

37. Hint: What would instantiation amount to in a universe with a single object? (See Answer No. 86.)

38. b. $(\forall x)(\forall y)(\sim Rx \lor \sim Ry \lor (x=y))$
    c. $(\exists x)(Rx \land (\forall y)(\sim Ry \lor (x=y)))$ The conjunction of the PL forms given for a. and b. is an equivalent answer.
    d. $(\exists x)(\exists y)(Rx \land Ry \land \sim(x=y))$
    e. $(\forall x)(\forall y)(\forall z)(\sim Rx \lor \sim Ry \lor \sim Rz \lor (x=y) \lor (x=z) \lor (y=z))$
    f. $(\exists x)(\exists y)(Rx \land Ry \land \sim(x=y) \land (\forall z)(\sim Rz \lor (x=z) \lor (y=z)))$ The conjunction of the PL forms given for d. and e. is an equivalent answer.

39. The abstractions of the conclusions would be as follows:
    a. (3) $\sim(\forall z)(\sim(\sim Cz) \lor Rz)$ $\qquad \sim(\text{CON})$
    b. (3) $\sim(\exists z)(\sim Wz \land \sim(\sim Cz))$ $\qquad \sim(\text{CON})$
    c. (3) $\sim(\forall z)(\sim(\sim Wz) \lor \sim Rz)$ $\qquad \sim(\text{CON})$
    d. (3) $\sim(\exists z)(\sim Cz \land Rz)$ $\qquad \sim(\text{CON})$
    e. (3) $\sim(\exists z)(\sim Wz \land \sim Wz)$ $\qquad \sim(\text{CON})$

40. First, try some simple examples. (See Answer No. 73.)

41. Answers to the questions of this chapter depend upon a careful discussion of context, and cannot easily be given. Instead of answers as such, in many cases comments will be provided which should enable the reader to determine whether he has noticed the difficulties. In a. through d. of this first question, notice that the attitudes expressed may be contrasted either to

opposite attitudes, or to the state of having neither positive attitude. For example, a person may believe something, may not believe it (because he believes it false), or he may have neither positive belief (because he hasn't thought about it or because he thinks the evidence warrants neither positive belief). In suitable contexts, negation may be taken contextually as citing the other positive attitude rather than as citing the disjunction of the other positive attitude and the neutral attitude. Further, in some specialized contexts, the negation of a statement like b. could be that someone else wants to go. In other words, the subject may be contrasted with other subjects, instead of contrasting different attitudes of the same subject. Clearly, both contrasts cannot be abstracted by negation of a single SL capital letter in the same context.

(See Answer No. 78.)

42. No. It might seem that the argument should be valid because the premise cannot be true, but the abstracted logical form is that of an invalid argument.

43. a.   (1) $(\forall x)(Wx \supset Rx)$
       (2) $(\forall y)(\sim Cy \supset Wy)$
       (3) $\sim (\forall z)(\sim Cz \supset Rz)$ $\sim$ (CON)
    b.   (1) $(\forall x)(\sim Rx \supset \sim (\sim Cx))$
       (2) $(\exists y)(\sim Wy \wedge \sim Ry)$
       (3) $\sim (\exists z)(\sim Wz \wedge \sim (\sim Cz))$ $\sim$ (CON)
    c.   (1) $(\forall x)(\sim Cx \supset \sim Rx)$
       (2) $(\forall y)(\sim Wy \supset \sim Cy)$
       (3) $\sim (\forall z)(\sim Wz \supset \sim Rz)$ $\sim$ (CON)

(See Answer No. 70.)

44. Proofs may be developed in different ways. If you have made the correct assessment of validity, make sure your proof is equivalent to the answer given. For convenience, we give just the lines of proof which come after the first lines which are given as part of the problem.

    a.   (4) $\sim A \wedge \sim B$ (1) DM_5
       (5) $\sim A$ (4) CS_1
       Proof blocks; the original argument is valid.
    b.   (4) M (2) D
       Proof simplifies without blocking; argument SL invalid.
    c.   (5) P (3) CS_1
       (6) $\sim Q$ (3) CS_2
       (7) ~~$F \wedge \sim G$~~   (1) , (5) DS_3

(8) F	(7) CS_1
(9) $\sim G$	(7) CS_2
(10) ~~$\sim (\sim G \vee R)$~~	(2) , (5) DS_4
(11) $G \wedge \sim R$	(10) DM_6
(12) G	(11) CS_1

Proof blocks, the original argument is valid. Notice that line (6) could be omitted.

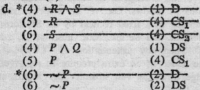

d. | *(4) ~~$R \wedge S$~~ | ~~(1) D~~ |
(5) ~~R~~	~~(4) CS_1~~
(6) ~~S~~	~~(4) CS_2~~
(4) $P \wedge Q$	(1) DS
(5) P	(4) CS_1
*(6) ~~$\sim P$~~	~~(2) D~~
(6) $\sim P$	(2) DS

Proof blocks; the original argument is valid. The lines erased before optimal use of D is obtained have been left to enable a careful check of proof development.

e. Proof completely simplifies without blocking; the original argument is SL invalid.

f. Proof blocks; the original argument is valid.

g. Proof simplifies without blocking; the original argument is SL invalid.

45.
(1) Q	
(2) $Q \supset ((R \supset \sim R) \wedge (\sim R \supset \sim P))$	
(3) $\sim (\sim P)$	$\sim$ (CON)
(4) $(R \supset \sim R) \wedge (\sim R \supset \sim P)$	(1) , (2) MP
(5) $R \supset \sim R$	(4) CS_1
(6) $\sim R \vee \sim R$	(5) MC
(7) $\sim R$	(6) DS*
(8) $\sim R \supset \sim P$	(4) CS_2
(9) $\sim P$	(7) , (8) MP

46.
(1) $(\forall x)(\exists y)(Lxy)$	
(2) $(\exists z)(\exists t)(Lzt \wedge Szt)$	$\sim$ (CON)
(3) $(\exists t)(L1t \wedge S1t)$	(2) $\exists$ - elimination
(4) $L12 \wedge S12$	(3) $\exists$ - elimination
(5) $(\exists y)(L1y)$	(1) $\forall$ - elimination
(6) $L13$	(5) $\exists$ - elimination

PL invalid.

47. A universe consisting of a blue, non-cubical block and a red, cubical block.

48. All of the pairs are equivalent.

49. This problem touches on an often discussed epistemological

question. As matters stand, the logical forms of the argument are just like those of arguments about belief, and the argument is PL invalid. Many philosophers have held that knowledge is different from belief in that if someone knows something, that something must be so, for we would retract the knowledge claim if it were to turn out that that something were not so. We can attempt to abstract a principle about knowledge claims as follows. Let "α" be a special variable which is instantiated in a fixed context by an SL form abstracting a statement, and we let "$Kx\alpha$" abstract "x, a man, knows that α." Then any instantiation of "$(\forall x)(\sim Kx\alpha \lor \alpha)$" may be added as an extra premise to an argument about knowledge, and we can abstract the argument as follows:

(1) KjP
(2) $Kj \sim P \lor Q$
(3) $(\forall x)(\sim KxP \lor P)$
(4) $(\forall x)((\sim Kx \sim P \lor Q) \lor (\sim P \lor Q))$
(5) $\sim Q$ $\sim$ (CON)

Instantiation of "α" takes us beyond PL techniques, but it is clear that we could extend PL techniques to show that this argument was valid by proof development. See [K2] for a discussion and bibliography.

50. Hint: We have seen that (Ax1) and (Ax2) *could* be interpreted as true in a universe of one object, or in the universe of the positive integers. Try some claim about the number of individuals in the universe.   (See Answer No. 77.)

51. a. $\sim P \land \sim Q$
    b. $\sim P \land (Q \lor \sim R)$
    c. $(\sim P \lor Q) \land (\sim P \lor Q)$
    d. $(P \land Q) \lor (P \land \sim Q)$

Using the observations of Exercise 8, c. and d. could be further simplified to "$(\sim P \lor Q)$" and "P."

52. a. $(\forall x)(Yx)$
    b. $(\exists x)(Yx) \land (\exists y)(Ry)$
    c. $(\forall x)(\sim Yx \lor Cx)$
    d. $(\exists x)(Rx \land \sim Cx)$
    e. $(\exists x)(Rx \lor Cx)$
    f. $(\exists x)(Rx) \lor (\exists y)(Cy)$
    g. $(\forall x)(Rx) \land (\forall y)(Cy)$
    h. $(\forall x)(Rx \land Cx)$

i. $(\forall x)((Cx \wedge Bx) \vee (\sim Cx \wedge \sim Bx))$; or
   $(\forall x)((Cx \wedge Bx) \vee \sim (Cx \wedge Bx))$

j. $(\forall x)(Bx) \vee (\forall y)(Cy)$

k. $(\forall x)(Bx \vee Cx)$

l. $(\forall x)(\sim Bx \vee Cx)$

m. $(\forall x)(\sim Bx \vee Cx) \wedge (\forall y)(\sim Ry \vee Cy)$; or
   $(\forall x)(\sim (Bx \vee Rx) \vee Cx)$; or
   $(\forall x)((\sim Bx \wedge \sim Rx) \vee Cx)$

   Notice that "$(\forall x)(\sim Bx \vee \sim Rx \vee Cx)$" would be
   wrong because it would abstract a statement that all
   blue *and* red blocks are cubical, but no block is blue
   and red.

n. $(\exists x)(Cx \wedge Bx)$

o. $(\forall x)(Cx \vee Yx \vee Rx)$

p. $(\forall x)(\exists y)(Lxy)$

q. $(\forall x)(\exists y)(Sxy)$

r. $(\forall x)(\forall y)(\sim Lxy \vee \sim Sxy)$

s. $(\forall x)(\sim Sxx)$ This statement is clearly false.

t. $(\exists x)(\forall y)(Lxy)$

u. $(\forall x)(\forall y)(\sim (\sim Lxy \wedge \sim Lyx) \vee Sxy)$; or
   $(\forall x)(\forall y)(Lxy \vee Lyx \vee Sxy)$

   This sentence may be taken as ambiguous, but the reading that every two blocks the same size weigh the same
   seems preferable to the claim that there are at least two
   blocks the same size which weigh the same.

v. Not possible. We can abstract statements that two blocks
   do not weigh the same as each other, but not that one
   block weighs more than another.

53. c. (1) $\sim Wa \wedge \sim Ca$
   (2) $(\forall x)(\sim (\sim Cx) \vee Lbx)$
   (3) $\sim Lba$ $\qquad\qquad\qquad\qquad\qquad$ $\sim$ (CON)

   d. (1) $(\exists x)(\sim Rx \wedge (\forall y)(\sim Wy \vee Lxy))$
   (2) $(\forall r)(\sim Rr \vee (\forall s)(\sim (\sim Cs) \vee \sim Lrs))$
   (3) $(\exists z)(Wz \wedge \sim Cz)$ $\qquad\qquad\qquad$ $\sim$ (CON)

   e. (1) $(\forall x)(\sim (\sim Cx) \vee (\forall y)(\sim Ry \vee Sxy))$
   (2) $(\exists r)(Wr \wedge (\forall s)(\sim Rs \vee \sim Srs))$
   (3) $(\forall z)(\sim Wz \vee (\exists t)(\sim Ct \wedge \sim Szt))$ $\quad$ $\sim$ (CON)

   f. (1) $(\forall x)(\sim (\sim Rx \wedge \sim Cx) \vee (\forall y)(\sim Ry \vee Lxy))$
   (2) $(\exists z)(\sim Rz \wedge Szc)$
   (3) $(\exists t)(Rt \wedge \sim Lct)$ $\qquad\qquad\qquad$ $\sim$ (CON)

54. There are several possible explanations. The most reasonable

seems to be that the second statement of the professor is in-
appropriately abstracted. As the abstraction stands, it incorrectly suggests there is no connection between passing and a
paper, and between passing and an exam. But this isn't what
the professor said. What he said is more appropriately ren-
dered as "$(C \land \sim P) \lor (C \land \sim E)$."

55. The conclusion of a. would seem to be a tautology. As a result, a. would seem to be valid; but strictly speaking, this
probably rests upon assuming in context that only one possible trip to New York is being talked about. Argument b. is
invalid on any abstraction except where "I sing the blues" is
taken as the negation of "I sing for joy." This abstraction,
however, seems to violate plain fact about singing.

56. g. (1) $(\forall x)(\sim (\exists z)(Fxz) \lor (\exists y)(Fyx))$
    (2) $\sim (\forall s)(\sim (\exists t)(\exists u)(Fst \land Ftu) \lor (\exists r)(\exists w)$
         $(Fsr \land Fws))$ $\sim$ (CON)
    The argument is PL (hence PL(=)) valid.

  h. (1) $(\forall x)(\forall y)(\sim (\sim (x=y)) \lor (\exists z)(Bxzy))$
    (2) $(\forall r)(\forall s)(\forall t)(\sim Brst \lor ((Lrs \land Lst) \lor$
         $(Lts \land Lsr)))$
    (3) $(\forall x')(\sim (x'=1) \lor Lx'1)$
    (4) $\sim (\exists y')(\exists z')(Ly'z')$ $\sim$ (CON)
    The argument is PL (hence PL(=)) valid.

57. c. (1) $(P \lor F) \lor (\sim (I) \land C)$
    (2) $\sim (P) \land \sim (F)$; or $\sim (P \lor F)$
    (3) $\sim (C)$ $\sim$ (CON)

  d. (1) $\sim (S) \lor (B \land \sim (M))$
    (2) $\sim (M) \lor W$
    (3) B (In context, this is probably all right.)
    (4) $\sim (S)$ $\sim$ (CON)

58. a. (1) $(\exists x)(\forall y)((Kx \land Lx) \land (\sim Ky \lor (x=y)))$
    (2) $\sim (\exists z)(Kz \land Lz)$
                                                          $\sim$ (CON)
    (3) $(\forall z)(\sim (Kz \land Lz))$
                                                          (2) QN
    (4) $(\forall y)((K1 \land L1) \land (\sim Ky \lor (1=y)))$
                                                          (1) $\exists$ - elimination
    (5) $(K1 \land L1) \land (\sim K1 \lor (1=1))$
                                                          (4) $\forall$ - elimination
    (6) $K1 \land L1$
                                                          (5) CS$_1$

$(7) \quad \sim (K1 \wedge L1)$

$(3) \quad \forall \text{-elimination}$

The proof blocks; the original argument is valid by PL proof development. (1) may be crossed out.

b. Hint: The second premise is equivalent to a statement that exactly one man wrote the *King Porter Stomp* and his name was Jelly Roll Morton.

(See Answer No. 72.)

59. The unsimplified switch is this:

$(P \wedge Q \wedge \sim R) \vee (P \wedge \sim Q \wedge R) \vee (\sim P \wedge Q \wedge R)$

Any two of these disjuncts can be grouped so as to eliminate one simple switch. By means of a suitable diagram, it is possible to find a way of eliminating one further simple switch.

60. a. The proof blocks; the original argument is PL valid.

b. The proof doesn't block; the original argument is not PL valid. Compare the results of a. and b. with your intuitions about the original arguments.

c. The proof blocks; the original argument is PL valid.

d. $(4) \quad \sim R1 \wedge (\forall y)(\sim Wy \vee L1y)$

$(1) \quad \exists \text{-elimination}$

(Notice that $\forall$-elimination cannot be directly applied to line (4).)

$(5) \quad \sim R1$

$(4) \quad CS_1$

$(6) \quad (\forall y)(\sim Wy \vee L1y)$

$(4) \quad CS_2$

$(7) \quad \sim R1 \vee (\forall s)(\sim (\sim Cs) \vee \sim L1s)$

$(2) \quad \forall \text{-elimination}$

$(8) \quad W2 \wedge \sim C2$

$(3) \quad \exists \text{-elimination}$

$(9) \quad \sim W2 \vee L12$

$(6) \quad \forall \text{-elimination}$

$(10) \quad W2$

$(8) \quad CS_1$

$(11) \quad L12$

$(9) , (10) \quad DS_3$

$(12) \quad \sim R1$

$(7) \quad DS*$

The proof does not block. Compare your intuition about the argument.

e. The proof does not block.

     f. The proof does not block.
61. Only a.
62. a. (not S) and E
     b. not (S and E)
     c. C or not (S and E)
     d. not (not (not P or C))
     e. (not S and E) or not (S and E)

     In a., b., c., and e., the parts in parentheses should be read about as quickly as words or symbols that lie outside any parentheses. Pronounce d. "not-not-not P or C," with the three indicated segments having equal length.

63. e. (1) $(\sim G \supset \sim O) \wedge ((G \wedge D) \supset L)$
        (2) E $\sim$ (CON)

       The argument is invalid as abstracted. Now add the premise "God is omnipotent." To do justice to the context, this can be taken as equivalent to "God is omnipotent and good, so that if he does no evil, there is none."

     f. The trap is to abstract the argument this way:
        (1) $\sim (\sim D \vee I)$
        (2) $\sim D$ $\sim$ (CON)

       If you do, you obtain the absurd result that the argument is valid. The premise should be taken as equivalent to "If I had diabetes, then I would not be glad to have it" in most conceivable contexts.

     g. (1) $\sim T \vee (\sim B \vee (F \wedge C \wedge R))$
        (2) $\sim U \vee (C \wedge \sim R)$
        (3) $\sim (\sim (T \wedge B) \vee \sim U)$ $\sim$ (CON)
       The argument is valid as abstracted.

     h. The first premise of this argument cannot be appropriately abstracted as a truth-function. For an interesting account of the philosophical problems involved in abstracting subjunctive conditionals, see the first chapter of [G3].

64. b., c., e., f., k., q., and r.
65. An axiomatic system which is (simply) inconsistent is trivially (simply) complete, since *every* sentence of the associated formal language is a theorem.
66. b., c., and d. are logical truths.
67. Argument a. might be considered valid in ordinary discourse. The reason it is SL invalid is related to the fact that whereas we know in an ordinary context that South Africa is neither Australia nor England, this geographical fact would have to

be added as an explicit premise to make the argument logically valid. This argument shows how logical systems can expose the presence of implicit assumptions. In the other arguments, intuition should agree with the logical test. Argument c. may not appear valid unless you "think it through." Notice that the logical test gives an answer that does not depend on "thinking it through." It should be clear that logical tests may save a great deal of intellectual effort in assessing more complex arguments.

68. a. $(\exists x)(\sim(\sim Rx \lor \sim Tx))$
b. Not applicable.
c. $(\forall y)(\sim(\sim(Ry \land Ty)))$
d. One application yields "$(\exists x)(\sim(\exists y)(\sim Rxy \lor Ty))$." After applying $\exists$-elimination in the course of developing a proof, QN could be applied to the resulting instantiation.

69. b.

(5)	$\sim R$	(2) CS_1
(6)	Q	(2) CS_2
(7)	$T \lor R$	(3), (6) MP
(8)	T	(7) DS*
(9)	$\sim T \lor \sim P$	(4) DM_5
(10)	$\sim P$	(8), (9) DS_3

c.

(5)	B	(1), (4) DS_2
(6)	$\sim(B \lor C) \lor (P \land Q)$	(2) MC
(7)	$P \land Q$	(6) DS*
(8)	P	(7) CS_1

d. should completely simplify with "E," "$\sim P$," and "$\sim Q$" as final lines.

70. a. (1) $(\forall x)(\forall y)(Lxy \supset \sim Lyx)$
(2) $\sim(\forall z)(\sim Lzz)$ $\sim$(CON)

b. (1) $(\forall x)(\forall y)(Sxy \supset Syx)$
(2) $\sim(\forall z)(\sim Szz)$ $\sim$(CON)

d. (1) $(\exists x)(\sim Rx \land (\forall y)(Wy \supset Lxy))$
(2) $(\forall r)(Rr \supset (\forall s)(Cs \supset \sim Lrs))$
(3) $\sim(\forall z)(Wz \supset \sim(\sim Cz))$ $\sim$(CON)

e. (1) $(\forall x)(\sim Cx \supset (\forall y)(Ry \supset Sxy))$
(2) $(\exists r)(Wr \land (\forall s)(Rs \supset \sim Srs))$
(3) $\sim(\exists z)(Wz \land (\forall t)(\sim Ct \supset Szt))$ $\sim$(CON)

71. b. Yes. A simple interpretation in the domain of a single integer will show this.

    c. No. Once again, an axiom may be added expressing information about the size of the universe.

    d. No.

    e. No. This statement is not true on the intended interpretation where the universe consists of the positive integers. It is true, along with all of the previous axioms, if the universe consists of all of the integers.

72. (1) $(\forall x)(\sim Kx \lor Px)$

    (2) $(\exists y)(Ky \land My \land (\forall z)(\sim Kz \lor (y = z)))$

    (3) $\sim (\exists u)(Mu \land Pu)$ $\sim$ (CON)

73. Let Γ be the dual of Δ. Replace every SL capital letter with the negation of the same SL capital letter. The result is Θ.

74. a. (1) $\sim (J \lor S) \lor (C \land V)$

       (2) $\sim (\sim J \lor C)$ $\sim$ (CON)

      The argument is valid.

    b. (1) $\sim C \lor R$

       (2) $\sim T$

       (3) $\sim \sim C$ $\sim$ (CON)

      It may be questioned whether the conclusion of the argument is correctly abstracted. Notice that Jack could borrow a shirt for the parade, so that the second premise is *not* abstracted appropriately as *"R"* except in an unusual context. The argument is SL invalid as abstracted.

    c. (1) $W \supset C$

       (2) C $\sim$ (CON)

      As abstracted, the argument is invalid, probably contrary to intuition. In ordinary speech, we would say that the premise is false unless there is some cheese in the pantry. Wanting cheese does not make any difference to there being some, i.e., no connection exists between merely wanting and having it. The first premise is probably not appropriately abstracted in context. SL is impervious to the sort of presupposition illustrated in this argument.

    d. (1) $(\sim L \lor \sim S) \land (L \lor J)$

       (2) $\sim \sim S \lor \sim J$

       (3) $\sim L$ $\sim$ (CON)

      The argument is valid as abstracted.

                    (See Answer No. 63.)

75. Example d. cannot be added as a derived rule of proof, but e. could be added. The substitutions *"$P \lor (\sim P \land Q)$"* and *"Q"* are sufficient to condemn d.

76. a. (1) $(\forall x)(\forall y)(\sim Fxy \lor \sim Fyx)$
       (2) $(\exists z)(Fzz)$ $\sim$ (CON)

   b. (1) $(\forall x)(\forall y)(\forall z)(\sim Fxy \lor \sim Fyz \lor Fxz)$
       (2) $(\forall u)(\sim Fuu)$
       (3) $(\exists v)(\exists w)(Fvw \land Fwv)$ $\sim$ (CON)

   The proof development of a. and b. is easy.

   c. Hint: Set the three conditions down as the first three lines of a proof, and then show that a proof developed from them would block, proving that the three lines could not be jointly true. Notice that "$\sim$ (CON)" does not appear on the right-hand side of any line.

77. Either "$(\forall x)(\exists y)(\sim (x = y))$" or its negation will do. It is easy to verify that neither is a theorem of the axiomatic system whose axioms are (Ax1) and (Ax2), and the axiomatic system defined by adding either as (Ax3) is (simply) consistent.

78. Example e. is fairly complex. The fossil might not be interesting, or it might have been found some time ago. Example f. is interesting because in such value contexts, *bad* often contrasts with *good,* that is, it is slightly odd not to recognize one's own tastes. Of course, the statement may also be negated in another context by pointing out that *this* is used to make the wrong reference. The ways of negating h. are almost as numerous as those for the example discussed in the chapter.

79. No.

80. d. and e.

81. b. Not simplified by convention.
   c. $((\sim (P) \lor \sim (Q)) \land R)$
   d. One can obtain "$\sim (P) \land Q \land R,$" but this cannot be grouped, so that this form is not simplified by convention.
   e. $(\sim (\sim (P)) \lor P)$

82. a. (1) $(P \land Q) \lor (\sim P \land R) \lor \sim R$
       (2) $(P \land Q) \lor \sim R \lor (\sim P \land R)$ (1) FE$_4$
       (3) $(P \lor Q) \lor \sim R \lor (R \land \sim P)$ (2) FE$_4$
       (4) $(P \land Q) \lor \sim R \lor \sim P$ (3) FE$_{12}$
       (5) $(P \land Q) \lor \sim P \lor \sim R$ (4) FE$_4$
       (6) $\sim P \lor (P \land Q) \lor \sim R$ (5) FE$_4$
       (7) $\sim P \lor Q \lor \sim R$ (6) FE$_{12}$

   b. (1) $(P \land \sim Q) \lor Q \lor (P \land R)$
       (2) $Q \lor (P \land \sim Q) \lor (P \land R)$ (1) FE$_4$

  (3) $Q \lor (\sim Q \land P) \lor (P \land R)$ (2) FE_3

  (4) $Q \lor P \lor (P \land R)$ (3) FE_{11}

  (5) $Q \lor P$ (4) FE_{10}

 c. $\sim R \land P \land Q$

 d. $R \land (P \lor Q)$

 e. $\sim R \land (P \lor Q)$ Hint: Use FE_2 to add a switch before simplifying.

83. a. (1) $(\forall x)(\sim Wx \lor Rx)$

   (2) $(\forall y)(\sim (\sim Cy) \lor Wy)$

   (3) $(\exists z)(\sim Cz \land \sim Rz)$ $\sim$(CON)

  Note: The denial of a sentence like "All *A*'s are *B*'s" is "Some *A* is not a *B*."

 b. (1) $(\forall x)(\sim (\sim Rx) \lor \sim (\sim Cx))$

   (2) $(\exists y)(\sim Wy \land \sim Ry)$

   (3) $(\forall z)(\sim (\sim Wz) \lor \sim Cz)$ $\sim$(CON)

 c. (1) $(\forall x)(\sim (\sim Cx) \lor \sim Rx)$

   (2) $(\forall y)(\sim (\sim Wy) \lor \sim Cy)$

   (3) $(\exists z)(\sim Wz \land Rz)$ $\sim$(CON)

  Note: The denial of a sentence like "No *A*'s are *B*'s" is "Some *A*'s are *B*'s." Be sure you understand this fact and the related one mentioned in the note to a.

              (See Answer No. 36.)

84. These are established just as in the example at the end of the chapter. The proofs developed from the axioms and the negation of a theorem as the first three lines will all block.

85. Parts a., b., c., and d. should be easy. For e., notice that the argument is *not*, strictly speaking, deductively valid. The argument shows that either "*S*" or "$\sim S$" abstracts a verifiable assertion. It is tacitly assumed in stating the conclusion that if "$\sim S$" is verifiable, then "*S*" must be also, a claim which does not follow from the explicit premises of the argument. Could one reasonably deny that if "$\sim S$" is verifiable, then "*S*" must be also, so that this assumption should be explicitly added as a premise of the argument? For f., either "$(S \land O_1) \lor \sim O_2$" or "$S \land (O_1 \lor \sim O_2)$" is such a truth-function. Notice that these are not equivalent, but can differ in truth-value in the same possible world.

86. An OS sentence is interpreted in the domain $D_1 = \{1\}$ as follows. First, make the OS sentence (and *not* its negation) line (1) of a proof. Then continue as though developing a proof, except that "1" should be used to instantiate each variable in

a step of ∀-elimination or ∃-elimination. This restriction is a violation of our rules of proof, brought about by the fact that we are not attempting to see whether the OS sentence is true in some interpretation in some domain, but whether it is true on an intended interpretation in a universe with a single individual. Simplify the proof completely. This will happen since each quantifier can only be instantiated once. Each final line after simplification will be one of these four expressions: "$(1=1)$," "$(1 \leqslant 1)$," "$\sim (1=1)$," or "$\sim (1 \leqslant 1)$." Call the first two *true simple statements* and the last two *false simple statements*. It should be clear on reflection that the original OS sentence is true on this interpretation if and only if the proof can be simplified (by using D appropriately) so that only true simple statements appear after simplification. The axioms of the axiomatic system are true on this interpretation, and the OS ordering sentence to be considered is false. We show the interpretation for (Ax1):

(1) $(\forall x)(\forall y)(\forall z)(((x \leqslant y) \land (y \leqslant z)) \supset (x \leqslant z))$

(2) $(\forall y)(\forall z)(((1 \leqslant y) \land (y \leqslant z)) \supset (1 \leqslant z))$

(3) $(\forall z)(((1 \leqslant 1) \land (1 \leqslant z)) \supset (1 \leqslant z))$

(4) $((1 \leqslant 1) \land (1 \leqslant 1) \supset (1 \leqslant 1))$

(5) $\sim ((1 \leqslant 1) \land (1 \leqslant 1)) \lor (1 \leqslant 1)$

(6) $(1 \leqslant 1)$

87. The answer is the same as that given for the original argument. We can see that line (5) and line (6) will block if "P" is chosen from line (5) by D. Development can now be shorter and no lines need to be erased.

88. Hint: Use a substitution into FE_9 on "$(P \land \sim R)$." The switch will then simplify.

INDEX

INDEX

(Note: Proper names of authors have been omitted from this index. In each section corresponding to a letter of the alphabet, capital letter abbreviations have been placed first, and then followed by phrases. For example, "SL" is placed before "Simplest constituent assertions." A few special symbols have been placed at the end of the index. The page numbers cited refer to definitions, characterizations, or to important discussion of the terms and symbols indexed, not simply to pages where they appear.)